PORSCHE

PRECISION, BALANCE, AND STYLE

Paul W. Cockerham

SMITHMARK

This edition published in 1996 by
SMITHMARK Publishers, a division of U.S. Media Holdings, Inc.,
16 East 32nd Street, New York, NY 10016.

SMITHMARK books are available for bulk purchase for sales promotion and premium use.
For details write or call the manager of special sales,
SMITHMARK Publishers, 16 East 32nd Street, New York, NY 10016; (212) 532-6600.

This book was designed and produced by
Todtri Productions Limited
P.O. Box 572, New York, NY 10116-0572
FAX: (212) 279-1241

Printed and bound in Singapore

Library of Congress Catalog Card Number 97-066051

ISBN 0-7651-9231-4

Author: Paul W. Cockerham

Publisher: Robert M. Tod
Editorial Director: Elizabeth Loonan
Book Designer: Mark Weinberg
Senior Editor: Cynthia Sternau
Project Editor: Ann Kirby
Photo Editor: Edward Douglas
Picture Researchers: Meiers Tambeau, Laura Wyss
Production Coordinator: Jay Weiser
Desktop Associate: Paul Kachur
Typesetting: Command-O design

Photo Credits

Ron Kimball
4–5, 12, 14, 17, 24–25, 27, 42 (bottom), 43, 48, 55 (bottom), 56–57

John Lamm
*11, 22, 23 (top & bottom), 34, 35 (bottom), 38, 39 (top & bottom), 40–41, 42 (top), 46, 47 (top left, top right, bottom), 49, 50
53 (top, center & bottom), 54, 55 (top), 58, 59 (top & bottom), 60 (top & bottom), 61, 62, 63, 64 (left & right), 65,
66 (top & bottom), 67 (top & bottom), 68, 69, 70, 71, 72–73, 74 (top & bottom), 75, 76, 77 (top & bottom), 78, 79*

National Motor Museum
6 (top), 7, 8–9, 10, 15 (bottom), 26, 29 (top), 32, 36, 37, 44, 45, 51 (top & bottom), 52

Denis L. Tanney
6 (bottom), 15 (top), 18 (top & bottom), 19, 20, 28, 29 (bottom), 30, 31

Nicky Wright
16, 21 (top & bottom), 35 (top)

Contents

Introduction

Two momentous events defined the summer of 1996 for Porsche AG.

In June, Porsche-powered cars reigned supreme at the 24 Hours of LeMans, capturing the top three finishing positions, and all three class titles.

Then on July 15, the one-millionth Porsche sports car rolled out of the company's assembly plant at Stuttgart-Zuffenhausen, to considerable fanfare. Sports-car enthusiasts who noted the occasion no doubt observed, with considerable irony, that the 285-horsepower vehicle was a police version of the venerable Porsche 911, and would be utilized by the German state of Baden-Wurttemberg, where it would patrol the autobahn for speeders.

Still, the police could not be blamed for wanting to level the playing field. Porsche AG has had a long and proud tradition of designing and producing high-performance vehicles exclusively for the sports car market.

The First Million

The first sports car to carry the Porsche name, the 356, was built forty-nine years ago in Austria. Production was quickly moved to the suburbs of Stuttgart after the first fifty examples were manufactured, and over the next fifteen years, approximately 77,000 356 coupes and convertibles were delivered to customers around the globe.

The 356 was replaced in 1963 with the vehicle that defines the Porsche legend: the 911. Over 419,000 units of the 911 and its derivatives have been produced to date, and it remains one of the most desired of automotive conveyances.

From 1969 to 1975, the company made 118,000 Porsche 914 mid-engined cars, which, because of its powerplant, was looked down upon by so-called true Porschephiles as being little more than a glorified Volkswagen. The 914 was replaced by the front-engined 924; it, and its successors, the 944 and 968, have accounted for 325,000 cars over the years.

The 356 was a responsive car with excellent road manners; with engine mass in the rear, however, drivers had to be vigilant about turning under acceleration.

Because of limited capacity at the Stuttgart plant, these 4-cylinder models have nearly all been built at Audi's factory in Neckarsulm.

Rounding out the company's million-car tally is the prestigious 928. The only sports car of its time to be awarded the accolade of "Car of the Year," the Porsche 928 was bought by 61,000 customers during its 1977–95 production run.

The company's achievements over the past fifty years are hard to ignore, and a flood of innovations have emerged from the engineering concepts underlying the original 356, many first found on the company's racing machinery. As time has progressed, the concept of what constitutes the ultimate Porsche driving experience has been refined.

Dr. Porsche

But it all began with the genius of Ferdinand Porsche (1875–1951). He was the son of a tinsmith, born into a world built upon centuries of respect for craftsmanship. At the time of his death, only the first few production examples of the 356 had rolled off the assembly line, but by then he had established himself as a true visionary, one of the few great designers who was able to visualize and create a car in its entirety.

His name first appeared on a vehicle that created a sensation at the Paris Exposition of 1900. The Lohner-Porsche was a battery-powered two-seater, with electric motors driving its front hubs. Porsche had designed those motors, as well as the car's lightweight chassis. Even then, his designs had a sporting purpose, and there were plans for a racing version of the car, targeted for a then-incredible 37-miles-per-hour top speed.

By 1906, the thirty-one-year-old designer moved on to Daimler Motor Co., where he served as technical director. Thus began an association that lasted for two decades. He designed several notable automobiles, and ultimately was rewarded with the position of chief engineer in 1923. The company was known

Dr. Ferdinand Porsche, the son of a tinsmith, was born into a world built upon centuries of respect for craftsmanship.

A stripped-down racing version of the magnificent, supercharged Mercedes SSK, a Porsche design that became one of the most coveted automobiles ever built, on both sides of the Atlantic.

Porsche was a noted race car designer during the 1930s. Here, an Auto Union grand prix car, with a monstrous V-16 engine located in the rear, is shown in-flight at Britain's Donington Park race course in 1937.

by then as Daimler-Benz, and one of Dr. Porsche's Mercedes designs brought fame to the factory when it won the Targa Florio race in 1924.

Later that decade Porsche designed some of the most incredible automobiles ever created—the Mercedes-Benz S series. Coveted by gentlemen and sportsmen seeking speed and comfort, the great S, SS, and SSK models graced roads on both sides of the Atlantic. They were particularly popular with Hollywood celebrities, such as Zeppo Marx, who owned one of the thirty-one rare, supercharged SSK roadsters that were produced.

But a breach between Porsche and the Daimler-Benz board of directors soon developed. Porsche wanted to engineer a Mercedes-Benz for the common man, mass produced and affordable. Then, as now, conscious of its image as a maker of prestigious transportation, Daimler-Benz turned the request down; Porsche, frustrated by the company's conservatism, quit.

"My father found that when he signed a contract with a firm, they could live another ten years on his designs, but he couldn't," said Ferry Porsche, the son and successor of Dr. Ferdinand, many years later.

FOLLOWING PAGE: Displacement of the 911's base engine had been raised to 3.0 liters by 1973. Such an engine powers this 1976 Carrera Targa.

Everyman's Car

Rounding up backing from a group of investors, Dr. Porsche went into business for himself, and the Porsche Konstruktionburo für Motoren-Fahrzeug-Luftfahrzeug und Wasserfahrzeug-bau came into being on March 6, 1931. The Stuttgart-based firm readily found work for the design of car, aircraft, and ship engines from Germany's reawakening military sector, which had already coalesced around the deadly charisma of Adolf Hitler.

Hitler himself became an enthusiastic backer for Porsche's pet project, the car for Everyman, and soon Porsche and his designers were creating sketches for the car that would ultimately become known as the Volkswagen. Prototypes emerged through the mid-1930s—proto-types that reflected the creator's philosophy of starting with a radical design, and then slowly, through painstaking evolution, affirming the engineering integrity underlying each component.

The engine for what would later be known as the "Bug" is an example of this. Porsche's original vision saw a 4-cylinder, horizontally opposed, air-cooled engine, mounted in the rear, powering the people's car, an engine that was sturdy and simple to maintain. Still, Porsche designed, built and tested twenty different engines before returning to his original concept. The integrity of this process can be seen in the overwhelming popularity the Volkswagen achieved in the 1950s and 1960s, a popularity largely attributed to the car's sturdiness. Sixty years later, "Bugs" are still being manufactured in Volkswagen's Latin America facilities.

And it was in the Volkswagen that the seed for the idea of today's Porsche sports cars grew. Aerodynamic coupes of the cars, three of them, were built to compete in the Berlin-Rome rallies of the 1930s, and the visual similarities between these vehicles and today's Porsches are so striking that some historians consider them prototypes.

World War II and Beyond

The year 1938 saw Porsche relocate his company to new facilities in Zuffenhausen, just outside of Stuttgart. As the war broke out, the company moved from designing tractors to engines for the feared "Tiger" tanks that filled the Panzer divisions.

At war's end, Porsche was finally freed of distractions from his central dreams. Work on the "people's car" continued under a separate company, largely directed by British personnel; as for Porsche's own company, his son, Ferry, and daughter, Louise Piech, were, by now, involved with his plans for a sports car based on the Volkswagen design.

The Porsche Type 32, shown here in a 1934 photo, was a prototype for a "people's car" that would ultimately evolve into the beloved Volkswagen.

The Porsche Speedster, introduced in 1954, ignited America's love affair with the marque. A 1956 edition in the rear is shown with a Speedster of 1990 vintage—an ele-gant illustration of how the company is constantly building on tradition.

*The 356 benefited from constant refine-
ments in engine, transmission, braking,
and bodywork components being per-
formed "on the fly" on the assembly line.*

Chapter One

The 356, and Its Evolution Into the 911

Performance was always a paramount concern when Dr. Ferdinand Porsche took on an automobile design, and the first car to bear his name, the legendary Type 356, had it in spades. Production began in the spring of 1948 in Gmund, Austria, where the company had temporarily relocated towards the end of World War II.

The Birth of the 356

The 356's rounded aluminum bodywork itself was designed by Erwin Komenda, who would ultimately pen many of the company's future works. It was a light, aerodynamic, shape; underneath, Porsche had created a rear-engine configuration off of an independently suspended floorpan. The car was very responsive and had excellent road manners, although it, and nearly every rear-engine Porsche since, demanded a degree of vigilance on the driver's part when turning under acceleration, lest the rear location of the engine mass encourage lurid slides that Porschephiles have always considered part of the car's considerable charm.

The soundness of these performance characteristics was soon demonstrated. The company's first motorsports victory came in 1948 in a race at Innsbruck, Austria— a first-in-class for the 1,500-cubic-centimeter car.

The following year saw the car prominently displayed at the Geneva Salon, which generated orders for forty-six 356 coupes that were produced at Gmund. The company soon returned to Zuffenhausen and started accepting outside contracts for design work, a practice that supported the company in its infancy and one that continues to this day.

By 1950, the 356 was setting class endurance records at 4,000 and 10,000 kilometers, reaffirming the car's reputation for ruggedness. Variations in the design started to emerge, including steel-bodied coupes, and convertibles, built by the adjacent coach-building firm, Reutter.

Dr. Porsche died the following year at seventy-six years of age, and his son, Ferry, took control of the company. The 356 competed for the first time at the 24 Hours of LeMans, taking victory in the 1,100-cubic-centimeter class, and also set a new world record in a seventy-two-hour endurance test, at an average speed of 94.6 miles per hour. This car was immediately rushed to the Paris Salon—dead flies, dirt, and all— and drew huge crowds to the Porsche exhibit.

America and Porsche: A Love Affair

Another, more significant, event for the company happened in 1951: Max Hoffman, an American car dealer based on the East Coast, who helped create the American sports-car craze, first imported the Type 356. The American love affair with Porsches was launched.

Hoffman's first imports sported some significant design alterations, including a two-spoke steering wheel that would become a company trademark. In its center was the company's new crest, which Ferry Porsche had originally sketched on a cocktail napkin; the crest carries a symbol of the family's love for Stuttgart.

Meanwhile, the company's design-consultancy work helped Porsche land a half-million-dollar contract with Studebaker, the American car concern. With the proceeds, the company began construction on a modern factory at Zuffenhausen.

Porsche 356 SL 1.1s took first in class at LeMans and the Mille Miglia in 1952, while a specially modified private car, the Glockler-Porsche, won the German sports-car championship. Inspired, the factory created a new race car for the

This Porsche 356 SL 1.1 is shown as it might have competed in SCCA E-production class events.

following year, the Type 550, unique among the company's offerings in that it utilized a spaceframe design.

The 550 had a phenomenal 1953 season, and inspired a production prototype, the 550/1500RS, which was shown at the Paris Salon in October. Produced for sale in 1954 and christened the Spyder, the car was as aerodynamic a car as could be bought by the motoring public. James Dean bought one, and soon was competing with it in amateur road races in California.

A milestone was reached in 1954 when the 5,000th Porsche rolled off the assembly line. Now in its sixth year, the 356 saw refinement in engine, transmission, braking, and body-work components "on the fly," being constantly improved by the company without the customary wait for model-year changeovers.

An additional model, targeting American customers, was launched—the Speedster—and the country's love affair with the little German car became truly passionate. Inspired by the company's success on racetracks worldwide, American fans established Porsche clubs across the country, celebrating the car's unique road capabilities, and campaigning Porsches in local club races. The young Sports Car Club of America, which by now had created a series of races centered around production cars (classes are dictated by engine displacement), awarded Porsche F Production class honors in both 1954 and 1955, and E, F, and G Production titles in 1956.

The coachbuilding firm of Reutter produced cabriolet bodies for the rugged little 356, as with this 1952 model.

Race on Sunday . . .

Such is Porsche's story through the rest of the decade. Racetrack adventures caused sales to soar past the 10,000 mark in 1956; 25,000 units were produced by 1958. Buyers were

The Porsche 550, with its 1,498-cc engine, had a phenomenal race season in 1953. It was unique among the company's offerings inasmuch as it utilized a spaceframe chassis.

also attracted to the technical refinement of Porsche's coupes and convertibles. The company's reputation for using the latest technological developments to develop cars was typified by the use of a computer to design a "high-lift" racing camshaft—this in 1957!

As the new decade got underway, Porsche was well positioned to capitalize on its success. Always great believers in the old saw, "win on Sunday, sell on Monday," the company decided to tackle the ultimate motorsports challenge: Formula One grand-prix racing. Porsche developed a rear-engined, 8-cylinder car in time for the 1962 season, and found some success. The Porsche, with American Dan Gurney behind the wheel, won the 1962 French Grand Prix at Rouen, but the company felt the returns from such an expensive program were limited, and withdrew from the sport the same year.

Meanwhile, a replacement for the venerable 356, now getting a tad long in the tooth, was developed. The new model, named the 901, an evolution of the car it would ultimately replace, debuted at the 1963 International Automobile Show in Frankfurt. The air-cooled, 2-liter engine, sporting 6 cylinders, was still located at the rear.

This 550A berlinetta competed in the 1957 season. Note the ventilation louvres on the deck lid and the quarterpanels that promoted breathing for its air-cooled engine.

A lovely 1955 Speedster shares a bucolic setting with some English sheep. The car's roadholding capabilities won it legions of fans in Europe and in the United States.

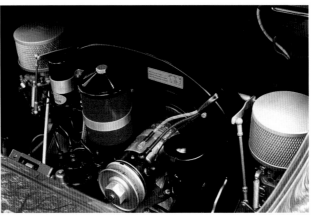

Optimal space utilization was always problematic in cars of this size; still, this 356A could provide all the utility a couple could want for a weekend getaway.

At the heart of the 356: a 1.5-liter, horizontally opposed, air-cooled, 4-cylinder engine, noted for its simplicity, economy, and performance.

In 1958, the year this 356A coupe was produced, Porsche reached the milestone of having produced 25,000 units.

With 75,000 units of the 356 produced, the car was finally retired in 1965. The car that had grown out of the prototype 901, now called the 911 (and its 4-cylinder twin, the 912), came to the fore as Porsche's standard-bearer, and firmly established the company as the world's leading manufacturer of sports cars.

The first 911 engines had a pair of triple-choke Solex carburetors, and power was put to the road through a five-speed gearbox. Sports-car races and rallying continued to fuel interest among the public in the company's offerings, and class wins occurred in the famed Monte Carlo Rally, as well as at Monza, LeMans, and in SCCA championships in the U.S.

The 356's rounded aluminum bodywork was penned by Erwin Komenda, who gave the car a light, aerodynamic shape.

The 911S was introduced in 1966 and was the most powerful variant of the 911 class to date.

A two-spoke wheel would become a design hallmark for the company. The crest in its center was a design created by Dr. Porsche on a cocktail napkin.

This 1965 904 prototype sports racer did battle against the Ford GT40s and Ferraris of the day, and could outperform the larger prototypes on twisty road courses.

The 100,000th Porsche, a 912 dressed up for police duty, left the factory in 1966, leading local observers to believe "that in Germany, there are no getaway cars," according to the company's official history.

The year 1966 also saw the introduction of the most powerful 911 variant to date, the 911S. Weber carburetors replaced the Solex units, and the engine was now good for 160 horsepower. Several innovations were featured, such as radial cooling passages that were cast into the brake rotors. It was also fitted with distinctive, five-spoke Fuchs wheels, which became a visual trademark of the model.

Mindful that many customers were going to want to race their new, rear-engine toys, the company offered a variety of gear-ratio sets for the 911S. The designations suggested, to these racer customers, potential applications: Airport (old World War II airfields proved to be popular locations for club racing, their long runways providing opportunities to hear the air-cooled Porsche engines at full song); Hillclimb; Nürburgring (a fabled road circuit of more than 40 miles' length that runs through Teutonic forests); and Fast Circuit. The trademark of the 911S was an engine shroud painted red; hereafter, red would signify the most powerful engines that could be found in the 911 series.

FOLLOWING PAGE: A 1960 356 cabriolet at rest. Buyers were attracted to the technical refinement of Porsche's coupes and convertibles.

Artistry in metal: the air cleaners, carburetor, intake manifold, and valve covers of the 904 prototype racer's 6-cylinder engine.

The 6,500 r.p.m. redline on this 904 prototype's tachometer is testimony to how much torque the car's engine could produce relatively low in its powerband.

Variations on a Theme

By 1967, Porsche had commenced production of the 911 Targa, which had a re-movable hardtop and a soft rear window that could be lowered. Two other new 911s also debuted: the 911T, a replacement for the 912, with a 110-horsepower engine; and the 911L, a model designation replacing the "plain" 911. The year also is notable for the launch of a four-speed "Sportomatic" transmission option.

Another 2-liter model, the 911E, debuted in August 1968, replacing the 911L and now boasting 140 horsepower. Output on the 911S is now up to 170, thanks to the use of mechanical fuel injection.

At this point in its history, the company developed a growing awareness that its highly refined products had become an indulgence that only the financially secure could afford. Remembering that populist concerns were always in the mind of Ferdinand Porsche, the company developed a radically different, squared-off, two-seater coupe based on Volkswagen mechanicals. Boasting a removable Targa top, the 914 debuted in 1969 in both 4-cylinder (the 914/4) and 6-cylinder (914/6) variants.

Porsche's racing prototype for the 1966 sports car championship for under 2-liter cars was the 906.

The Porsche 912 was a 4-cylinder twin of the 911 line. A 1967 model is shown.

A 1973 911 custom cabriolet. Bosck K-Jetronic fuel injection was now featured to meet customer concerns about fuel efficiency and pollution.

The car was immediately controversial. Longtime Porschephiles looked down on the new offering, contending it was not a "real Porsche" because of the low output of its VW powerplant. The engine, while still located behind the driver, was situated in front of the rear wheels (a "mid-engine" configuration); if anything, the 914's overall balance was superior to that of its upscale older brother. The concept never really caught on, however, and was dropped after a few years.

The engines in these early 911s were high revvers, with power that just kept on coming as they roared to the red line (tachometers, which indicate engine rpm, have a red line that warns drivers not to attempt to blow up the engine). Improvements in carburation and ignition brought steady reliability to the platform, so the engineers next turned their attention to torque. In August 1969 the engine was enlarged to 2.2 liters, which made the engine more flexible in the low end; the E and T models benefited most from this improvement.

Drivers of the 911S, which now boasted 180 horsepower, had to keep revs above the 5,500 mark to really make use of the engine. A neat feature on the racetrack, but perhaps a bit of an impediment in daily driving; enthusiast publications went so far as to suggest that the T was actually a better car, because of its flexibility.

Displacement was again increased in 1972 to 2.4 liters, and to the minds of many enthusiasts, this made for the classic production 911. New camshafts and improved engine breathing came with the bigger engine, while the underside enjoyed some suspension tweaks that improved handling at high speeds.

A desire by the racing department to participate in Group 4 Special GT racing led to the development in 1971 of the Carrera RS. The word "Carrera" was used by the company to designate its sportiest cars, and comes from the Mexican Carrera Panamerican road races of the 1950s, an event in which Porsche gained a class victory in 1953. "RS" stood for RennSport, signifying the racing

The Carrera RS was the hottest-performing Porsche available to the public until the Turbo variant bowed. A 1973 model is shown.

The side view of this 1973 911 cabriolet clearly shows how well the car's new energy-absorbing bumpers integrate into the overall design.

This 911S was the second such model imported into Great Britain in 1973. Depending on a customer's racing inclinations, Porsche offered four different gear ratio sets for the car.

department. The new car's engine was bored out to 2.7 liters, good for 210 horsepower, and lightweight aluminum pistons were used.

In 1973 the RS was enlarged to 3 liters, although these cars really weren't any quicker than their predecessors, because the factory had run out of the original's lightweight body parts.

Now nine years into its production run, the 911 series had set in place developing expectations among customers, both new and old, as to how each generation of the car would perform. But what ultimately shaped the development of Porsche's products from this point on had less to do with customer demands than it did with global political realities.

Engine displacement for the 911S had been increased to 2.4 liters by 1972; combined with better breathing and a new camshaft, this made for the classic production 911 in the minds of many enthusiasts.

The 4-cylinder 924 was Porsche's first production front-engined car. Its transaxle was attached to the engine via a hollow drive shaft, which made for a very well-balanced chassis.

Chapter Two

It's What's
Up Front

Porsche, at various points in its history, has considered optional platforms to the rear-engined, air-cooled vehicles that dominate its history. The first to see the light of day was the 924.

The 924: Fun *and* Affordable

A replacement for the extinct 914, the 924 took its predecessor's role in the model lineup as a relatively low-cost, entry-point car. When it came out in 1976, Porsche observers were stunned. The car had a small, inline 4-cylinder engine, the company's first, and the engine was cooled by water, another first.

The 924 was also a front-engined car, but what was truly unique was the placement of the transmission as part of a rear transaxle, connected to the engine by a hollow drive shaft. This created a very well balanced platform.

The new car featured a smoothly contoured body, retractable headlamps, and a large rear window that functioned as a back hatch. The body was notable for a lack of spoilers and fender flares, which contributed to the car's image as a gimmickless, plain, inexpensive, but fun and sporty drive.

Its mechanical capacities included a 2-liter, Bosch Jetronic-injected engine that produced 143 horsepower. The transmission was a five-speed manual, although automatics would be offered as a later option. The suspension in front had MacPherson struts with lower A-arms, coil springs, and an anti-roll bar; in back were found semi-trailing arms, torsion bars, tube shocks, and another anti-roll bar.

When it hit the market, potential customers were those who were considering the Datsun Z sport coupes, Mazda RX-7s, or Triumph TR7s. The car's totally neutral handling characteristics were welcomed by the public, particularly those who had always wanted a Porsche but were intimidated by the 911's incipient tail-happiness. Speed was not the 924's strong suit—sportiness was. The flexible engine allowed for easy runs up and down the gears, and the car was very pitchable into corners and curves. Best of all, it was affordable.

But within three years, the 924 had already become something of an old dog, not having quite the distinctive performance cachet that usually marked Porsches. Turbocharging breathed new life into the car, and a turbo-assisted variant, quite a fast car, was available for the 1980 model year. It also offered better brakes than the base model, and had some distinguishing styling characteristics: a NACA duct on the hood, four new front vents, and a wraparound spoiler on the back hatch.

More Power

The 924 carried on until the 1983 model year, when its more powerful successor, the 944, was introduced. Interestingly enough, the company brought the body style back four years later, when it felt that the base 944 was still too expensive a car to provide an entry-point Porsche experience. The 1987 924S basically saw a ten-year-old body being attached to the 944's chassis bits, including the latter's 2.5-liter engine. Technically, the only real difference between the two lay in the steering control arm; stamped in the 924S, forged for the 944.

About 20 pounds lighter than the 944, the 924S was also about 3 miles per hour faster than its sibling, and cost about $4,500 less—no doubt causing consternation among 944 owners.

Still, the 944, when introduced, was all the car the original 924 could very well have been. It was an instantly successful design for the Stuttgart concern, boasting a new, larger, 2.5-liter engine and more aggressive bodywork. The body shell was actually the same as the 924's, but it incorporated flared fenders, a rear spoiler, and an air dam in front.

The car also boasted some technical refinements. The steering wheel was moved further away from the driver's seat, ameliorating a space problem in the 924. The eight-valve engine also had a balance shaft, which smoothed out noise levels and vibrations.

A few production Porsches were modified by outside firms to receive the "slant-nose" treatment found in the company's racers of the late '70s to early '90s.

Over its history, the 944 saw minor performance and appearance upgrades. In 1987 the engine's compression ratio was raised to 10.2:1, which added 8 more horsepower. Two years later, the engine size was boosted to 2.7 liters, and the compression was raised again; horsepower increased by 4. A new dashboard and instrument panel were offered halfway through the 1985 model year.

The year 1987 saw the introduction of the 944S model, which featured a 16-valve engine and an antilock braking system. An impressive car, it was still overshadowed in desirability by what Porsche had wrought the previous year: the 944 Turbo.

When the 944 debuted, it possessed a 2.5-liter engine and aggressive bodywork that immediately made it one of the company's most popular offerings.

NEVADA
12-86
1662
SILVER STATE

The hatch lid for the Porsche 924, made entirely from glass, helped make the front-engined car a practical little grand tourer.

As this photo so elegantly implies,
covering a lot of ground with the top
down is the essence of Porsche cabriolet
motoring. A 16-valve 944S is shown.

Just in case you couldn't
tell what model Porsche
you were following . . .

Hello, Turbo

The Turbo variant was a totally re-engineered automobile, with new engine and brakes, a beefed-up suspension, 15-inch alloy wheels, a rear chin spoiler, and a new front cap that integrated bumper and fog lights. Enthusiasts feel that it was perhaps the most underrated car Porsche ever made, a fast, elegant touring car that could be civilized in drives around town and an absolute beast on the highway.

The only giveaway that you were driving a Turbo, as opposed to a normally aspirated 944, was the presence of a boost gauge, directly under the tachometer. That changed when one stepped on the gas, for the addition of turbocharging boosted engine horsepower levels by 50 percent! It accelerated through the quarter-mile a full 2 seconds faster than did the base car.

FOLLOWING PAGE:
The Turbo was a totally re-engineered variant on the 944 model, with new engine and brakes, body cladding, and a beefed-up suspension.

This 1985 Turbo offered performance to match its looks, and was the basis for many privateer sports car team's racing activities. The "slant-nose" became an official factory option in 1981.

Turbocharging boosted the output of the 944's 4-cylinder inline engine by a good fifty percent and provided 2 seconds faster acceleration through the quarter-mile.

The lineup of Porsches for the 1986 model year showed the company had offered a broad range of approaches to the sports car driving experience.

The culmination of the normally aspirated 944 was the S2 model, introduced in 1989. It had a new 3-liter engine in it, good for 208 horsepower. Its bodywork was identical to that of the Turbo's. The following year a cabriolet version became available, which many consider to be the best-looking front-engined car Porsche ever made.

The 944 made an indelible impression on the motoring public, making a convincing case that owning a front-engine Porsche did not mean any loss in prestige or performance. But the model line wound down for the 1991 model year.

Porsche had originally considered that the 944's replacement would be known as the 944S3, but, after realizing that there was so much that was new about the car, the company positioned it, legitimately, as an all-new model: the 968.

Monster on the Loose

In appearance, the 968 had the same basic shape as the 944, but by rounding edges and substituting covered retractable headlights with pop-up ones, the 968 appeared to be a more proper member of the Porsche family. Its bumper sections were fully integrated into the bodywork, its sill extensions resembled those of the Carrera 2 that was also introduced in 1992. Air intakes were rearranged from those found on the 944, and a "968" badge was prominently displayed in the center of the rear deck lid.

The 968, which ended production in 1995, was one of the most balanced Porsches ever made. It retained the 944's 50/50 weight distribution, with the transaxle located in the rear, but offered more power. The 3-liter engine produced 240 horsepower, making it the most powerful normally aspirated 4-cylinder engine ever made. The engine had a variable profile camshaft, which Porsche called Variocam; this was essentially an adjustable tensioner on the camshaft's chain drive that retarded intake valve actuation up to 7.5 degrees. This allowed the engine to burn cleaner while producing more torque and horsepower.

The engine from this "flat nose" Turbo had its air intake system integrated into the bodywork of the car's spoiler.

Porsche reintroduced the "Speedster" moniker to the product line in the late '80s when it produced a modified version of the 911 cabriolet. Note the hard shell covering the convertible top.

Two different transmissions were available in the 968. A six-speed manual was standard, and it was a true six-speed, fifth and sixth gears being separated by only 500 rpms, but top speed could only be obtained in sixth. The other unit was Porsche's revolutionary four-speed Tiptronic unit. Outwardly a standard automatic unit with the normal P/R/N/D/3/2/1 selections, it could also be used as a manual unit, thanks to electronic controls. When in "drive," the lever could be moved horizontally to the right into a second, parallel slot. There the driver could "tip" the unit forward to upshift a gear, or back to downshift. Stand on the gas and get too close to the engine's red line, and a computer would shift to a proper gear on its own.

The 968 weighed in at 3,086 pounds. Its wheelbase was 94.5 inches long; the overall length, 170.9 inches. At 68.3 inches wide overall, wheel track was relatively narrow at 58.2/57.1 inches front/rear. Care needed to be taken with bumps, as the car rode only 4.9 inches off the ground. The 968 was also available in a Turbo version. Already a quick car, turbocharging, along with twin NACA hood ducts, huge, three-piece wheels, a front chin spoiler, and a

The final iteration of Porsche's experiment with front-engine cars was the 968, one of the most well-balanced cars the company ever produced.

speed-sensitive retractable rear wing signified a car that was lightning fast. The rear badge simply read "Turbo S."

Go-power came from a four-valve-per-cylinder, 3-liter 4, tweaked by a water-cooled KKK turbocharger, equipped with a bypass valve that had its own separate gate (to reduce dreaded "turbo lag"); this in turn boosted a sequential multiple-port fuel system and gave the four-banger a stupendous 305 horsepower A six-speed manual shifter and a limited-slip differential interceded between powerplant and pavement.

Braking was through power-assisted, four-piston, aluminum-alloy fixed-caliper units, which grabbed internally vented, cross-drilled discs. The wheels were indeed quite large for a car this size—18 inches in diameter, 8 inches wide in front and 10 inches wide in back. They boasted Dunlop Sport 8000 series Z-rated tires, 235/40s in front, 265/35s aft. Top speed was electronically limited to 175 miles per hour.

Seating was matched to the body color, and heavily bolstered to keep the driver in place. This no doubt helped with feelings of driver security, especially since he or she would be looking at a speedometer that registered up to 190 miles per hour.

The chassis was lowered .8 inch and fitted with stiffer springs and shocks, and the transmission received a stronger clutch. Chassis undercoating and electric accessory actuators (for windows, locks, and seats) were removed to keep weight down to a mere 2,867 pounds. This meant that each unit of horsepower had only 9.5 pounds of car to move around (standard family sedans of the time had weight to horsepower ratios in the area of 20:1), so startling performance would come as no surprise.

At Last, a V-8

As car enthusiasts will always attest, more is better, so it's appropriate that Porsche's ultimate front-engined automobile would be the one fitted with a nice, big V-8 engine: the 928.

Porsche's 8-cylinder 928 was the largest Porsche the company had built by 1978; in terms of power and luxury, it was the company's flagship design. A 1984 928S2 is shown here.

The 928's design was spurred by factory concerns that its traditional car technology might be legislated out of existence.

Ahead of its time from day one, the 928 was produced for seventeen years, from 1978 through 1995. During that period, this was the ultimate Porsche, both in power and luxury. It was only available as a two-door coupe.

Porsche's engineers first conceptualized what would be the 928 in 1971, and it was six years before the fruits of their efforts rolled off the production line. It debuted at the Geneva Auto Show of 1977, causing a sensation, and production began in September of that year.

Initially, the 928's engine was a 90-degree, 4.5-liter V-8, with dual overhead cams and four valves per cylinder. It produced 219 horsepower, putting power to the road through a either a five-speed manual or three-speed automatic transaxle in the back of the car. This configuration was first seen in the 924 coupe, but as the 928 was actually an earlier design, it earns the distinction of being the first front-engined Porsche.

Its appearance was in stark contrast to the boxier sedans that tooled the world's highways at the time. Its curvy shape was comparatively amorphous, almost alien, and produced a slippery drag coefficient of only 0.34 cd. Its long hood, pop-up headlights, sloping greenhouse, raked B-pillars, and wraparound rear taillights contributed to a muscular sinuousness.

The 928 was certainly the largest Porsche built to date. The body was a tad over 178 inches long, and it rode a 98.4-inch wheelbase. The width was 74.4 inches, and wheel track was 61.1/63.6 inches front/rear. The car stood just 50.5 inches tall and had a ground clearance of only 4.5 inches. Altogether, the "big" Porsche weighed in at 3,593 pounds, but it still maneuvered with the responsiveness of a much smaller automobile, and it was very much the equal of the 911 in terms of all-around performance.

The car was rich with technical innovations. A timing belt that seemed to go on forever drove all those camshafts and the power accessories. The cylinder block and what would normally have been combustion heads were but a single unit, made of an alloy Porsche

called "Alusil." The cylinder bores were etched to expose hard silicon particles that reduced wear.

Underneath, the car's near-perfect weight distribution was borne by a sophisticated multiple-link "Weissach" suspension layout in the back, unique at the time in its use of a form of passive rear-wheel steering. The rear suspension toed in under braking or deceleration to counter trailing-throttle oversteer. This was the first rear-steering technology ever unleashed on the public.

Aluminum was everywhere in the 928: in the doors, the hood, and in all the large castings. The interior was strikingly modern, of the finest materials, and boasted a full complement of electronic comfort and convenience features. One striking extra was the mounting of the instrument "pod" on top of the steering column, which kept it perfectly in view no matter how the steering-wheel height was adjusted. Interiors were finished either in leather or a striking "op art" velour cloth.

The 928 driving experience was both civilized and invigorating. There was always more than enough power available (particularly for drivers of the final 1995 928GTS, which boasted a 5.4-liter, 345-horsepower engine good for 369 pound-feet of torque). Stand on the gas, and the power simply kept coming and coming, even in the automatic cars, all the way through the rpm range. The automatic unit shifted most efficiently, without any hesitation, until it was called into action again by the next engine redline. Should the driver simply be cruising along lazily, mashing the pedal would result in his being mashed back into the seat. For the manual-shifting crowd, all that power was just more controllable. It was far too simple a proposition to run all the way through the gears, only to look down at the speedometer and realize that the needle was pointed beyond the 140-miles-per-hour mark.

For all that fury, the 928 was eminently controllable and contained. Even at speed, engine noise was so low as to provide an eerie sensation. The Pirelli P7–clad 17-inch wheels kept the 928 firmly grounded on the pavement, and steering input was firm and secure—perhaps not as sharp as that found in the 944, but more than suited to the task.

Speed and luxury were perhaps never as artfully joined as they were in Porsche's ultimate front-engine machine. Still, it was in rear-engined cars that the company's brilliance would shine most brightly.

Power for the 928 was significantly upgraded for the S4 model. Its engine displaced 4.9 liters and could produce 316 h.p.

The 928 was an unprecedented Porsche, as the company's top-of-the-line car was now powered by a front-mounted 4.5-liter V-8 engine producing 219 h.p.

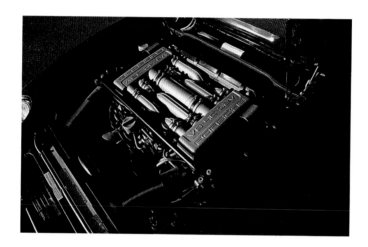

An interior shot of the 928S4. The instrument cluster was mounted directly on top of the adjustable steering column so that the driver's view of the gauges would always be unobstructed.

In Germany, aftermarket manufacturers offer the truly wealthy customer their own particular spin on the Turbo theme.

Chapter Three

Of Turbos, Four-Wheel-Drives, and Other Exotica

The world market for performance automobiles took a major hit in 1973 when the first global fuel crisis occurred. Although fuel was still cheap in absolute terms, skyrocketing gasoline prices and long queues at the fuel pump shook the public's belief in the infinite availability of fuel, and with Porsche's 911S getting 15 miles per gallon, the company, and others like it, was put on the defensive.

Meanwhile, American sports-car enthusiasts flat out wondered if their country wasn't going completely nuts. Laws were being formulated on the federal level, as well as with particular zeal in California, that would mandate improvements in automotive crash resistance as well as make their engines less toxic to the atmosphere.

Fortunately for Porsche, it had always placed a great emphasis on engineering research and development. The company anticipated that emissions regulations might threaten the future of the company's air-cooled boxer engines; these concerns, as well as others on crashworthiness and occupant protection, helped stimulate the development of a four-seat sports-car design that would ultimately be known as the 928. But this initiative did not necessarily mean that Porsche was going to close the book on its namesake. Iterations on the 911 designs still figured very strongly in the company's future plans; all this meant was that the staff at the new Research and Development Center in Weissach, just west of the company's Stuttgart headquarters, would have to turn their considerable talents to more than just performance issues.

Adapting to the Times

In the meantime, production-car advances grew out of the company's ongoing involvement in racing. Development of engine turbocharging commenced in 1971, and the first turbo racer, the 917/10, won the Can-Am sports prototype championship in 1972; its successor, the legendary 917/30, won all

Battling across the ages, a 917 prototype from the late 1960s (left), in the John Wyer/Gulf racing colors, shows up a 962 campaigned nearly twenty years later by the BF Goodrich team.

The 911S Targa offered the rigidity of a coupe with the open-air pleasures normally associated with convertibles.

eight races the following year, with Mark Donohue driving to victory in six. The company drew on the development of the 917/30 as it created the 2.8-liter Turbo Carrera, which was introduced in the U.S. in 1975 as a 1976 model.

The company's involvement in rallying, which often takes place on open desert, forest roads, or in blizzards, led it to investigate four-wheel drive. Porsche introduced a special all-wheel-drive 911 prototype in 1984; the car won that year's Paris–Dakar rally. The production car that evolved from this was the Carrera 4, which debuted in 1988.

Porsche had already made inroads into making their cars cleaner running, as could be seen in the 1973 911T built for the U.S. market. This was the first Porsche to use the Bosck K–Jetronic fuel-injection system, which was particularly efficient and burned cleanly. Other alterations to engine flow, particularly to the exhaust, typified modifications that car companies made to their creations in the name of enviro-friendliness and fuel economy, but these often resulted in a loss of horsepower. Porsche remedied this by enlarging the base

Four wheel drive ultimately became available in Porsche's mainstream 911 line; such cars received the designation Carrera 4. A 1989 model is shown.

Porsche's first Turbo Carrera was powered by a 3.0-liter engine that could put out 234 h.p., providing speeds in excess of 155 m.p.h.

engine size in the 911 to 2.7 liters as of August 1973; not only was power loss offset, but the resultant engine was also more flexible, with more torque at low engine speeds—a particularly useful characteristic on roads that were becoming ever more crowded.

Other changes made to the car at this time primarily concerned the creation of energy-absorbing bumpers that would meet new, low-speed-crash-resistance standards. Car companies had less success with this than they did with engine compliance, as the appearance of a car could be radically affected. MG, for example, placed huge, molded-rubber caps on the nose and tail of its MGB; its looks ruined and ride compromised (the car was raised to meet bumper-height standards), the MGB soon faded to unglorified obscurity and death.

Porsche, in meeting this challenge, actually managed to improve the appearance of the 911. Perhaps because the 911 had always been a car in which form followed function, Porsche stylists, particularly Wolfgang Möbius, took the opportunity to lower the car's appearance, making it seem that much more aggressive.

A warm, dry day in the desert provides a perfect motoring environment for this 1984 Carrera convertible.

Four-wheel drive in the Carrera 4 goes a long way towards eradicating the 911's legendary penchant towards tail-happiness under throttle.

The business office of a Carrera 4. The grouping of five instrument dials directly in front of the driver has been a Porsche design trait since the beginning.

The technology underlying the Carrera 4 (foreground) is an outgrowth of Porsche's work on the legendary 959 (background).

The 911 cabriolet rides on cast-aluminum suspension pieces that are mounted to an aluminum subframe with rubber bushings, creating a quiet ride.

FOLLOWING PAGE: This nostalgic background provides a stark contrast to the 930 Carrera Turbo in its role as a manifestation of state-of-the-art automotive technology.

Current Offerings

The Porsche mantle is primarily held by the 993, now known simply as the Carrera. Its air-cooled, 6-cylinder engine generates 282 horsepower; coupled with the six-speed manual transmission the car can reach 60 miles per hour in just 5.3 seconds. Should traffic jams be too much of an everyday reality, the driver can order the car with Porsche's Tiptronic-S transmission. Available as a coupe or cabriolet, the Carrera rides on cast-aluminum suspension pieces, mounted to an aluminum subframe with rubber bushings, creating a quiet ride.

The company still offers a Targa model, which now has a sensational sliding glass panel roof. Retracting at the touch of a button, the large, double-thick glass slides beneath the backlight. The Targa also boasts both a power-operated sunshade to keep the cabin cool, and a power-operated wind deflector that minimizes interior wind buffeting when the roof is retracted.

The Carrera coupe and cabriolet are also available as four-wheel-drive models under the Carrera 4 banner. The most obvious benefit from all-wheel drive in a rear-drive Porsche is that the car's legendary tail-happiness is totally eradicated. Porsche purists may tell you that tail-sliding is part of the car's charm, but not everyone has the same degree of solid will it takes to master a conventional (if there is such a thing) Porsche.

Thanks to improvements in the exhaust system, the 1992 911 Turbo was the fastest and cleanest-burning regular production Porsche available to date.

Next stop—anywhere you want. A 1995 911 Cabriolet, its top down, beckons the adventurous driver to take command.

In fact, the less conventional the Porsche, the more indelible an impression it makes. The 930 Carrera Turbo, in its extreme performance capabilities, is perhaps the most unconventional Porsche currently offered.

The 930's legacy dates back to 1976, when the first Turbo Carrera was offered. A very special 911, the new car had the 3-liter engine, wide fender flares, trick suspension parts, and its most recognizable characteristic: the whaletail. This Porsche developed 234 horsepower and 246 pound-feet of torque, could go from 0 to 60 in 6.7 seconds, and could cruise at speeds in excess of 155 miles per hour. It was Porsche's fastest car to date and extremely tail-happy, and marked the first significant application of turbocharging in a production automobile.

Today's 911 variant is known internally at Porsche as the 993, to the consumer it is simply the Carrera. A 6-speed manual transmission is mated to the 282-h.p. flat six; the Tiptronic-S automatic shifter is optional.

This was merely the beginning. Within two years the first real 930 came out, boasting a 3.3-liter, intercooled engine that could propel the whaletail to 60 in just 4.9 seconds, up to a top speed of nearly 170 miles per hour. The badge on the back of said tail now simply said "Turbo."

Such a bright star had but a brief history, and 1979 was the final year of 930 availability in the United States. Well, actually, no. The car was reintroduced seven years later, virtually unchanged, with the same four-speed manual shifter (rare in a Porsche) and the same penchant to wiggle under throttle. But by 1989 several modifications had refined the beast; these included a five-speed

Top down, deck up: A 911 cabriolet, circa 1988 vintage, at rest.

The interior of this 911 cabriolet is representative of German high-performance cars: clean lines and luxurious leather bucket seats.

Turbos were unavailable in the United States from 1980 to 1986. As engine output increased, the car received further improvements in suspension and braking.

The dash panel of a 1988 911 Turbo shows, in the tachometer just above the driver's thumb, the all-important boost gauge.

With engine displacement boosted to 3.3 liters by 1978, the 911 Turbo could reach 60 m.p.h. in just 4.9 seconds, assuming one could get through its 4-speed shifter quickly enough.

transmission, an upgraded 285-horsepower engine, a better suspension, improved brakes, and wider road rubber. Special-order conversions of a slant-nose variant had been available since 1981, but this only became an official option with 1987 models.

Turbo sales took a year off in 1990, and a new 911 Turbo was on the scene the following year. Thanks largely to improvements in the exhaust system, this car was the fastest and cleanest-burning Porsche yet.

By 1993, the engine size had grown to 3.6 liters, providing more power (360 horsepower, to be exact) and greater speed, mandating further improvements in suspension and braking. The car was now called the 911 Turbo 3.6, but it was offered for only two years, to be replaced by the current 993 variant, the 930 Carrera Turbo.

It can safely be said that this final manifestation of Porsche's turbocharging tendencies puts the company in the class of truly elite car manufacturers. This is a production car that reaches 60 miles per hour a tenth of a second faster than the million-dollar Ferrari 333SP, a full-blown racing machine. But is this the ultimate Porsche? Probably not. For the ultimate Porsche is no more.

The 930 Carrera Turbo is offered with four-wheel drive in its home German market, and is as close as contemporary buyers can come to enjoying the performance of the legendary 959.

Porsche's revolutionary Tiptronic transmission provides the ease of use of an automatic system with the driver control of a manual. The lever is moved to the right-hand gate while the car is in drive; the driver simply flicks the lever forward and back for up- and downshifts.

Porsche's engineering magicians have, in the 930 Carrera Turbo, produced a production automobile engine that makes the car out-accelerate full-blown racing Ferraris.

The Pirelli rubber found on the 930 Carrera Turbo is aggressive in profile and bears V-shaped channels in the tread design to make the most of the car's four-wheel-drive capability.

Between its fender bulges, wheel flares, and the traditional "whale tail" spoiler, the 930 Carrera Turbo provides a sinuously aggressive appeal.

The business office of the 911 Turbo 3.6 places controls and information in immediate proximity to the driver.

The power-plant of this 1994 911 Turbo 3.6 produced 360 h.p. The car was the immediate predecessor to the 930 Carrera Turbo.

For all of its refinement
in engineering and finish,
the 911 Turbo 3.6 is not
a drive for amateurs, de-
manding vigilance, quick
reflexes, and strength from
those behind the wheel.

The integrated headrest of
the Porsche seat, here in a 911
Turbo 3.6, provides a pleasing
line. Note the position of
the seat adjustment controls.

King of the Hill

The ultimate Porsche was the 959. Its first prototype debuted in 1983 at the Frankfurt Auto Show, drawing intense scrutiny because of its comparatively outrageous appearance (that of a Carrera RS on steroids) and the fact that motive power was administered through all-wheel drive. Running prototypes were being tested three years later, and production was underway by 1987.

Only 230 959s saw the light of day. Two-hundred were divided among "Comfort" and "Sport" models; another 30 Sports were created specifically for the American market. The two models differ in the lack of a passenger-side mirror, automatic ride-height control, air conditioning, electric windows and seats, and soundproofing in the Sport.

Why was the 959 the ultimate Porsche? Simply put, no other production car, built either before or since, could out-accelerate a 959. Zero-to-60 was a matter of only 3.6 seconds' time, and a top speed in excess of 210 miles per hour was possible. There are faster cars in terms of top-end speed (220 is attainable in a Jaguar XJ220, McLaren F1, and special Lamborghinis), but none get there quicker than the 959, and none of these alternatives are truly production automobiles.

Speeds at this range demand particular ride characteristics of an automobile, and the 959 was unique in that it adapted to road conditions automatically. The car had a normal ride height of 4.7 inches, but one of a pair of shock absorbers at each wheel could vary the height to either 5.9 or 7.1 inches, depending on conditions, doing so at set increments.

It is not very easy to catch up to a Porsche 959 and get this view of it. It was said that your grandmother could drive this car at 200 m.p.h. and feel perfectly safe.

Despite a top speed in excess of 210 m.p.h., the 959 was one of the most manageable Porsches ever built, thanks to full-time four-wheel drive.

Presenting the undefeated, fastest-accelerating production car of all time—the four-wheel-drive Porsche 959, which could reach 60 m.p.h. in just 3.6 seconds.

The 959 was also one of the most manageable Porsches ever built, thanks to its full-time all-wheel-drive system. The steering column had a switch that the driver could set to a corresponding road condition: dry, wet, snow, or traction. The final setting had both multidisc clutches (one for the front wheels, one for the back) locking up solid, providing maximum traction on slippery surfaces. Backing off to the "snow" setting, for example, would distribute forty percent of the drive power to the front wheels, and sixty percent to the rear, a ratio that matched perfectly with the car's weight distribution. "Dry" and "wet" modes both had a variable front/rear torque split range from 40/60 at constant speeds, to about 20/80 under full acceleration, depending on dynamic weight distribution.

The end result was a car which, it was said, your grandmother could drive in a rainstorm at 200 miles per hour and feel perfectly safe. Of course, a pressure loss at these speeds could do Grandma in, so the cast-magnesium wheels were fitted with pressure sensors to detect hairline cracks.

Such capacities were obviously suited to race conditions, and indeed, the 959 was an adaptation of a car Porsche had developed for rallying (thus the all-wheel drive). The racing regulations led to the development of a truly unique powerplant, a *water-cooled*, 2.9-liter flat 6 with twin sequential turbochargers. Even with this relatively small engine, the 959 was good for 450 horsepower.

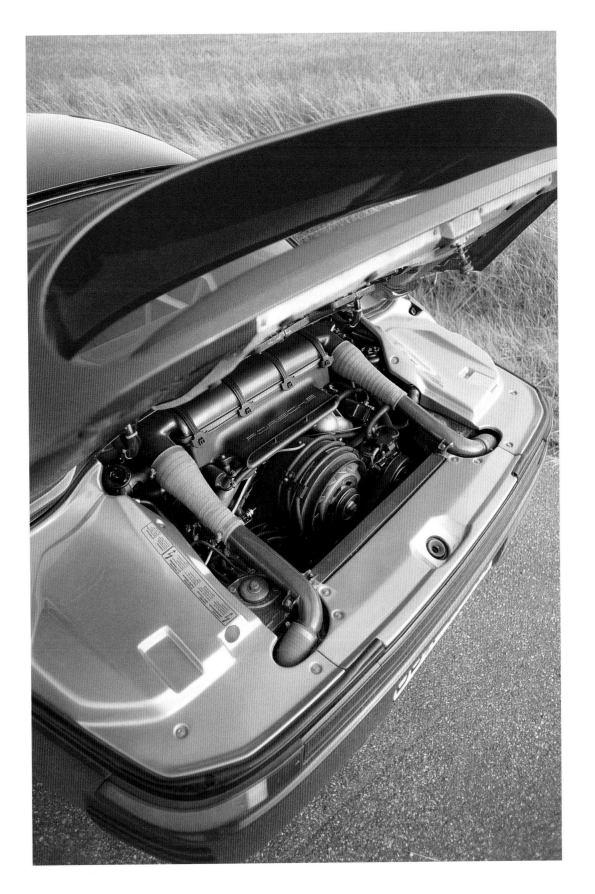

FOLLOWING PAGE: The interior of the 959 coddles passengers in typical Porsche creature comforts; the dash includes a switch that adjusts the ride height of the car according to conditions.

A unique Porsche powerplant—a water-cooled, twin-turbocharged flat-six displacing 2.9 liters—provided 450 h.p. in the 959.

The rear decklid of this Boxster
prototype opens to reveal—
surprise!—luggage space.
A separate cover in the floor
is removed to provide access to
the low-maintenance engine.

An interesting update to the
company's traditional dashboard
design is found in the showcar
prototype of the Porsche Boxster.

Today's Top Banana . . .

For this writer, the ultimate Porsche produced today is one that draws on the company's past, in terms of styling cues, and blends these with state-of-the-art technology. Ironically, it is also the most affordable Porsche: the 986 Boxster.

Designed and developed in just over three years, the new Boxster is a sensational little two-seat roadster whose lines bring back memories of the original Boxsters of the 1950s. Created with a goal to list under $40,000, the car's first-year allotment was immediately accounted for following its late-1996 introduction.

The Boxster has a mid-engine configuration, providing a degree of safety and balance not found in the 911 and its successors. The 2.5-liter, 6-cylinder engine is also water cooled, and, working through either a five-speed manual or a new five-speed Tiptronic gearbox (actuated by thumb through steering-wheel mounted buttons, like a Formula One car), it can propel the little Porsche to a top speed of 155 miles per hour.

A mid-engined car, the Boxster's lines are strongly reminiscent of the company's 550 Spyder from the 1950s.

The cast wheels of the Porsche Boxster have specially shaped spokes that promote cooling of the braking system.

The engine is designed to be virtually maintenance free. It uses hydraulic tappets, long-life spark plugs, direct ignition, and automatic belt tighteners. Still, should fluid levels need to be checked and replenished, the engine is accessible through a service panel in the rear cargo bay.

The mid-engine layout offers a low center of gravity, which makes for agile and secure handling. Steering automatically adjusts axially, according to the needs of the driver at the moment, providing a remarkable degree of precision. The lightweight front-strut and multilink rear suspension uses a variation of the Weissach axle first found in the 928. Toe-out in front and toe-in in back encourage mild understeer (being a Porsche, the car has to be a little tail-happy) at the limit, while keeping a lid on lift-off oversteer. With the wheels mounted wide and in the corners, the chassis is very well mannered.

The Boxster is also the most functional Porsche yet, as the engine configuration allows for large storage compartments. Two suitcases will fit in the nose, and two sets of golf clubs can fit in back. An optional roof storage system that can be used with the top up or down (it attaches to the rear side panels) is available, and can hold up to 165 pounds of gear.

Speaking of the top, it's soft and fully retractable by electrics in 12 seconds. An optional removable hardtop nicely harmonizes with the car's appearance.

The chassis is Kevlar reinforced for safety and strength. The car was designed with programmed deformation zones and an integrated roll-protection system, and uses monoblock brake calipers, based on racing units, that bring the car to a dead halt time after time with very little fading.

The 993 series updates Porsche's long-held "bug-eye" appearance by fairing the headlamps more gradually into the fender.

The Boxster prototype provides a showcase for hints as to what Porsche's future designs might incorporate. The ovoid brushed aluminum cover for the shift gate is particularly attractive.

. . . And Tomorrow's

And the ultimate Porsche of tomorrow? As this book was going to press, the newest bearer of the 911 legacy, the 996 series, was set to be unveiled. The first offering, the 996 Carrera Coupe, was to be released in September 1997, with its cabriolet mate hitting the showrooms four months later. The 996 is a larger car than the current 993 in almost every respect, and was to do away with Porsche's air-cooled engine forever.

Longtime Porschephiles might shed a tear at this development, but the company isn't giving up on tradition entirely. The 290-horsepower, 3.4-liter unit will still be found in the car's tail, confounding rationalists and delighting enthusiasts, as its predecessors have for the past forty or so years.

The 2.5-liter six found in the Porsche Boxster uses hydraulic tappets, long-life spark plugs, direct ignition, and automatic belt tighteners to minimize maintenance.

The Porsche Boxster, in production guise, varies only slightly in appearance from the prototype, but still shows its shared heritage with the Spyder (rear).

Index

JORGE LUIS BORGES

Modern Critical Views

These and other titles in preparation

Modern Critical Views

JORGE LUIS BORGES

Edited and with an introduction by
Harold Bloom
Sterling Professor of the Humanities
Yale University

CHELSEA HOUSE PUBLISHERS ◇ 1986
New York ◇ New Haven ◇ Philadelphia

Library of Congress Cataloging-in-Publication Data
Main entry under title:

Jorge Luis Borges.

   (Modern critical views)
   Bibliography: p.
   Includes index.
   1. Borges, Jorge Luis, 1899–   – Criticism and
interpretation – Addresses, essays, lectures.
I. Bloom Harold.   II. Series.
PQ7797.B635Z7394 1986   863   85-29056
ISBN 0-87754-721-1 (alk. paper)

Contents

Editor's Note

This book offers a representative selection of the best criticism so far devoted to the writings of the Argentine master, Jorge Luis Borges. It begins with the editor's introduction, originally published in 1969, but presenting a view of both the strength and limitations of Borges' achievement that still seems valid today.

The volume then reprints, in chronological order of publication, a major sequence of what can be called Borgesian receptions. This begins with Thomas R. Hart, Jr.'s account of Borges' own literary criticism, emphasizing the powerful skepticism that the criticism shares with Borges' fictions. Paul de Man's astute, characteristically ironic apprehension of Borgesian irony follows, setting a standard that subsequent criticism of Borges has failed to attain, but then de Man increasingly is seen as one of the handful of major critics in our time.

The readings of "Death and the Compass," "Emma Zunz" and "The God's Script" by Louis Murillo, and of "The Immortal" by Ronald J. Christ, share a concern for Borgesian hermeticism, whether metaphysical or literary. Ultimate hermeticism, the Jewish Kabbalah, is charted by Jaime Alazraki, who finds in Kabbalah the principle of reading old texts afresh that generates Borgesian writing. James E. Irby, studying the Borgesian idealism in relation to the vision of Utopia, centers upon the story "Tlön, Uqbar, Orbis Tertius," which he reads in the mode of his epigraph from Derrida: "There is nothing outside the text."

The later phase of Borges' stories, from 1966 on, is the subject of Carter Wheelock's essay, which finds both gain and loss in the later, more direct mode of narration. Emir Rodríguez-Monegal, the leading authority on Borges, also emphasizes issues of transition in Borgesian symbolism, as its maker himself wearies of such prevalence and yet cannot write in its absence.

Borges, as the precursor of post-Structuralist criticism, has inspired such criticism from the early response of Paul de Man through the recent comparison of Borges to Derrida by the Cuban-American deconstructionist Roberto

González-Echevarría. Two such commentaries, by Alicia Borinsky on Borgesian repetition, and by John Sturrock on disjunctions and doublings in Borges, complement one another in advancing our awareness of Borges' labyrinthine language-traps.

In a reading of three Borgesian sonnets, Nancy B. Mandlove returns us to Borges' conviction that only the most traditional metaphors are valid, a conviction featured also in Shlomith Rimmon-Kenan's examination of doubles and counterparts in the crucial tale "The Garden of Forking Paths." A brief analysis of the Borgesian labyrinth, by Ricardo Gutiérrez-Mouat, reaches a parallel conclusion that there never can be an arrival at the center in Borges' work.

With the account of Borges' early Ultraist poetry by Thorpe Running, we are returned to the question of Borgesian origins. Finally, the essay by Roberto González-Echevarría, translated by the author and published here in English for the first time, brings together Borges and Derrida as heroic reconstructors of literature, despite all appearances otherwise.

Introduction

For the gnostic in Borges, as for the heresiarch in his mythic Uqbar, "mirrors and fatherhood are abominable because they multiply and disseminate that universe," the visible but illusory labyrinth of men. Gnostics rightly feel at ease with Jung, and very unhappy with Freud, as Borges does, and no one need be surprised when the ordinarily gentlemanly and subtle Argentine dismisses Freud "either as a charlatan or as a madman," for whom "it all boils down to a few rather unpleasant facts." Masters of the tale and the parable ought to avoid the tape-recorder, but as Borges succumbed, an admirer may be grateful for the gleaning of a few connections between images.

The gnostic gazes into the mirror of the fallen world and sees, not himself, but his dark double, the shadowy haunter of his phantasmagoria. Since the ambivalent God of the gnostics balances good and evil in himself, the writer dominated by a gnostic vision is morally ambivalent also. Borges is imaginatively a gnostic, but intellectually a skeptical and naturalistic humanist. This division, which has impeded his art, making of him a far lesser figure than gnostic writers like Yeats and Kafka, nevertheless has made him also an admirably firm moralist, as these taped conversations show.

Borges has written largely in the spirit of Emerson's remark that the hint of the dialectic is more valuable than the dialectic itself. My own favorite among his tales, the cabbalistic "Death and the Compass," traces the destruction of the Dupin-like Erik Lönnrot, whose "reckless discernment" draws him into the labyrinthine trap set by Red Scharlach the Dandy, a gangster worthy to consort with Babel's Benya Krik. The greatness of Borges is in the aesthetic dignity both of Lönnrot, who at the point of death criticizes the labyrinth of his entrapment as having redundant lines, and of Scharlach, who just before firing promises the detective a better labyrinth, when he hunts him in some other incarnation.

The critics of the admirable Borges do him violence by hunting him as Lönnrot pursued Scharlach, with a compass, but he has obliged us to choose his own images for analysis. Freud tells us that: "In a psychoanalysis the physician always gives his patient (sometimes to a greater and sometimes to a lesser extent) the conscious anticipatory image by the help of which he is put in a position to recognise and to grasp the unconscious material." We are to remember that Freud speaks of therapy, and of the work of altering ourselves, so that the analogue we may find between the images of physician and romancer must be an imperfect one. The skillful analyst moreover, on Freud's example, gives us a single image, and Borges gives his reader a myriad; but only mirror, labyrinth, compass will be gazed at here.

Borges remarks of the first story he wrote, "Pierre Menard, Author of the Quixote," that it gives a sensation of tiredness and skepticism, of "coming at the end of a very long literary period." It is revelatory that this was his first tale, exposing his weariness of the living labyrinth of fiction even as he ventured into it. Borges is a great theorist of poetic influence; he has taught us to read Browning as a precursor of Kafka, and in the spirit of this teaching we may see Borges himself as another Childe Roland coming to the Dark Tower, while consciously not desiring to accomplish the Quest. Are we also condemned to see him finally more as a critic of romance than as a romancer? When we read Borges—whether his essays, poems, parables, or tales—do we not read glosses upon romance, and particularly on the skeptic's self-protection against the enchantments of romance?

Borges thinks he has invented one new subject for a poem—in his poem "Limits"—the subject being the sense of doing something for the last time, seeing something for the last time. It is extraordinary that so deeply read a man-of-letters should think this, since most strong poets who live to be quite old have written on just this subject, though often with displacement or concealment. But it is profoundly self-revelatory that a theorist of poetic influence should come to think of this subject as his own invention, for Borges has been always the celebrator of things-in-their-farewell, always a poet of loss. Though he has comforted himself, and his readers, with the wisdom that we can lose only what we never had, he has suffered the discomfort also of knowing that we come to recognize only what we have encountered before, and that all recognition is self-recognition. All loss is of ourselves, and even the loss of falling-out of love is, as Borges would say, the pain of returning to others, not to the self. Is this the wisdom of romance, or of another mode entirely?

What Borges lacks, despite the illusive cunning of his labyrinths, is precisely the extravagance of the romancer; he does not trust his own vagrant impulses. He sees himself as a modestly apt self-marshaller, but he is another Oedipal self-destroyer. His addiction to the self-protective economy and overt knowingness of his art is his own variety of the Oedipal anxiety, and the pattern of his tales betrays throughout an implicit dread of family-romance. The gnostic mirror of nature reflects for him only Lönnrot's labyrinth "of a single line which is invisible and unceasing," the line of all those enchanted mean streets that fade into the horizon of the Buenos Aires of his phantasmagoria. The reckless discerner who is held by the symmetries of his own mythic compass has never been reckless enough to lose himself in a story, to our loss, if not to his. His extravagance, if it still comes, will be a fictive movement away from the theme of recognition, even against that theme, and towards a larger art. His favorite story, he says, is Hawthorne's "Wakefield," which he describes as being "about the man who stays away from home all those years."

THOMAS R. HART, JR.

Borges' Literary Criticism

Outside the Spanish-speaking world, Jorge Luis Borges is known almost exclusively as a writer of short stories. His books of essays, with a few exceptions, have not yet been translated. Yet the short stories, as Ana María Barrenechea has pointed out, form a relatively small part of Borges' work; most of them were written during a period of some fifteen years, from the middle thirties to the early fifties. Borges' career as an essayist, on the other hand, begins with the publication of *Inquisiciones* [*Inquisitions*] in 1925 and continues without a breakdown to the publication of *El hacedor* [*Dreamtigers*] in 1960. Though he has written, or at least published, hardly any new works of fiction in the past ten years, he remains active as a poet and essayist.

The value of Borges' essays has been, and continues to be, hotly debated by critics. There is surely much less agreement about their worth than about that of his short stories. While the lasting value of the essays may well be largely in the light they throw on the mind of the artist who created the stories, they are, nevertheless, of considerable interest in themselves. Many of the themes found in Borges' poems and stories appear also in the essays; some, already present in his youthful writings, recur again and again in his later books. Borges' thought, however, has not remained static. In this paper I shall attempt to trace the development of some of his central ideas on the nature of literature and of literary criticism.

The most important influence on Borges' literary criticism is doubtless that of Benedetto Croce. Borges, however, has not followed Croce slavishly. Some superficially Crocean passages in his essays reveal important differences in point

From *MLN* 78, no. 5 (December 1963). © 1963 by The Johns Hopkins University Press.

of view, and Borges has not hesitated to make explicit his disagreement with Croce on particular issues. It is, nevertheless, true that Croce is mentioned in Borges' essays more often than any other critic; true, too, that, while Borges' attitude toward certain features of Croce's doctrine has changed with the years, his critical practice has remained consistently true to Crocean principles.

Borges' first book of essays, *Inquisiciones*, published in 1925, presents an apparent exception. Croce is not mentioned and the idea of poetry which Borges defends does not seem specifically Crocean. There are, however, as we shall see, a number of passages in the book which, if not drawn from Croce himself, do suggest substantial agreement with his views.

Borges explicitly declares his adherence to Croce's theory of art as expression in an essay, "La simulación de la imagen" ["The Simulation of the Image"], first published in the Buenos Aires newspaper *La Prensa* on December 25, 1927, and incorporated in his second book of essays, *El idioma de los argentinos* [*The Language of the Argentines*], in the following year: "Indagar ¿qué es lo estético? es indagar ¿qué otra cosa es lo estético, qué única otra cosa es lo estético? Lo expresivo, nos ha contestado Croce, ya para siempre. El arte es expresión y sólo expresión, postularé aquí [To ask, what is aesthetics?, is to ask, what single other thing is aesthetics? The expressive element, has been Croce's answer. Art is expression and only expression, I will propose here]." In another essay included in the same collection, "Indagación de la palabra" ["Inquiry into the Word"], Borges is just as explicit in *dissenting* from Croce's theory that the ultimate unit of speech is not the word but the sentence and that the latter must be understood, not in the usual grammatical way, but as an expressive organism whose meaning is complete, and which, therefore, may extend from a single exclamation to a long poem. Such a view, Borges insists, is

> psicológicamente. . . insostenible [y] una equivocación psicológica no puede ser un acierto estético. Además, ¿no dejó dicho Schopenhauer que la forma de nuestra inteligencia es el tiempo, línea angostísima que sólo nos presenta la cosas una por una? Lo espantoso de esa estrechez es que los poemas a que alude reveren-cialmente Montolíu-Croce alcanzan unidad en la flaqueza de nuestra memoria, pero no en la tarea sucesiva de quien los escribió ni en la de quien los lee. (Dije espantoso, porque esa heterogeneidad de la sucesión despedaza no sólo las dilatadas composiciones, sino toda página escrita.)

> [psychologically . . . unsustainable (and) a psychological error cannot be a good aesthetic judgment. Besides, did not Schopenhauer say that the shape of our intelligence is time, narrowest of lines that

only presents things to us one by one? The horror of this narrowness is that the poems to which Montolíu-Croce allude reverentially attain unity in the feebleness of our memory, but not in the successive labor of the writer or the reader. (I said "the horror" because that heterogeneity of succession fragments not only the extensive compositions, but any written page.)]

Twelve years later, in the short story "Tlön, Uqbar, Orbis Tertius," we find Borges writing that on his imaginary planet Tlön, "hay poemas famosos compuestos de una sola enorme palabra. Esta palabra integra un *objeto poético creado* por el autor [there are famous poems made up of one enormous word, a word which in truth forms a poetic *object*, the creation of the writer]" (*Ficciones*; [*Ficciones*, tr. A. Reid]).

Croce's identification of art with expression which Borges accepts in this essay is questioned in "La postulación de la realidad" ["The Postulation of Reality"], published in the review *Azul* in 1931. The difference in tone between the two essays is striking. "Hume notó para siempre," Borges begins,

> que los argumentos de Berkeley no admiten la menor réplica y no producen la menor convicción; yo desearía, para eliminar los de Croce, una sentencia no menos educada y mortal. La de Hume no me sirve, porque la diáfana doctrina de Croce tiene la facultad de persuadir, aunque ésta sea da única. Su defecto es ser inmanejable; sirve para cortar una discusión, no para resolverla.
>
> Su fórmula — recordará mi lector — es la identidad de lo estético y de lo expresivo. No la rechazo, pero quiero observar que los escritores de hábito clásico más bien rehuyen lo expresivo.
>
> [Hume noted for all time that Berkeley's arguments do not admit the slightest reply and do not produce the slightest conviction. I would like, in order to eliminate Croce's arguments, a no less gracious and mortal sentence. Hume's does not serve my purpose because Croce's diaphanous doctrine has the power of persuasion, if nothing more. The result is unmanageability: it serves to cut short a discussion, not to resolve it. Croce's formula, my reader will recall, is the identity of the aesthetic and the expressive.]
>
> (*Discusión*; [*Borges, A Reader*, tr. E. R. Monegal and A. Reid])

"Classical" here, as Borges goes on to explain, does not designate the writers of a particular historical period. The classical writer is one who has confidence in the power of the accepted language to say anything he may wish to say: "Distraigo aquí de toda connotación histórica las palabras *clásico* y romántico,

entiendo por ellas dos arquetipos de escritor (dos procederes). El clásico no
desconfía del lenguaje, cree en la suficiente virtud de cada uno de sus signos
[I diverge here from all historical connotations of the words 'classicist' and
'romantic'; by them I understand two archetypes of the writer (two approaches).
The classicist does not distrust language, he believes in the adequate virtue
of each one of its signs]." The classical writer "no escribe los primeros contactos
de la realidad, sino su elaboración final en conceptos [does not write of initial
contacts with reality, but rather of their final conceptual elaboration]"; as
examples, Borges cites Gibbon, Voltaire, Swift, and Cervantes. Such a view
is obviously very different from the Crocean doctrine of intuition, as Borges
himself makes clear: "Pasajes como los anteriores, forman la extensa mayoría
de la literatura mundial, y aun la menos indigna. Repudiarlos para no incomodar
a una fórmula, sería inconducente y ruinoso. Dentro de su notoria ineficacia,
son eficaces; falta resolver esa contradicción [Passages like the previous one
make up the greater part of world literature, even of that which is least
unworthy. To repudiate them in order to accommodate a formula would be
misleading and ruinous. Within their notorious inefficacy, they are efficacious;
that contradiction must be resolved]." Borges attempts to resolve it with the
argument that

> la imprecisión es tolerable o verosímil en la literatura, porque a ella
> propendemos siempre en la realidad. . . . El hecho mismo de percibir,
> de atender, es de orden selectivo: toda atención, toda fijación de
> nuestra conciencia, comporta una deliberada omisión de lo no
> interesante. . . . Nuestro vivir es una serie de adaptaciones, vale decir,
> una educación del olvido.
>
> [imprecision is tolerable or plausible in literature because we are
> always inclined to reality. . . . The very act of perceiving, of heeding,
> is of a selective order; every attention, every fixation of our con-
> science, implies a deliberate omission of that which is uninteresting.
> . . . Our lives are a series of adaptations, that is to say, the educating
> of forgetfulness.]

Readers of Borges' stories may recall the case of Funes *el memorioso* [*the
memorious*], who was incapable of forgetting anything he had once experienced
and equally incapable of grouping his experiences—we might say, in Crocean
language and not without a certain malice, his *intuizioni*—into any more general
categories. As a result poor Funes "no era muy capaz de pensar. Pensar es olvidar
diferencias, es generalizar, abstraer. En el abarrotado mundo de Funes no había
sino detalles, casi inmediatos [was not very capable of thought. To think is
to forget a difference, to generalize, to abstract. In the overly replete world

of Funes there were nothing but details, almost contiguous details]" (*Ficciones*; [*Ficciones*, tr. A. Kerrigan]).

One consequence of Croce's theory of poetry as a perfectly realized expression of an immediate intuition is his rejection of allegory as a literary form. "For Croce," as Orsini explains, "allegory is essentially a kind of cryptography . . . . By an act that is purely arbitrary, and therefore belongs to the sphere of the practical will and not that of the imagination, a writer decides that a certain sign shall stand for a certain thing with which it is not usually connected." Borges presents Croce's argument, with appropriate quotations from the *Estetica* and from *La poesia*, in an essay of 1949, "De las alegorías a las novelas" ["From Allegories to Novels"]. To Croce's denial that allegory can ever be aesthetically successful, Borges opposes Chesterton's view that language is not an adequate instrument for the representation of reality: "Declarado insuficiente el lenguaje, hay lugar para otros; la alegoría puede ser uno de ellos, como la arquitectura o la música [With one form of communication declared to be insufficient, there is room for others; allegory may be one of them, like architecture or music]" (*Otras inquisiciones* [*Borges, A Reader*]). Though Borges begins his essay with the assertion that he believes Croce to be in the right, he later shifts his position and declares that "no sé muy bien cuál de los eminentes contradictores tiene razón; sé que el arte alegórico pareció alguna vez encantador . . . y ahora es intolerable [I am not certain which of the eminent contradictors is right. I know that at one time the allegorical art was considered quite charming . . . and is now intolerable]." Borges' explanation of how allegory came to lose favor with both readers and writers need not concern us here. It will be enough to remark that his sympathy with Chesterton's position is probably greater than it appears to be in this essay; we shall return to this point a little later in connection with Borges' views on the nature of language.

Another, more detailed exposition of Croce's attack on allegory and Chesterton's defense of it may be found in the long essays on Nathaniel Hawthorne, also of 1949. Here again Borges' own position is somewhat ambiguous, though he is, I think, rather more sympathetic to Chesterton than to Croce:

> La alegoría, según esa interpretación desdeñosa [that of Croce,] vendría a ser una adivinanza, más extensa, más lenta y mucho más incómoda que las otras. Sería un género bárbaro o infantil, una distracción de la estética. Croce formuló esa refutación en 1907; en 1904, Chesterton ya la había refutado sin que ayuel lo supiera.
>
> [By that derogatory definition (that of Croce) an allegory would be a puzzle, more extensive, boring, and unpleasant than other

puzzles. It would be a barbaric or puerile genre, an aesthetic sport. Croce wrote that refutation in 1907; Chesterton had already refuted him in 1904 without Croce's knowing it.]

(*Otras inquisiciones;* [*Other Inquisitions*, tr. R. Simms])

Borges, however, still refuses to commit himself fully: "No sé si es válida la tesis de Chesterton; sé que una alegoría es tanto mejor cuanto sea menos reductible a un esquema, a un frío juego de abstracciones [I don't know if Chesterton's thesis is valid; I know that an allegory is the more effective the less it is open to reduction into a schema, into a cold game of abstractions]." There are, he declares, two kinds of writers: those who think in images (Shakespeare, Donne, Victor Hugo) and those who think in abstractions (Julien Benda, Bertrand Russell). Neither group is inherently superior to the other, but difficulties arise when a writer attempts to change groups:

Cuando un abstracto, un razonador, quiere ser también imaginativo, o pasar por tal, occure lo denunciado por Croce. Notamos que un proceso lógico ha sido engalanado y disfrazado por el autor. . . . Es, para citar un ejemplo notorio de esa dolencia, el caso de José Ortega y Gasset, cuyo buen pensamiento queda obstruído por laboriosas y adventicias metáforas.

[When an abstract man, a reasoner, also wants to be imaginative, or to pass as such, then the allegory denounced by Croce occurs. We observe that a logical process has been embellished and disguised by the author. . . . A famous example of that ailment is the case of José Ortega y Gasset, whose good thought is obstructed by difficult and adventitious metaphors.]

Hawthorne is an example of the opposite tendency. It is worth noting that Borges' division of writers into two groups may not be simply a matter of difference in temperament; indeed, his choice of examples suggests that the distinction is rather between creators of imaginative literature and writers who cultivate discursive forms, with the implicit corollary that what is appropriate in one kind of writing will be out of place in another.

Croce's sharp distinction between the poetic and the "practical" personality of the writer has fared much better in Borges' hands than his summary dismissal of the aesthetic possibilities of allegory. There is, however, no evidence that Borges considers the distinction peculiarly Crocean. We find it already in an essay of 1922, "La nadería de la personalidad" ["The Nothingness of Personality"], in which Borges declares that yo, al escribir [estas inquietudes,] sólo soy una certidumbre que inquiere las palabras más aptas para persuadir tu atención. Ese propósito y algunas sensaciones musculares y la visión de la límpida enramada que ponen frente a mi ventana los árboles construyen mi yo actual. . . .

Fuera vanidad suponer que ese agregado psíquico ha menester asirse a un yo para gozar de validez absoluta, a ese conjetural Jorge Luis Borges en cuya lengua cupo tanto sofisma y en cuyos solitarios paseos los atardeceres del suburbio son gratos.

[I upon writing (these uneasy thoughts) am only a certainty that searches for the right words to capture your attention. This goal, and some muscular sensations, and the vision of the clear arbor of trees in front of my window constitute my present self. . . . It would be vanity to suppose that this psychological aggregate needed to take hold of an *I* in order to enjoy absolute validity, to take hold of that conjectural Jorge Luis Borges in whose words could be found such sophistries and who finds such pleasures in his solitary suburban strolls.]

(Inquisiciones)

Borges here insists that many things a writer has said and done may have no bearing at all on his work. There are, however, some books in which the reader's interest is centered on the personality of the writer himself. Whitman is a case in point; another, less obvious perhaps, is Valéry. In an essay, "Valéry cómo simbolo" ["Valéry as Symbol"], written on the occasion of the French poet's death in 1945, Borges compares him with Whitman and declares that although the two seem wholly unlike each other, they are, nevertheless, linked by the fact that "la obra de los dos es menos preciosa como poesía que como signo de un poeta ejemplar, creado por esa obra [the work of the two is less precious as poetry than as a sign of an exemplary poet, created by that work]" (*Otras inquisiciones*). In a later essay, "Nota sobre Walt Whitman" ["Note on Walt Whitman"] of 1947, Borges returns to the same theme and develops it in considerably more detail. His point of departure is Robert Louis Stevenson's remark that "the whole of Whitman's work is deliberate," an observation which, as Borges is careful to point out, has also been made by a number of other critics. The protagonist of *Leaves of Grass* must not be equated with the poet: "Imaginemos que una biografía de Ulises. . . indicara que éste nunca salió de Itaca. La decepción que nos causaría ese libro, felizmente hipotético, es la que causan todas las biografías de Whitman [Imagine that a biography of

Ulysses...indicated that he never left Ithaca. Such a book is fortunately hypothetical, but its particular brand of deception would be the same as the deception in all the biographies of Whitman]" (*Otras inquisiciones;* [*Other Inquisitions*]). Borges has recently returned to the same theme of the distinction between the writer as a man and as a figure in his own works in a brilliant and witty essay, "Borges y yo" ["Borges and I"], where he asserts that

> al otro, a Borges, es a quien le ocurren las cosas....Me gustan los relojes de arena, los mapas, la tipografía del siglo XVIII, el sabor del café y la prosa de Stevenson; el otro comparte esas preferencias, pero de un modo vanidoso que las convierte en atributos de un actor. Sería exagerado afirmar que nuestra relación es hostil; yo vivo, yo me dejo vivir, para que Borges pueda tramar su literatura y esa literatura me justifica....Poco a poco voy cediéndole todo, aunque me consta su perversa costumbre de falsear y magnificar. ...No sé cuál de los dos escribe esta página.

> [It's the other, it's Borges, that things happen to.... I like hour glasses, maps, eighteenth-century typography, the taste of coffee, and Stevenson's prose. The other one shares these preferences with me, but in a vain way that converts them into the attributes of an actor. It would be too much to say that our relations are hostile; I live, I allow myself to live, so that Borges may contrive his literature and that literature justifies my existence.... Little by little I am yielding him everything, although I am well aware of his perverse habit of falsifying and exaggerating....I do not know which of us two is writing this page.]
>
>   (*El hacedor;* [*Dreamtigers*, tr. M. Boyer and H. Morland])

Both in his theoretical writings and in his practical criticism, Croce lays great stress on what he calls "characterization" (*caratterizzazione*). In his studies of individual writers, "the method," as René Wellek has remarked, "is always one and the same. Croce selects what he considers poetry, pushes aside what is something else, and tries to define a leading sentiment, something like Taine's *faculté maîtresse*, which allows him to characterize by constant qualification." Here again, Borges' critical practice is much like Croce's, though, as with the distinction between the poetic and the practical personality of the writer, there is no reason to speak of the influence of Croce on Borges. Borges himself sets forth the critic's problem in an essay, "Menoscabo y grandeza de Quevedo" ["The Littleness and Greatness of Quevedo"], published in 1924 in the *Revista de Occidente*:

Aquí está su labor [that of Quevedo], con suaparente numerosidad
de propósitos, ¿cómo reducirla a unidad y curajarla en un símbolo?
La artimaña de quien lo despedaza según la varia actividad que
ejerició no es apta para concertar la despareja plenitud de su obra.
Desbandar a Quevedo en irreconciliables figuraciones de novelista,
de poeta, de teólogo, de sufridor estoico y de eventual pasquinador,
es empeño baldio si no adunamos luego con firmeza todas esas
vislumbres.

[Here is his work (that of Quevedo), with its apparent multiplicity
of intentions—how can we reduce it to a unity and sum it up in
a symbol? The artifice of whoever analyzes it according to Quevedo's
various activities, is not adequate to harmonize the uneven plenitude
of his work. To break up Quevedo into the irreconcilable roles
of novelist, poet, theologian, stoic sufferer and occasional satirist
is a futile task if afterwards we do not bring these glimmerings firmly
together.]

(Inquisiciones)

He concludes that the unity of Quevedo's work lies not in its subject matter,
which is immensely varied, but in the author's constant preoccupation with
exploiting the resources offered him by language: "Casi todos sus libros son
cotidianos en el plan, pero sobresalientes en los verbalismos de hechura [Almost
all of his books are quotidian in their project, but outstanding in their verbal
workmanship]" (*Inquisiciones*). The same method is employed in many of Borges'
later essays. Thus, the essay on Whitman, to which we have already referred,
is centered on the conception of Whitman as a conscious artist who deliberately
creates his own personality as poet in the same way that a novelist might create
a personality for his protagonist. Nor is the method limited solely to studies
of individual writers; the *caratteristica*, to use Croce's term, of the *gaucho* poetry
of the nineteenth century is that it presents the life of the cowboy as it appeared
to a sophisticated observer from Buenos Aires or Montevideo:

Derivar la literatura gauchesca de su materia, el gaucho, es una
confusión que desfigura la notoria verdad. No menos necesario para
la formación de ese género que la pampa y que las cuchillas fue
el carácter urbano de Buenos Aires y de Montevideo. . . . De la
azarosa conjunción de esos dos estilos vitales, del asombro que uno
produjo en otro, nació la literatura gauchesca.

[To derive "gauchesca" literature from its subject, the "gaucho," is
a confusion that distorts the well-known truth no less necessary

for the formation of this genre than the "pampa" and the knives
was for the urban character of Buenos Aires and Montevideo.
. . . From the fortuitous conjunction of these two vital styles, from
the wonder that one produced in the other, "gauchesca" literature
was born.]

(*Discusión*)

Since, for Croce, art is a perfect realization of the artist's intuition, form
and content are inseparable. Croce has no interest in the forms of poetic
language, since the forms—not only metrical and stanzaic forms, but also such
things as metaphor and simile—are not poetic in themselves; they become so
only when they are used to express the artist's intuition, that is, when they
are combined with an appropriate content. Borges' position is identical with
Croce's, and he does not hesitate to acknowledge his debt. In *El idioma de
los argentinos*, surely the most consistently Crocean of all his books, he declares
that "la metáfora no es poética por ser metáfora, sino por la expresión alconzada.
No insisto en la disputa; todo sentidor de Croce estará conmigo [metaphor
is not poetry because it is a metaphor, but because of the achieved expression.
Any reader of Croce will agree with me]." In an essay of 1931, "La supersticiosa
ética del lector" ["The Superstitious Ethic of the Reader"], Borges returns to
the same point and develops it at much greater length. Most readers today,
he argues, "entienden por estilo no la eficacia o la ineficacia de una página,
sino las habilidades aparentes del escritor: sus comparaciones, su acústica, los
episodios de su punctuación y de su sintaxis [understand by style not the efficacy
or inefficacy of a page, but the apparent abilities of the writer: his comparisons,
his acoustics, the episodes of his punctuation and syntax]" (*Discusión*).

If those who insist that "la numerosidad de metáfores [es] una virtud [the
plurality of metaphors is a virtue]" (*Idioma*) are in the wrong, so are those who
consider the number of words in a particular language a valid index of its
possibilities as an instrument of aesthetic expression, a fault, incidentally, which
Borges finds particularly common among peninsular Spanish critics. Here again,
just as with metaphors, "la numerosidad de representaciones es lo que importa,
no la de signos [the plurality of representations is what matters, not that of
signs]," and we find Borges once more proclaiming the unity of form and content:
"la sueñera mental y la concepción acústica del estilo son las que fomentan
sinónimos: palabras que sin cambiar de idea cambian de unido [the mental
drowsiness and the acoustic conception of style are what encourage synonyms:
words that change sound without a change in idea]."

The same point, combined with another which is of great importance for
Borges' thinking about the nature of literary language, is made in the essay,
"Indagación de la palabra," of 1927:

Es una sentencia de Joubert, citada favorablemente por Matías Arnold.... Trata de Bossuet y es así: *Más que un hombre es una naturaleza humana, con la moderación de un santo, la justicia de un obispo, la prudencia de un doctor y el poderío de un gran espíritu.* Aquí Joubert jugó a las variantes no sin descaro; escribió (y acaso pensó) *la moderación de un santo* y acto continuo esa fatalidad que hay en el lenguaje se adueñó de él y eslabonó tres cláusulas más, todas de aire simétrico y todas rellenadas con negligencia. Es como si afirmara... *con la moderación de un santo, el qué sé yo de un quién sabe qué y el cualquier cosa de un gran espíritu*.... Si la prosa, con su mínima presencia de ritmo, trae estas servidumbres, ¿cuáles no traerá el verso?

[It is a pronouncement of Joubert, quoted favorably by Matthew Arnold.... It deals with Bossuet and it goes as follows: "More than a man, he is a human nature, with the moderation of a saint, the justice of a bishop, the prudence of a doctor, and the might of a great spirit." Here Joubert gambled unashamedly with the variants; he wrote (and perhaps thought) "the moderation of a saint" and immediately that fatalism that exists in language took hold of him and he forged three more clauses, all with asymmetrical flavor, and all stuffed with carelessness. It is as if he affirmed... "with the moderation of a saint, the what have you of a who knows what and the anything of a great spirit...." If prose with the minimal presence in it brings these bondages, does not verse bring them with it?]

(*Idioma*)

Borges here sees language as a dangerous invitation to the writer to exploit the resources which it offers him without regard for what he himself wishes to say. The danger is obviously greater in verse than in prose, a point to which Borges returns again and again. In his prologue to *Indice de la nueva poesía argentina [Index of the New Argentine Poetry]*, of 1926, we already find him saying that "la rima es aleatoria. Ya don Francisco de Quevedo se burló de ella por la esclavitud que impone al poeta [rhyme is fortuitous. Don Francisco de Quevedo already made fun of it for the servitude that it imposes on the poet]." In "La supersticiosa ética del lector," he declares that "ya se practica la lectura en silencio, *sintoma venturoso* [italics mine]. Ya hay lector callado de versos. De esa capacidad sigilosa a una escritura puramente ideográfica—directa communicación de experiencias, no de sonidos—hay una distancia incansable, pero siempre menos dilatada que el porvenir [reading is now practiced in silence, *'felicitous symptom.'* There now exist silent readers of verse. From that silent capacity to a purely ideographic writing—direct communication of experience and not of sound—there is an enduring distance, but always less vast than the future]" (*Discusión*). The danger, however, is present in prose, too, as Borges demonstrates in his analysis of the sentence he quotes from Joubert; it is a consequence, not simply of the need to fit one's thought into a given metrical scheme, but of the need to express it in a pre-existing language.

Every language, Borges insists, represents an attempt to inject some order into our perceptions of the reality which surrounds us, to simplify it and make it intelligible; we should not be too much surprised if this collective vision, the project of centuries of development, should fail to correspond exactly to the pattern imposed upon reality by the will and needs of any individual. Here Borges, by stressing the writer's subservience to language, his inability to say precisely what he wants to say, differs sharply from Croce, who contends that the writer creates his own language anew, on the basis of his private intuitions. Borges' conception of language as a check upon the writer's freedom has important consequences for his theory of literature. Since the writer's ability to create something wholly new is, for Borges, limited by the language he uses, he may as well resign himself to repeating, with minor variations, things others have said before him:

> Ni [Spinoza] con su metafísica geometrizada, ni [Lulio] con su alfabeto traducible en palabras y éstas en oraciones, consiguió leudir el lenguaje. . . . Sólo pueden soslayarlo los ángeles, que conversan por especies inteligibles: es decir, por representaciones directas y sin ministerio alguno verbal.
>
> ¿Y nosotros, los nunca ángeles, los verbales, los que en este bajo relativo suelo escribimos, los que sotopensamos que ascender a letras de molde es la máxima realidad de las experiencias? Que la resignación, virtud a que debemos resignarnos—sea con nosotros. Ella será nuestro destino: hacernos a la sintaxis, a su concatenación traicionera, a la imprecisión, a los talveces, a los demasiados énfasis, a los peros, al hemisferio de mentira y de sombra en nuestro decir. . . .
>
> No de intuiciones originales—hay pocas—, sino de variaciones y casualidades y travesuras, suele alimentarse la lengua. La lengua: es decir humilladoramente el pensar.
>
> [Neither Spinoza with his geometricized metaphysics nor Lull with his alphabet which translates into words, and these into prayers, managed to escape language. . . . Only the angels who converse by

means of intelligible species can evade language: that is to say by means of direct representations and without any verbal aid.

And we, the never angels, the verbal ones, we who in these lower regions write, we who understand that to ascend to printed letters is the highest of experience? Let resignation, a virtue to which we should resign ourselves—be with us. This will be our destiny: to adapt ourselves to syntax, to the traitorous concatenations, to imprecision, to uncertainty, to overemphasis, to the reservations, to the hemisphere of deceit and shadows in our speech.

Not with original intuitions—of which there are few—but with variations and coincidences and playfulness, language tends to nurture itself. Language: that is to say, humbly, thought.]

(*Idioma*)

The idea that the writer cannot hope to create anything wholly new becomes increasingly frequent in Borges' later essays. In *Inquisiciones*, he had defined the creation of a metaphor as "la inquisición de cualidades comunes a los dos terminos de la imagen, cualidades que son de todos conocidas, pero cuya coincidencia en dos conceptos lejanos no ha sido vislumbrado hasta el instante de hacerse la metáfora [inquisition of qualities common to two aspects of an image, qualities which are widely known, but in which coincidence of two distant concepts is not realized until the moment in which they become metaphor]." In an essay on Norse poetry, "Las kenningar," first published as a separate book in 1933 and later included in the collection of essays *Historia de la eternidad* [*History of Eternity*], he adopts a somewhat different position. Though he praises certain kennings because they can awaken a sense of wonder in the reader ("nos extrañan del mundo [they make the world alien to us]"), he is aware that the kennings do not in most cases represent original poetic intuitions, but simply the use of a learned language; their apparent originality is an illusion created by our ignorance (*Eternidad*). In the lecture on Hawthorne, of 1949, we find him doubting whether a really new metaphor can be found at all: "es quizá un error suponer que puedan inventarse metáforas. Las verdaderas, las que formulan íntimas conexiones entre una imagen y otra, han existido siempre; las que aún podemos inventar son las falsas, las que no vale la pena inventar [perhaps it is a mistake to suppose that metaphors can be invented. The real ones, those that formulate intimate connection between one image and another, have always existed; those we still can invent are the false ones, which are not worth inventing]" (*Otras inquisiciones*; [*Other Inquisitions*]). "La esfera de Pascal" [Pascal's Fearful Sphere"] of 1951, begins with the suggestion that "quizá la historia universal es la historia de unas cuantas metáforas [perhaps universal history is the history of a few metaphors]" and ends with a slightly more precise statement of the same theme: "quizá la historia universal es la historia de la diversa entonación de algunas metáforas [perhaps universal history is the history of the diverse intonation of some metaphors]" (*Otras inquisiciones*). Borges thus reaffirms his adherence to a point of view fundamentally identical with that he had expressed in "Indagación de la palabra" nearly a quarter of a century earlier: "No de intuiciones originales—hay pocas—, sino de variaciones y casualidades y travesuras, suele alimentarse la lengua [Not with original intuitions—of which there are few—but with variations and coincidences and playfulness, language tends to nurture itself]" (*Idioma*).

Borges' criticism has been attacked on the ground that it rarely aims primarily at the interpretation of a given work but rather uses the work as a point of departure for reflections on all sorts of philosophical problems. The charge is not without foundation; one might perhaps counter it by saying that Borges is less a literary critic than a theorist of literature. Indeed, I think it can be argued that the remarks on books and writers scattered throughout Borges' essays do add up to some clearly definable and coherent ideas on the nature of literature and the function of criticism. These ideas may be expressed in the form of three postulates, though, of course, any such schematization of Borges' thought, expressed in dozens of essays and over a period of almost forty years, runs a grave risk of distorting it by making it seem more systematic than it really is.

The first postulate is that a work of literature is an indivisible whole; the critic cannot profitably consider form and content in isolation from one another. But this does not mean that the union of form and content is always perfectly realized; Borges' objection to the sentence from Joubert, already cited, is that the four parallel phrases do not correspond to a fourfold development of the writer's thought. It does mean that the critic must be concerned, not with form in itself, but in its relation to the whole work.

The second postulate is that a work of literature is self-contained; its critical corollary is that the critic's interest should be centered on the work itself. From this comes Borges' distinction between the writer as a man and as a "mask" in his own writings. (I use this somewhat unsatisfactory term rather than "character" since I wish it to include the implicit "speaker" of an essay or lyric.)

The last, and most important, of the three postulates is closely bound up with the second; it is that a work of literature may best by understood, not as an assertion about something outside itself, but as a hypothesis about something whose existence is neither affirmed nor denied. Borges' critical position here comes quite close to that of Northrop Frye, for whom literature is "a body of hypothetical creations which is not necessarily involved in the worlds of truth and fact, nor necessarily withdrawn from them, but which may enter into any kind of relationship to them, ranging from the most to the least explicit."

Borges' theory of the autonomy of the literary work is a consequence of his more general theory that man can never truly know reality:

> Notoriamente no hay clasificación del universo que no sea arbitraria y conjetural. La razón es muy simple: no sabemos qué cosa es el universo . . . . Cabe sospechar que no hay universo en el sentido orgánico, unificador, que tiene esa ambiciosa palabra. Si lo hay, falta conjeturar su propósito; falta conjeturar las palabras, las definiciones, las etimologías, las sinonimias, del secreto diccionario de Dios.

> [Obviously there is no classification of the universe that is not arbitrary and conjectural. The reason is very simple: we do not know what the universe is. . . . We must suspect that there is no universe in the organic, unifying sense inherent in that ambitious word. If there is, we must conjecture its purpose; we must conjecture the words, the definitions, the etymologies, the synonymies of God's secret dictionary.]

> (*Otras inquisiciones;* [*Other Inquisitions*])

Borges' philosophical position is thus fundamentally skeptical, as he himself recognizes. In the epilogue to *Otras inquisiciones* he declares that in reading the proofs he has noted "una [tendencia] a estimar las ideas religiosas o filosóficas por su valor estético y aun por lo que encierran de singular y de maravilloso. Esto es, quizá, indicio de un escepticismo esencial [a (tendency) to evaluate religious or philosophical ideas on the bases of their aesthetic worth and even for what is singular and marvelous about them. Perhaps this is an indication of a basic skepticism]." Borges surely would agree with those librarians mentioned in his story "La biblioteca de Babel" ["The Library of Babel"] who "repudian la supersticiosa y vana costumbre de buscar sentido en los libros y la equiparan a la de buscarlo en los sueños o en las líneas caóticas de la mano [repudiate the vain superstitious custom of seeking any sense in the books and compare it to looking for meaning in dreams or in the chaotic lines of one's hands]" (*Ficciones;* [*Ficciones*, tr. A. Kerrigan]). He is like the metaphysicians of his own imaginary Tlön who "no buscan la verdad ni siquiera la verosimilitud: buscan el asombro. Juzgan que la metafísica es una rama de la literatura fantástica [are not looking for truth, nor even for an approximation of it; they are after a kind of amazement. They consider metaphysics a branch of fantastic literature]"

(*Ficciones*; [*Ficciones*; tr. A. Reid]). The remark applies with equal force to Borges'
own, often fantastic, stories, and to his criticism of other men's writings, of
whatever kind. But it is worth stressing that Borges' critical principles, despite
the fanciful way in which they are usually presented, are sound enough, and
that they do form a coherent, if not a comprehensive, theory of literature.

PAUL DE MAN

A Modern Master

Empty eyeballs knew
That knowledge increases unreality, that
Mirror on mirror mirrored is all the
Show

—W. B. YEATS

Although he has been writing poems, stories, and critical essays of the highest quality since 1923, the Argentinian writer Jorge Luis Borges is still much better known in Latin America than in the U. S. For the translator of John Peale Bishop, Hart Crane, E. E. Cummings, William Faulkner, Edger Lee Masters, Robert Penn Warren, and Wallace Stevens, this neglect is somewhat unfair. There are signs however, that he is being discovered in this country with some of the same enthusiasm that greeted him in France, where he received major critical attention, and has been very well translated. Several volumes of translations in English have recently appeared, including a fine edition of his most recent book *El hacedor* (*Dreamtigers*) and a new edition of *Labyrinths*, which first appeared in 1962. American and English critics have called him one of the greatest writers alive today, but have not as yet (so far as I know) made substantial contributions to the interpretation of his work. There are good reasons for this delay. Borges is a complex writer, particularly difficult to place. Commentators cast around in vain for suitable points of comparison and his own avowed literary admirations add to the confusion. Like Kafka and contemporary French existential writers, he is often seen as a moralist, in rebellion against the times. But such an approach is misleading.

It is true that, especially in his earlier works, Borges writes about villains:

From *New York Review of Books* 3, no. 6 (November 5, 1964). © 1964 by the Estate of Paul de Man.

The collection *History of Infamy* (*Historia universal de la infamia, 1935*) contains an engaging gallery of scoundrels. But Borges does not consider infamy primarily as a moral theme; the stories in no way suggest an indictment of society or of human nature or of destiny. Nor do they suggest the lighthearted view of Gide's Nietzschean hero Lafcadio. Instead, infamy functions here as an aesthetic, formal principle. The fictions literally could not have taken shape but for the presence of villainy at their very heart. Many different worlds are conjured up—cotton plantations along the Mississippi, pirate-infested South seas, the Wild West, the slums of New York, Japanese courts, the Arabian desert, etc.—all of which would be shapeless without the ordering presence of a villain at the center.

A good illustration can be taken from the imaginary essays on literary subjects that Borges was writing at the same time as the *History of Infamy*. Borrowing the stylistic conventions of scholarly critical writing, the essays read like a combination of Empson, Paulhan, and *PMLA*, except that they are a great deal more succinct and devious. In an essay on the translations of *The Thousand and One Nights*, Borges quotes an impressive list of examples showing how translator after translator mercilessly cut, expanded, distorted, and falsified the original in order to make it conform to his own and his audience's artistic and moral standards. The list, which amounts in fact to a full catalogue of human sins, culminates in the sterling character of Enna Littmann, whose 1923–1928 edition is scrupulously exact: "Incapable, like George Washington, of telling a lie, his work reveals nothing but German candor." This translation is vastly inferior, in Borges' eyes, to all others. It lacks the wealth of literary associations that allows the other, villainous translators to give their language depth, suggestiveness, ambiguity—in a word, style. The artist has to wear the mask of the villain in order to create a style.

So far, so good. All of us know that the poet is of the devil's party and that sin makes for better stories than virtue. It takes some effort to prefer *La nouvelle Héloise* to *Les liaisons dangereuses* or, for that matter, to prefer the second part of the *Nouvelle Héloise* to the first. Borges' theme of infamy could be just another form of *fin-de-siècle* aestheticism, a late gasp of romantic agony. Or, perhaps worse, he might be writing out of moral despair as an escape from the trappings of style. But such assumptions go against the grain of a writer whose commitment to style remains unshakable; whatever Borges' existential anxieties may be, they have little in common with Sartre's robustly prosaic view of literature, with the earnestness of Camus' moralism, or with the weighty profundity of German existential thought. Rather, they are the consistent expansion of a purely poetic consciousness to its furthest limits.

The stories that make up the bulk of Borges' literary work are not moral fables or parables like Kafka's, to which they are often misleadingly compared, even less attempts at psychological analysis. The least inadequate literary analogy would be with the eighteenth-century *conte philosophique*: their world is the representation, not of an actual experience, but of an intellectual proposition. One does not expect the same kind of psychological insight or the same immediacy of personal experience from *Candide* as from *Madame Bovary*, and Borges should be read with expectations closer to those one brings to Voltaire's tale than to a nineteenth-century novel. He differs, however, from his eighteenth-century antecedents in that the subject of the stories is the creation of style itself; in this Borges is very definitely post-romantic and even post-symbolist. His main characters are prototypes for the writer, and his worlds are prototypes for a highly stylized kind of poetry or fiction. For all their variety of tone and setting, the different stories all have a similar point of departure, a similar structure, a similar climax, and a similar outcome; the inner cogency that links these four moments together constitutes Borges' distinctive style, as well as his comment upon this style. His stories are about the style in which they are written.

At their center, as I have said, always stands an act of infamy. The first story in *Labyrinths*, "Tlön, Uqbar, Orbis Tertius," describes the totally imaginary world of a fictitious planet; this world is first glimpsed in an encyclopedia which is itself a delinquent reprint of the *Britannica*. In "The Shape of the Sword," an ignominious Irishman who, as it turns out, betrayed the man who saved his life, passes himself off for his own victim in order to tell his story in a more interesting way. In "The Garden of the Forking Paths" the hero is a Chinese who, during World War I, spies on the British mostly for the satisfaction of refined labyrinthine dissimulation. All these crimes are misdeeds like plagiarism, impersonation, espionage, in which someone pretends to be what he is not, substitutes a misleading appearance for his actual being. One of the best of his early stories describes the exploits of the religious impostor Hakim, who hides his face behind a mask of gold. Here the symbolic function of the villainous acts stands out very clearly: Hakim was at first a dyer, that is, someone who presents in bright and beautiful colors what was originally drab and gray. In this, he resembles the artist who confers irresistably attractive qualities upon something that does not necessarily possess them.

The creation of beauty thus begins as an act of duplicity. The writer engenders another self that is his mirror-like reversal. In this anti-self, the virtues and the vices of the original are curiously distorted and reversed. Borges describes the process poignantly in a later text called "Borges and I" (it appears in *Labyrinths* and also, in a somewhat better translation, in *Dreamtigers*). Although he is aware of the other Borges' "perverse habit of falsifying and exaggerating," he yields more and more to this poetic mask "who shares [his] preferences, but in a vain way that converts them into the attributes of an actor." This act, by which a man loses himself in the image he has created, is to Borges inseparable from poetic greatness. Cervantes achieved it when he invented and became Don Quixote; Valéry achieved it when he conceived and became Monsieur Teste. The duplicity of the artist, the grandeur as well as the misery of his calling, is a recurrent theme closely linked with the theme of infamy. Perhaps its fullest treatment appears in the story "Pierre Ménard, Author of the Quixote" in *Labyrinths*. The work and life of an imaginary writer is described by a devoted biographer. As the story unfolds, some of the details begin to have a familiar ring: even the phony, mercantile, snobbish Mediterranean atmosphere seems to recall to us an actual person, and when we are told that Ménard published an early sonnet in a magazine called *La conque*, a reader of Valéry will identify the model without fail. (Several of Valéry's early poems in fact appeared in *La conque*, which was edited by Pierre Louys, though at a somewhat earlier date than the one given by Borges for Ménard's first publication.) When, a little later, we find out that Ménard is the author of an invective against Paul Valéry, as well as the perpetrator of the shocking stylistic crime of transposing "*Le cimetière marin*" into alexandrines (Valéry has always insisted that the very essence of this famous poem resides in the decasyllabic meter), we can no longer doubt that we are dealing with Valéry's anti-self, in other words, Monsieur Teste. Things get a lot more complicated a few paragraphs later, when Ménard embarks on the curious project of re-inventing Don Quixote word for word, and by the time Borges treats us to a "close reading" of two identical passages from Don Quixote, one written by Cervantes, the other by Pierre Ménard (who is also Monsieur Teste, who is also Valéry) such a complex set of ironies, parodies, reflections, and issues are at play that no brief commentary can begin to do them justice.

Poetic invention begins in duplicity, but it does not stop there. For the writer's particular duplicity (the dyer's image in "Hakim") stems from the fact that he presents the invented form as if it possessed the attributes of reality, thus allowing it to be mimetically reproduced, in its turn, in another mirror-image that takes the preceding pseudo-reality for *its* starting-point. He is prompted "by the blasphemous intention of attributing the divine category of *being* to some mere [entities]". Consequently, the duplication grows into a proliferation of successive mirror-images. In "Tlön, Uqbar, Orbis Tertius," for example, the plagiarized encyclopedia is itself falsified by someone who adds an entry on the imaginary region Uqbar, presenting it as if it were part of an imaginary country as *his* starting point, another falsifier (who, by the way, is a Southern segregationist millionaire) conjures up, with the assistance of a team of shady experts, a complete encyclopedia of a fictional planet called Tlön—a pseudo-reality equal in size to our own real world. This edition will be followed in turn by a revised and even more detailed edition written not in English but in one of the languages of Tlön and entitled *Orbis Tertius*.

All the stories have a similar mirror-like structure, although the devices vary with diabolical ingenuity. Sometimes, there is only one mirror-effect, as when at the end of "The Shape of the Sword" Vincent Moon reveals his true identity as the villain, not the hero, of his own story. But in most of Borges' stories, there are several layers of reflection. In "Theme of the Traitor and the Hero" from *Labyrinths* we have: (1) an actual historic event—a revolutionary leader betrays his confederates and has to be executed; (2) a fictional story about such an occurrence (though in reversed form)—Shakespeare's *Julius Caesar*; (3) an actual historic event which copies the fiction: the execution is carried out according to Shakespeare's plot, to make sure that it will be a good show; (4) the puzzled historian reflecting on the odd alternation of identical fictional and historical events, and deriving a false theory of historical archetypes from them; (5) the smarter historian Borges (or, rather, his duplicitous anti-self) reflecting on the credulous historian and reconstructing the true course of events. In other stories from *Labyrinths*, "The Immortal," "The Zahir," or "Death and the Compass," the complication is pushed so far that it is virtually impossible to describe.

This mirror-like proliferation constitutes, for Borges, an indication of poetic success. The works of literature he most admires contain this element; he is fascinated by such mirror-effects in literature as the Elizabethan play within the play, the character Don Quixote reading *Don Quixote*, Scheherazade beginning one night to retell *verbatim* the story of *The Thousand and One Nights*. For each mirrored image is stylistically superior to the preceding one, as the dyed cloth is more beautiful than the plain, the distorted translation richer than the original, Ménard's Quixote aesthetically more complex than Cervantes'. By carrying this process to its limits, the poet can achieve ultimate success—an ordered picture of reality that contains the totality of all things, subtly transformed and enriched by the imaginative process that engendered them. The imaginary world of Tlön is only one example of this poetic achievement; it recurs throughout Borges' work and constitutes, in fact, the central, climactic image around which each of the stories is organized. It can be the philosophically coherent set of laws that makes up the mental universe of Tlön, or it can be the fantastic world of a man blessed (as well as doomed) with the frightening gift of total recall, a man "who knows by heart the forms of the southern clouds at dawn on the 30th of April 1882" as well as "the stormy mane of a pony, the changing fire and its innumerable ashes" ("Funes the Memorious," in

Labyrinths). It can be vastly expanded, like the infinitely complex labyrinth that is also an endless book in "The Garden of the Forking Paths," or highly compressed, like a certain spot in a certain house from which one can observe the entire universe ("The Aleph"), or a single coin which, however insignificant by itself, contains "universal history and the infinite concatenation of cause and effect" ("The Zahir"). All these points or domains of total vision symbolize the entirely successful and deceiving outcome of the poets irrepressible urge for order.

The success of these poetic worlds is expressed by their all-inclusive and ordered wholeness. Their deceitful nature is harder to define, but essential to an understanding of Borges. Mirror images are indeed duplications of reality, but they change the temporal nature of this reality in an insidious fashion, even—one might say especially—when the imitation is altogether successful (as in Ménard's Quixote). In actual experience, time appears to us as continuous but infinite; this continuity may seem reassuring, since it gives us some feeling of identity, but it is also terrifying, since it drags us irrevocably towards an unknowable future. Our "real" universe is like space: stable but chaotic. If, by an act of the mind comparable to Borges' will to style, we order this chaos, we may well succeed in achieving an order of sorts, but we dissolve the binding, spatial substance that held our chaotic universe together. Instead of an infinite mass of substance, we have a finite number of isolated events incapable of establishing relations among one another. The inhabitants of Borges' totally poetic world of Uqbar "do not conceive that the spatial persists in time. The perception of a cloud of smoke on the horizon and then of the burning field and then of the half-extinguished cigarette that produced the blaze is considered an example of association of ideas." This style in Borges becomes the ordering but dissolving act that transforms the unity of experience into the enumeration of its discontinuous parts. Hence his rejection of *style lié* and his preference for what grammarians call parataxis, the mere placing of events side by side, without conjunctions; hence also his definition of his own style as baroque, "the style that deliberately exhausts (or tries to exhaust) all its possibilities." The style is a mirror, but unlike the mirror of the realists never lets us forget for a moment, that it creates what it mimics.

Probably because Borges is such a brilliant writer, his mirror-world is also profoundly, though always ironically, sinister. The shades of terror vary from the criminal gusto of the *History of Infamy* to the darker and shabbier world of the later *Ficciones*, and in *Dreamtigers* the violence is even starker and more somber, closer, I suppose, to the atmosphere of Borges' native Argentina. In the 1935 story, Hakim the impostor proclaimed: "The earth we live on is a mistake, a parody devoid of authority. Mirrors and paternity are abominable things, for they multiply this earth." This statement keeps recurring throughout the later work, but it becomes much more comprehensible there. Without ceasing to be the main metaphor for style, the mirror acquires deadly powers—a motif that runs throughout Western literature but of which Borges' version is particularly rich and complex. In his early work, the mirror of art represented the intention to keep the flow of time from losing itself forever in the shapeless void of infinity. Like the speculations of philosophers, style is an attempt at immortality. But this attempt is bound to fail. To quote one of Borges' favorite books, Sir Thomas Browne's *Hydrothapia, Urne-Buriall* (1658): "There is no antidote against the *Opium* of time, which temporally considereth all things. . ." This is not, as has been said, because Borges' God plays the same trick on the poet that the poet plays on reality; God does not turn out to be the arch-villain set to deceive man into an illusion of eternity. The poetic impulse in all its perverse duplicity, belongs to man alone, marks him as essentially human. But God appears on the scene as the power of reality itself, in the form of a death that demonstrates the failure of poetry. This is the deeper reason for the violence that pervades all Borges' stories. God is on the side of chaotic reality and style is powerless to conquer him. His appearance is like the hideous face of Hakim when he loses the shining mask he has been wearing and reveals a face worn away by leprosy. The proliferation of mirrors is all the more terrifying because each new image brings us a step closer to this face.

As Borges grows older and his eyesight gets steadily weaker, this final confrontation throws its darkening shadow over his entire work, without however extinguishing the lucidity of his language. For although the last reflection may be the face of God himself, with his appearance the life of poetry comes to an end. The situation is very similar to that of Kierkegaard's aesthetic man, with the difference that Borges refuses to give up his poetic predicament for a leap into faith. This confers a somber glory on the pages of *Dreamtigers*, so different from the shining brilliance of the stories in *Labyrinths*. To understand the full complexity of this later mood, one must have followed Borges' enterprise from the start and see it as the unfolding of a poetic destiny. This would not only require the translation into English of Borges' earlier work, but also serious critical studies worthy of this great writer.

LOUIS MURILLO

Three Stories

We (the undivided divinity which acts within us) have dreamt the world. We have dreamt it resistant, mysterious, visible, ubiquitous in space and firm in time; but we have consented in its architecture to tenuous and eternal interstices of non-reason in order to know that it is false.

The third-person narrative of "Death and the Compass" (1942), an under-handed concession to literary convention, is the surface manner of a structure attempting to displace the archetypal "mystery" of all detective fictions. It is one of Borges' most stylized efforts, the surface manner providing the reader with a relatively easy access to the perplexities of structure. I shall not go into an extended analysis of the story because a good discussion of it is available, and because I think I have already put before the reader the widest as well as the narrowest contexts of Borges' irony. The stories I take up [here] offer particular problems and degrees of refinement. My intent is to disclose, for each story, the central, pivotal point on which the whole irony rests, the point suspending the total "inevitability" of the structure.

In "Death and the Compass" we have an archetypal detective plot displace-able at the point where the reader can infer the total sense of Borges' allusions to an antinomy of symbolic knowledge, the point of irony suspending the mystery of "the names of God." The stylization is so complete that, in spite of the surface manner, a bare outline of the plot is impossible without a recital of the counterplot. For our purpose we need not attempt to extricate one from the other. We can safely approach the story as a particular stylization of the structure of consciousness. To get to the sense of the stylization, we shall have

From *The Cyclical Night: Irony in James Joyce and Jorge Luis Borges.* © 1968 by the President and Fellows of Harvard College. Harvard University Press, 1968.

to reduce the components of the detective fiction to an abstract meaning—in the last paragraph to an "invisible, unending line"—and to see the structure of an "inevitable" solution fitting the series of crimes as the structure of fallible human powers committed to reading the transcendental "content" of symbols. In the archetypal detective plot, Erik Lönnrot, the detective, and Red Scharlach, the gunman, are the "inevitable" antagonists, matching powers of cunning and intelligence, each dedicated to the eradication of the other. The basic clue exposing the reader's reactions to the tensions of an irresolvable antinomy is that the gunman traps and kills the detective. The antithetical points of similarity between them allude to one "criminal archetype." The rivalry is suspended in a conflict of antithetical and mutual displacements about the symbolic quantities *three* and *four*.

On the 4th of December, Doctor Yarmolinsky, the delegate from Podolsk to the Third Talmudic Congress, is found murdered in his room in the Hôtel du Nord. The detective's mind, eager to venture on the solution, is committed to proceed by the hypotheses of pure reason, to premise an "inevitable" solution corresponding to an "inevitable" cause and premeditated motive for the crime, and excluding a decisive intervention of chance. The inspector, Franz Treviranus, whose conjectures are commonplace, guesses the true state of affairs from the evidence—a matter of chance—and, later, the spurious nature of the third crime, which takes place on the night of February third, at a point southeast of the first. The second crime, the murder of Yarmolinsky's assassin, takes place on the night of January third, in a remote corner of the western suburbs. The three crimes, as the letter from "Baruch Spinoza" *alias* Red Scharlach, asserts, have a perfect symmetry of time and place. When superimposed on a map of the city, the three places form an equilateral triangle. Three crimes, or "sacrifices," give us one kind of mystical or symbolic unity.

A fourth crime at a point South, which "Baruch Spinoza" said would not take place, introduces a perplexing set of ironical relations. The fourth crime, "inevitable" by the compass at the villa of Triste-le-Roy, makes possible two equilateral triangles by the drawing of an "invisible" and displaceable line between points East and West. The two triangles are identical, in more than one sense, and are therefore one and the same. The same fourth point, of course, provides the rhombus figure of the paint shop, the harlequin costumes, and the window lozenges of the mirador of the villa of Triste-le-Roy. Now, if we focus our attention on the radical antithesis between the quantities three and four in their geometrical representation, the antithetical tensions of the story will reveal the irresoluble symbolic conflict activated and contained in the single, reiterated figure. This conflict is, again, a refraction of consciousness, as indicated in the dizzy moment Lönnrot fixes his perceptions on the rhomboid diamonds of the window, and Scharlach and his men appear from "nowhere" to kill him.

> By way of a spiral staircase he came to the mirador. The evening
> moon shone through the lozenges of the windows; they were yellow,
> red, and green. A frightening, bewildering memory halted him.
>   Two men of short stature, ferocious and stout, pounced on
> him and disarmed him.

The stylized effect is brought off by the abruptness of the transition between the two paragraphs; the men break upon Lönnrot abruptly at that moment in which his perceptions connect the lozenges of the window to the rhombs of the paint shop and the harlequin costumes, and to the moment he drew the rhombus figure on the map and determined the site of the fourth crime with the compass. Simultaneously, he has intuited that *he* is the victim of this "inevitable" fourth crime, and that this very intuition has displaced the idea that occurred to him on the train but that he rejected: that Scharlach himself might be the fourth victim. The men pounce on him as if they materialized from the intuition provoked and symbolized by the lozenges.

This is the point in the reading of the story, the center of the labyrinth, where the reader can displace the detective mystery and perceive the archetypal mystery of symbolic knowledge alluded to in the conflict of *three* and *four* and the "invisible, unending line" to which all quantities and the conflict itself can be reduced. The rhombuses simultaneously contain the triangles and are displaceable by them. The "predicament" of symbolic knowledge alluded to is that the same figure or symbol can contain two antithetical orders of meaning, a trinity and a tetragram, a mystic, equilateral triangle and the Tetragrammaton.

Lönnrot rejects Treviranus' conjecture that Yarmolinsky has been the victim of chance and mishap, but the evidence that magnetizes his mind, the unconcluded sentence, *The first letter of the Name has been uttered*, has come about precisely because of the element of chance he rejects. He extracts an "inevitable" motive from Yarmolinsky's book, the *History of the Hasidic Sect*. His purely "rabbinical explanation" produces the purely rabbinical motive which his mind premised and Scharlach deduced as that premise: the Hasidic sect has sacrificed Yarmolinsky in the hope of discovering the Secret Name. The detective's mind, then, is fallible from within its own reasoning. In Borges' dialectical conflict Lönnrot is simultaneously the detective proceeding according to the deductions of pure reason and the "inevitable" victim of those deductions as deduced by his antagonist. The fallibility of the detective's mind is expressed diagrammatically in the rhombus figure by the simultaneity of the relations between points three and four, the third crime and the fourth crime. The killing of the detective by the gunman is simultaneously the third crime and the fourth crime. The total irony indicates that Lönnrot was certain to be Scharlach's victim according to both orders of symbolic meaning in the "sacrifices"; he is the third victim of the triangle of crimes contained simultaneously in the rhombus or tetragram of crimes in which he is the fourth victim and Scharlach the sham third. Moreover, this antithetical symmetry is possible because it is perceptible to the pure intellect as the precise equilibrium, a mutual dislocation of one by the other, of chance and the "inevitable" solution.

The antithetical sense of this equilibrium is the symbolic "content" dislocated by the paradoxical situation in which the gunman solves the mystery of the crimes for the detective and for the reader. Scharlach read in the columns of the *Yidische Zaitung* that Lönnrot was studying the names of God in order to come across the name of Yarmolinsky's killer. The editor's simplification, without scrutiny, can pass as another occurrence of chance, but under pressure it will expose its antithetical content and a "fallible," atheistic editor to go with the fallible detective. In the popular edition of Yarmolinsky's *History of the Hasidic Sect* the gunman read that the fear of uttering the Name of God had given rise to the doctrine that the equilateral Name is all-powerful and secret, and learned that some Hasidim, in search of the Secret Name, had gone so far as to make human sacrifices. He deduced that Lönnrot would conjecture the Hasidim had sacrificed the rabbi, and set out to justify that conjecture. He executed a sequence of crimes which could be seen as a mysterious sequence of either three *or* four, but which are in fact three *and* four, or three *in* four, because the third one is a sham or simulacrum. In the murder taking place in the carnival atmosphere of February third, Scharlach played the part of the victim with the tripart identity, "Gryphius-Ginzberg-Ginsberg." The scrawled evidence left behind contained a plurality of meanings, any one of which can be read in an absolute, symbolic sense: *The last of the letters of the Name has been uttered*. The hoax deceived Lönnrot, who deduced, as Scharlach intended, that it was the third in the series of "sacrifices" and that a fourth was also inevitable, since the "purely rabbinical" explanation demanded a fourth crime to correspond to the fourth day of the month as computed by the Hebrews and the four points of the compass and the Tetragrammaton. The sham crime, then, is the ironical, displaceable quantity which gives us Lönnrot as the "inevitable," fallible victim in either the tri or tetra order of symbolical symmetries of time, place, and identities. Its function as the total irony is to dislocate from one "absolute" symbolic context the contrary symbolic context, and to sustain, in the reader's mind, the conflict of mutual dislocations from the one geometrical figure of the rhombus as the structural meaning of the story. The total irony can be activated at any point in the story; any given point of the structure, like the interconnected letters of the Secret Name, will reveal its infinite, simultaneous, and "inevitable" connections with all the others.

The archetypal detective mystery, to which the mysterious element in all detective fictions can be reduced by this catalytic irony, is the predicament of the human intellect committed to deciphering the enigmatic and ultimately elusive order of the universe. The predicament and its human reality is the mystery, and this is Borges' theme in the stylized play between the "dusty Greek word" and the outwitting of the detective. The effect of the dislocating irony is to create a constant play between the mystical inevitability of the four-letter secret Name and the total inevitability of the events of the story. The story, with all its complicating symmetries, is actually possible as a direct third-person narrative because Borges has managed to ironize from every direction his own techniques for producing the "total inevitability."

The order of the crimes, three *or* four, or three *in* four, within a period of ninety-nine *or* one hundred days, has been a secret collaboration between detective and gunman; the crimes are so precise as to place, time, and identity of the victims, even to the precise problematical adjustments between them dependent on the dislocating function of the "hiatus" of irony, that the perfect solution can hardly be other than the eradication of the reasoning mind which first prefigured them. The detective's powers, in the archetypal sense, are committed to reasoning order out of mystery. The gunman knew all along there was no mystery in the real events, but his hatred for the rival and the desire for vengeance compelled him to create a semblance, a simulacrum of mystery, no less authentic or ingenious than the efforts of authors of detective fiction. The mystery exists in the detective's mind as an ineludible reality to be grappled with and overcome. The detective is committed, on an ontological plane, as Yarmolinsky and the Hasidim on a mystical or superstitious plane, to fathom the absolute secret, "the Secret Name." He is the victim of Scharlach's simulacrum of a mystery because he intuits the everlasting, ineluctable symmetry or order of which their antithesis and rivalry is a symbol.

Our story, again, works out as if it were a riddle. The irony of Lönnrot's destiny is the symbolic "content" dislocated from the unutterable Name by the jarring implications of the sham crime. But the total irony is that the components with which we grasp that there is a riddle to be solved are reiterating the elusiveness and insolubility of the ultimate mystery. This is the antithetical sense with which every detail of the story is charged. The impression of a total inevitability can be traced to the completeness of the stylization playing for ironical effects between the chance "form" of Yarmolinsky's sentence and the absoluteness of its "content," the ineffable Name; between the journalistic sensationalism of human sacrifices committed to the end of learning the name of God and the even more sensational exposure of the theological, epistemological, and ontological postulates implicated in the intelligential act of the detective, the pure reasoner, who foresaw but failed to prevent the murder which would be his own.

Every detail about the crimes conveys the antithetical sense of the whole; every detail, like the unfinished sentence on Yarmolinsky's typewriter, can refract under pressure into a plurality of meanings: the stylized reiterating of the color red, the elusive character of the Hôtel du Nord, the contents of Yarmolinsky's books, Scharlach's brother, who corresponds to the second of the identical triangles, the vast impersonality of the city, a stylized version of Buenos Aires. Every fact about the crimes is charged with a potentially "infinite" meaning and relation to the others, offering the reader an inexhaustible source of surprises. To recite the inevitable connections of any one of them to all the others would amount to a total reconstruction of the story. The reader can undertake the task and abandon himself to it with the foreknowledge that he will find himself in a maze whose every point reiterates the center.

Finally, behind the third-person narrative of "Death and the Compass" we can discern the complete impersonality of the narrator. That impersonality, to the reader intimate with Borges' ways and sensibility, is conveyed in the quality of the perceptions which establish and release the metaphorical unity of, for instance, the odor of eucalypti, "the interminable odor of the eucalypti," or the images of Lönnrot's exploration of the villa of Triste-le-Roy. The narrator refers to himself and his locale only once. The self-reference is a signature stroke of irony: "To the south of the city of my story there flows a blind little river." The effect of the total irony dislocates the Buenos Aires of fact and relocates it as a creation of dream within our fiction. The supposed realistic reference is in the reverse direction, from dream to fact.

Between the plot and the counterplot, the triangle and the rhombus, the third day of the month and the fourth, and corresponding to the hiatus which, as the Hasidim reason, indicates the hundredth name of God and corresponds to the Absolute Name, lies the shifting, elusive expanse of irony on which Lönnrot was led to betrayal by his deductions. This area of unspecified bounds, activated by our reactions, is actually the indeterminate region, with its depth and surface, on which we construe and reconstruct the intuition and the conjecture of Borges' story. The indispensable requirement for grasping the quality of his irony is to perceive that the total inevitability of the plot is produced by construing or inferring the counterplot; thereon the reader discovers that the total irony releases from the simultaneity of his perceptions a sense of vast, primeval areas of meaning, stretching apart "doomsday and death." Then come counter-shocks of meaning to jar the events of the story into a final adjustment of an ironical reading.

II

In the volume *The Aleph*, a collection of stories from the period 1944–52, "Emma Zunz" is the farthest removed from elements of fantasy, unreality, or dream, a fact Borges emphasizes. The actions of Emma Zunz are related as a third-person narrative in the sense and order of a crime fiction striving for surprise, climax, and anticlimax by a narrator whose surreptitious presence, knowledge of certain facts, suppression or unexplained ignorance of others, constitute the decisive element in the concretion of the story's structure; that is, the decisive element in the structural antithesis of plot and counterplot, as apart from Emma Zunz's actions. The outcome of the structural antithesis, as apart from the outcome for Emma, gives us a total inevitability resulting from the interconnections of time, place, compulsion, motive, and identities. The story, then, may be seen as the subtle incorporation into a structure of consciousness of the requirements of both a crime fiction and the realistic, third-person narrative.

The total irony of the story awakens the reader's impulses to the vast disproportion between what Emma intended to accomplish in the exchange of her virginity, as just cause for killing the man responsible for the disgrace of her father, and the outcome of events for her. The structure of consciousness intrudes upon and displaces the crime story sense and technique at the points where we can infer the inevitable fallibility in the events corresponding to the fallibility of the motives of the eighteen-year old girl.

Emma works in the textile factory, in Buenos Aires, of which Aarón Loewenthal is part owner. On a Thursday afternoon she receives a letter, posted in Brazil, from a stranger informing her of the death of Manuel Maier, presumably by suicide. The stranger, a boardinghouse friend of the deceased, does not know that Maier's real name is Emanuel Zunz and that Emma is his daughter. Emma later destroys the letter, and evidently the Buenos Aires police remained completely oblivious to any connection between the death that motivated Emma's plan and the shooting of Loewenthal. For, again, the central character is the bearer of a secret, and the possession of this secret and the sense of power it provides expose her fallibility. The secret Emanuel Zunz confided to his daughter that "final night," six years previously (at the age of her puberty), was the sworn assertion that Loewenthal, at the time the manager of the factory, was the thief of the embezzled funds—of which Emanuel Zunz had been accused, convicted, and disgraced. Emma's obsession to inflict a just punishment on Loewenthal, her plan and its execution, are based entirely on her father's sworn word. We are probably right in assuming that she lost her mother at an early age. For Emma the bonds between her and her father are inviolate, but, as readers, we may allow ourselves the sophistication that incest in involved. In order to avenge her father in accordance with her plan and the justification for it, no connection must be suspected between the disgrace and death of her father and her shooting of Loewenthal on the part of anyone, not even her closest friends, except her victim (and the reader, the narrator, and God). For all concerned, as for God, she must have an inviolate reason for killing him.

"She did not sleep that night and when the first light of dawn defined the rectangle of the window, her plan was already perfected." Somewhere along the intricate workings of her mind that night, so intricate a part of the vigil of her consciousness that we can only express it crudely where Borges discreetly committed it to abstruse silence, her father's sworn word of innocency, his honor among men and before God, equated itself to her own purity before men and God, his blemished honor to her unblemished girlhood, according to the secret workings of her being, moved by the love and veneration, perhaps even the obsession, that only a daughter may keep for her father when she has repulsed any thought of him or feeling originating even remotely in sex; somewhere along the movement of her being it became evident to her that the intimate possession of her body was the thing to be sacrificed to the end of consummating the secret vengeance and the righteous triumph. She would submit to the horror of giving herself to a man in the way that would preserve the purity of her motive and cause. For it was essential that in killing Loewenthal and accusing him before the courts of human justice which had passed sentence on her father she have an unquestionable motive and its incontestable proof. The man to whom she will give herself in the hours immediately preceding an appointment with Loewenthal must not know who she is, nor care to know; he must be a man who cannot possibly connect her with the worker who shoots Loewenthal, as the newspapers are sure to report, after he deceived her outrageously and attacked her. She must not be punished for shooting him, for she is an instrument in the execution of divine justice. Her sacrifice is righteous in the sight of God. Her motive is secret and pure, a thing between her and her father.

She has conceived a plan and a justification for it as perfect as the rectangle of light at the window. The reader of Borges, by recognizing its symbolic "content," will read that too-exact realistic detail as an allusion to the labyrinth of consciousness on whose precarious paths she compels herself to an inexorable destiny. The events of Friday, as she had probably foreseen, provided two circumstances of utmost importance to her plan. There were rumors of a strike at the factory, and Emma, as before, made known that she was against all violence. After work she went with Elsa Urstein, her best friend, to enroll in an athletic club for women and underwent a medical examination. On Saturday morning the other circumstance on which her plan depended presented itself. She read in *La Prensa* that the ship *Nordstjärnan*, out of Malmo, would sail that night. Then she phoned Loewenthal and insinuated that she had some information about the strike she wanted to tell him without the other girls knowing, and promised to stop by his office at nightfall.

The narrator's careful compression of plot and counterplot, insuring the total inevitability of the outcome, has enclosed the psychological explanation of Emma's motive within a sociological circumstance. On the superficial plane apparent to the public, Emma was an employee on whose loyalty to her fellow workers Loewenthal infringed while violating the trust due to his position as owner. The truth, of course, is very much the reverse. Emma and Loewenthal are moral enemies, but with this in common: both assume God's righteousness to be their cause. "Loewenthal was very religious. He believed he had a secret pact with the Lord, which exempted him from doing good in exchange for prayers and piety." The antithesis between them has a theological context to which the unconcealed symmetries in the adventitious realism are to be referred: their claim to share God's righteousness is the exposed source of their fallibility as human beings because it is the source of their feeling of power. The public's disbelief in Emma's accusation, which the incontestable evidence will overcome, is based on the assumption that the bald, corpulent, respectable, and recently widowed factory owner cannot have had an erotic interest in the girl. Moreover, as his intimate friends know, his true passion is money.

In order to defend himself from thieves Loewenthal kept the iron gate to the factory yard locked and a dog in the yard and, as everyone knew, a revolver in the drawer of his desk. To shoot Loewenthal with his own revolver is Emma's stratagem. The symbolic "content" of that revolver, the indispensable prop of the crime story, is multiple and refractive along the lines of the dialectical symmetry. Once the absolute sense of Borges' realistic details lies exposed we can assume, quite rightly, their inevitability as their inevitable meaning. The revolver, of course, has a sexual significance, but it has lain innocently in Loewenthal's drawer for many years without the slightest suspicion of sexual symbolism. Could Emma have foreseen what the revolver, that instrument of justice prefigured by her consciousness making her plan possible, would become in the fateful moment she would point it at Loewenthal and force him to confess? Could she have foreseen that the revolver, like the money she tears up in her feelings of hate and loathsomeness, would resolve themselves into ineradicable reminders of her falling and of the guilt uniting her dishonor to her father's?

An interesting element about "Emma Zunz" is the inverse direction of its symbolism. The usual procedure for Borges is to compel the reader to dislocate a symbolic "content" from a particular disclosure as the counteracting effect of its dialectical opposite. Here we do not have an evident dialectical opposite provoking the antithetical tensions and their irony; we have only the subtlest allusion to one. Consequently we find the irony working directly on the realistic detail and upon our impulse to respond to the realism of the action. The peculiar refinement of the story is the subtlety of the dislocating effect of the irony on the realistic detail. For instance, the details which fix our attention on the objects, a letter, a revolver, hidden in drawers. Emma hides the letter in a drawer "as if in some way she already knew the ulterior facts"—that is, as if she were already guilty of the thing for which her guilt is going to be so great. The revolver in Loewenthal's desk drawer is the indispensable weapon in her plan. Before she thinks out her plan that night the revolver is "already" the inevitable connective back to the letter. "She had already become the person she would be." Where the symmetries of inevitability insinuate themselves, as the dialectical opposite of the adventitious realism, we are compelled to displace the realism of, for instance, the revolver and the money the sailor leaves for Emma, as symbols of her destiny, and, finally, by referring them to the outcome, to dislocate their "content." The process is all the more engaging because Borges has restricted himself to a bare minimum of props for staging a drama of dialectical tensions whose purpose it is to give us the inner, eternal structure of the action.

On Saturday afternoon Emma made her way to the waterfront and to the Paseo de Julio, the brothel district.

> To relate with some reality the events of that afternoon would be difficult and perhaps unrighteous. One attribute of the infernal is its unrealness, an attribute which seems to mitigate its terrors and which aggravates them perhaps. How can one make credible an action hardly believed in by the person who experienced it? How recover that brief chaos which today the memory of Emma Zunz repudiates and confuses?

In order to preserve the purity of the horror of what she was doing Emma chose from the men of the Nordstjärnan a coarse one for whom she could have no feelings of tenderness.

> The man led her to a door and then to a murky entrance hall and then to a tortuous stairway and then to a vestibule (in which there was a window with lozenges identical to those of a house she lived in as a child with her parents) and then to a passageway and then to a door that closed behind her.

Behind the closed door, as the space-time reiteration of the labyrinth theme suggests, Emma's girlhood presided over by the figure of her venerated father came to an end in the consummation of the act which cannot ever end in the desolation of her consciousness. In that room outside of time did Emma think *once* of her dead father? "My own belief is that she did think once, and in that moment her desperate undertaking was imperiled." In that moment she thought of her father *and* her mother, and the exposure of her parents to the bleakness of her action revealed their union as the origin of this horror she had inflicted upon herself. In that moment her father's sex blemished her purity and contaminated forever her womanhood. Emma could not have foreseen that her fallibility lay in exposing her virgin's motive to the successful execution of her plan to avenge her father.

> The man, a Swede or Finn, did not speak Spanish; he was an instrument for Emma as she was for him, but she served for pleasure and he for justice.

Her first act, after the man left, was to tear up the money "as before she had torn up the letter." The oblique meaning of the act consigns her father to the depths of her nausea and her hatred for men.

Having made her way to Loewenthal's office without being noticed, as her plan required, not her father's vengeance but her own was foremost in her obsessive compulsion, although she kept repeating to herself the accusation now pathetically devoid of meaning. Loewenthal, innocent in this matter, was to feel the brunt of her guilt and hatred. The Emma who shoots him more or less heedless of the motive that originally justified the act, fires the revolver to eradicate the man who now becomes, like her father, the indirect cause of her dishonor. Loewenthal dies before she finishes her accusation: "I have avenged my father and they cannot punish me . . ." She never knew whether he understood at all.

> The dog's barking reminded her that she could not, yet, rest. She disarranged the divan, unbuttoned the coat on the cadaver, took off the bespattered glasses and left them on the filing cabinet. Then she picked up the telephone and repeated what she would repeat so many times again, with these and with other words: *An incredible thing has happened . . . Mr. Loewenthal had me come over on the pretext of the strike . . . He abused me, I killed him . . .*

The story, in fact, was incredible, but it imposed itself on everyone because substantially it was true. True was Emma Zunz' tone, true her shame, true her hate. True also was the outrage she had suffered;

only the circumstances were false, the time, and one or two proper names.

The final paragraphs simultaneously release the multiple, interconnected ironies and position them in relation to the ironic destiny of guilt and humiliation Emma inflicted on herself in exchange for her chastity. Loewenthal probably died without knowing why Emma killed him, but then there is no one single, exact explanation as to why she did. Her motive was not the one for which she sacrificed her chastity; hence she murdered him for an offense he never committed, unless we can conjecture a metaphysical explanation in which he is more than the indirect cause of her dishonor. Emma's accusation is incredible, yet it imposed itself on everyone because it is "substantially" correct. The public, meanwhile, accepted Loewenthal's guilt for an outrage for which Emma's father is equally to blame. Loewenthal was killed by a revolver which he kept for his own defense, but Emma was betrayed and dishonored by the very thing by which she justified her act of violence. She exchanged her virginity not for righteousness but for guilt, and her secret (unknown to any persons but Borges and his reader) shall never cease to be the terrible thing it is because it is a reality between her and God.

The total inevitability of these interconnected ironies (and I have mentioned only enough of them to make my point) rests implicitly upon our understanding that Emma's chastity, as a metaphysical, not biologic, reality is her inviolate relation to God. The total irony assigns this absolute meaning to the outcome of her actions or no meaning at all. The inevitability of the ironical symmetries of time, place, names, and identities gives us either a meaning and a moral order in the events which can be seen as "infinite" and absolute and pointing to a meaning and order beyond themselves, or else a completely meaningless order, implicating the mind and imagination which conceives and gives it shape. The "reality" of the events of the story moves into the final focus in our apprehending that the ironies construct and sustain the irreconcilability of these two orders of interpretation.

III

"The God's Script" (1949), by all counts one of the most original, is—it may be said almost axiomatically—the most successful of Borges' stories. One or two others represent a greater effort in craftsmanship, but even "The Immortal" falls short of a total exactitude or equivalence in its effects. I am even tempted to call "The Script" the paradigm or archetype of Borges' accomplishments in the short prose fiction, if only to emphasize that it is the most nearly perfect fusion and compression of his themes, resources, and techniques conceivable, the dialectical tensions assuming a finely sharpened parabolic sense and direction. I shall leave to the end of my discussion what I have to say about it as a parable of this or that, because any such attempts depend on insights into the total irony of the structure.

The story takes place, if it can be said to take place at all, in Mexico at the time of the Spanish conquest of the Aztec empire. As in the case of "The Garden," we have a revelatory account in the first person, by a prisoner, Tzinacán, the Aztec magician-priest of the pyramid of the god Qaholom. Pedro de Alvarado, known to history as the ruthless and brutal lieutenant of Hernán Cortés, while searching for a fabulous and secret treasure, came upon the pyramid of Qaholom at dusk. His men captured and tortured the magician-priest; before his very eyes they wrecked the idol of the god, but Tzinacán did not reveal the location of the hidden treasure. They lashed him, deformed and broke his body, and threw him into a prison. The torture of his imprisonment, worse than death, has lasted many years. The narrative, an account of the effects on his body, mind, and spirit of these many years, reveals how Tzinacán deciphered the magical script of his god. Borges has fancied for Tzinacán an intuition and mentality, a *Weltanschauung*, that one could not, with any plausibility, attribute to an Aztec priest. Embedded in Tzinacán's cabalistic, theological, and mystical cogitation (see the Epilogue to *El Aleph*), for example, is this oblique reference to the existentialism of the twentieth-century Spanish philosopher, José Ortega y Gasset: "a man is, by and large, his circumstances."

Having developed a long analysis of "The Garden," which broke the splendid continuity of the very sequences under discussion, I shall not attempt a similar effort here, but shall provide the complete text of the brief account in a version as faithful to the quality of the effects of the original Spanish as I can manage. To get the full effect, one must be prepared to read "The Script" as an uninterrupted concatenation of symbols building up to a climax that, simultaneously, annuls and consummates itself. The opening phrase, *La cárcel es profunda y de piedra*, has the charge of emotive and symbolical connotations usually associated with poetry. The circular prison, a domed pit, is divided into two adjacent cells by a high wall, with an opening in it covered by an iron grating (evidently a gate that can be raised from above); his cell is one side of this underground pit; in the other side his jailers have put a jaguar that, but for the grating, can tear Tzinacán to pieces instantly.

THE GOD'S SCRIPT

The prison is deep and of stone; its form, that of a nearly perfect hemisphere, though the floor (also of stone) is somewhat less than a great circle, a fact which in some way aggravates the feelings of oppression and of vastness. A dividing wall cuts it at the center; this wall, although very high, does not reach the upper part of the vault; in one cell am I, Tzinacán, magician of the pyramid of Qaholom, which Pedro de Alvarado devastated by fire; in the other there is a jaguar measuring with secret and even paces the time and space of captivity. A long window with bars, flush with the floor, cuts the central wall. At the shadowless hour [mid-day], a trap in the high ceiling opens and a jailer whom the years have gradually been effacing maneuvers an iron sheave and lowers for us, at the end of a rope, jugs of water and chunks of flesh. The light breaks into the vault; at that instant I can see the jaguar.

I have lost count of the years I have lain in the darkness; I, who was young once and could move about this prison, am incapable of more than awaiting, in the posture of my death, the end destined to me by the gods. With the deep obsidian knife I have cut open the breasts of victims and now I could not, without magic, lift myself from the dust.

On the eve of the burning of the pyramid, the men who came down from the towering horses tortured me with fiery metals to force me to reveal the location of a hidden treasure. They struck down the idol of the god before my very eyes, but he did not abandon me, and I endured the torments in silence. They scourged me, they broke and deformed me, and then I awoke in this prison from which I shall not emerge in mortal life.

Impelled by the fatality of having something to do, of populating time in some way, I tried, in my darkness, to recall all I knew. Endless nights I devoted to recalling the order and the number of stone-carved serpents or the precise form of a medicinal tree. Gradually, in this way, I subdued the passing years; gradually, in this way, I came into possession of that which was already mine. One night I felt I was approaching the threshold of an intimate recollection; before he sights the sea, the traveler feels a quickening in the blood. Hours later I began to perceive the outline of the recollection. It was a tradition of the god. The god, foreseeing that at the end of time there would be devastation and ruin, wrote on the first day of Creation a magical sentence with the power to ward off those evils. He wrote it in such a way that it would reach the most distant generations and not be subject to chance. No one knows where it was written nor with what characters, but it is certain that it exists, secretly, and that a chosen one shall read it. I considered that we were now, as always, at the end of time and that my destiny as the last priest of the god would give me access to the privilege of intuiting the script. The fact that a prison confined me did not forbid my hope; perhaps I had seen the script of Qaholom a thousand times and needed only to fathom it.

This reflection encouraged me, and then instilled in me a kind of vertigo. Throughout the earth there are ancient forms, forms incorruptible and eternal; any one of them could be the symbol I sought. A mountain could be the speech of the god, or a river or the empire or the configuration of the stars. But in the process of the centuries mountains are leveled, the river changes its course, empires undergo mutations and havoc, and the configuration of the stars varies. There is change in the firmament. The mountain and the star are individuals, and individuals perish. I sought something more tenacious, more invulnerable. I thought of the generations of cereals, of grasses, of birds, of men. Perhaps the magic would be written on my face, perhaps I myself was the end of my search. That anxiety was consuming me when I remembered the jaguar was one of the attributes of the god.

Then my soul filled with pity. I imagined the first morning of time; I imagined my god confiding his message to the living skin of the jaguars, who would love and reproduce without end, in caverns, in cane fields, on islands, in order that the last men might receive it. I imagined that net of tigers, that teeming labyrinth of tigers, inflicting horror upon pastures and flocks in order to perpetuate a design. In the next cell there was a jaguar; in his vicinity I perceived a confirmation of my conjecture and a secret favor.

I devoted long years to learning the order and the configuration of the spots. Each period of darkness conceded an instant of light, and I was able thus to fix in my mind the black forms running through the yellow fur. Some of them included points, others formed cross lines on the inner side of the legs; others, ring-shaped, were repeated. Perhaps they were a single sound or a single word. Many of them had red edges.

I shall not recite the hardships of my toil. More than once I cried out to the vault that it was impossible to decipher that text. Gradually, the concrete enigma I labored at disturbed me less than the generic enigma of a sentence written by a god. What type of sentence (I asked myself) will an absolute mind construct? I considered that even in the human languages there is no proposition that does not imply the entire universe; to say *the tiger* is to say the tigers that begot it, the deer and turtles devoured by it, the grass on which the deer fed, the earth that was mother to the grass, the heaven that gave birth to the earth. I considered that in the language of a god every word would enunciate that infinite concatenation of facts, and not in an implicit but in an explicit manner, and not progressively but instantaneously. In time, the notion of a divine sentence seemed puerile or blasphemous. A god, I reflected, ought to utter only a single word and in that word absolute fullness. No word uttered by him can be inferior to the universe or less than the sum total of time. Shadows or simulacra of that single word equivalent to a language and to all a language can embrace are the poor and ambitious human words, *all, world, universe.*

One day or one night—what difference between my days and nights can there be?—I dreamt there was a grain of sand on the floor of the prison. Indifferent, I slept again; I dreamt I awoke and that on the floor there were two grains of sand. I slept again; I dreamt that the grains of sand were three. They went on multiplying in this way until they filled the prison and I lay dying beneath that hemisphere of sand. I realized I was dreaming; with a vast effort I roused myself and awoke. It was useless to awake; the innumerable sand was suffocating me. Someone said to me: *You have not awakened to wakefulness, but to a previous dream. This dream is enclosed within another, and so on to infinity, which is the number of grains of sand. The path you must retrace is interminable and you will die before you ever really awake.*

I felt lost. The sand burst my mouth, but I shouted: *A sand of dreams cannot kill me nor are there dreams within dreams.*

A blaze of light awoke me. In the darkness above there grew a circle of light. I saw the face and hands of the jailer, the sheave, the rope, the flesh, and the water jugs.

A man becomes confused, gradually, with the form of his destiny; a man is, by and large, his circumstances. More than a decipherer or an avenger, more than a priest of the god, I was one imprisoned. From the tireless labyrinth of dreams I returned as if to my home to the harsh prison. I blessed its dampness, I blessed its tiger, I blessed the crevice of light, I blessed my old, suffering body, I blessed the darkness and the stone.

Then there occurred what I cannot forget nor communicate.

There occurred the union with the divinity, with the universe (I do not know whether these words differ in meaning). Ecstasy does not repeat its symbols; God has been seen in a blazing light, in a sword or in the circles of a rose. I saw an exceedingly high Wheel, which was not before my eyes, nor behind me, nor to the sides, but every place at one time. That Wheel was made of water, but also of fire, and it was (although the edge could be seen) infinite. Interlinked, all things that are, were, and shall be formed it, and I was one of the fibers of that total fabric and Pedro de Alvarado who tortured me was another. There lay revealed the causes and the effects, and it sufficed me to see that Wheel in order to understand it all, without end. O bliss of understanding, greater than the bliss of imagining or feeling. I saw the universe and I saw the intimate designs of the universe. I saw the origins narrated in the Book of the Common. I saw the mountains that rose out of the water, I saw the first men of wood, the cisterns that turned against the men, the dogs that ravaged their faces. I saw the faceless god concealed behind the other gods. I saw infinite processes that formed one single felicity and, understanding all, I was able also to understand the script of the tiger.

It is a formula of fourteen random words (they appear random) and to utter it in a loud voice would suffice to make me all-powerful. To say it would suffice to abolish this stone prison, to have daylight break into my night, to be young, to be immortal, to have the tiger's jaws crush Alvarado, to sink the sacred knife into the breasts of Spaniards, to reconstruct the pyramid, to reconstruct the empire Forty syllables, fourteen words, and I, Tzinacán, would rule the lands Moctezuma ruled. But I know I shall never say those words, because I no longer remember Tzinacán.

May the mystery lettered on the tigers die with me. Whoever has seen the universe, has beheld the fiery designs of the universe, cannot think in terms of one man, of that man's trivial fortunes or misfortunes, though he be that very man. That man *has been he* and now matters no more to him. What is the life of that other to him, the nation of that other to him, if he, now, is no one. This is why I do not pronounce the formula, why, lying here in the darkness, I let the days obliterate me.

It was inevitable, in this drama of consciousness, that the prisoner Tzinacán should conclude that the god's script was writ there on the jaguar's fiery skin;

that, as he aged and his mind grew darker, his flesh and spirit weakened, the ordeal should sunder his personal being; inevitable, also, that a revelation of secret designs in the universe, with its illumination of love and pity, should justify his torturous existence, and reconcile him to the horror of death-in-life: for the ultimate meaning of the universe that a man may possess cannot be other than his own destiny.

The correlations between cause and effect, between beginning and outcome, in Tzinacán's ordeal are so exact, in his telling of it, that their sum total is one and the same with their inevitability. That is, their inevitability derives from the Borgian exactitude between the order of the experiences and events disclosed and the order in which they are narrated. The irony of the story coincides with and thus reiterates this inevitability, from the scale of the whole down to small details. It is suggested first in the details of the oppressive form of the stone chamber—the imperfection in the shape of the floor, the barred window, the total darkness with its instant of light at noon. Its implications begin to emerge as we learn the details of the prisoner's precarious existence next to the jaguar and the circumstantial process wherein he first recalls the tradition of the god, and determines that the secret, destined for a chosen one at the end of time, is writ there on the moving beast. Their totality heightens as we follow the prisoner's hallucinatory attempts to decipher that arcane "text," that "fearful symmetry" consisting of a design of lines and spots (*rosetas jeroglíficas*) which he sees always in motion, through the iron bars, for an instant of light. Then, totally evident, the implications focus on the crux of the matter: the problematical relation of the deciphering mind of the human subject to the absolute "content" of the magical script. The total irony of the story, one and the same with the totality of Tzinacán's destiny, can thus be seen as pivoting the absolute "content" of the god's script on the circumstantial process of decipherment.

The exactness between form and meaning in "The Script" has produced what one may call the Borgian paradigmatic structure of consciousness. By this I mean that at any level of interpretation the "content" of the displaceable symbols will be indivisible from the content of the story as a whole. Hence, in this paradigmatic structure, the fallibility of the hero inheres in the "totality" of the attempt of the powers of consciousness, will and understanding, memory and language, to compel their own transcendence. The consciousness of the hero attempts and accomplishes nothing less than the very annihilation of its powers through their consummation.

Reiterative, pervasive, the irony creates the effect of irreconcilable extremes between the starting point of the story and its close. But this effect is the result of tensions *progressively* elaborating an account whose total meaning is grasped *instantly* in the moment the story reaches its climax, in the disclosure: "This is why I do not pronounce the formula." The antithetical sense of the tensions, at their apex, is a concatenation of symbols revealing, or releasing, a meaning which simultaneously annuls and sustains, by means of the effect of a total reiteration, the entire dialectical design. The god's script, as conceived and deciphered by the prisoner, a formula of "forty syllables, fourteen words," containing the total meaning and power of the universe, and, of course, of language, is, therefore, Borges' paradigmatic symbol within the total symbolism of his story.

The most apparent of the antithetical tensions is the one we can perceive between the *ultimate sense* of the account and its *progressive*, or *sequential, sense*. The sequential sense conveys in ordered progression the when and why, where and how, the prisoner deciphered the all-powerful arcanum. The ultimate sense reveals that its discovery and possession is the reason for the account itself. Consequently, the antithetical sense of each disclosure is that each is simultaneously an evocation of the ordeal undergone by the prisoner, and a reiteration of the ultimate effect of possessing the script, and of the inner, eternal circumstance of his imprisonment. The inevitability of the sequential sense (its presciential order or concatenation) is determined by the ultimate sense, but the latter, once the final displacement comes about in a reader's mind and feelings, will be a retroaction, the sequential concatenation in reverse.

Upon completing the story, the reader perceives that its beginning is its inevitable ending, and, conversely, that the ending is the inevitable beginning. One is led to conclude that Borges has epitomized in the structure the thematic antithesis of being and its coming-to-be in time. In the piece "Borges and I" we read: "Spinoza understood that all things wish to persist in their being; the stone eternally wants to be a stone, and the tiger a tiger." But the time dimension in our story is suspended, like stormy spray in a still seascape, in the infinite space-time present of mystical illumination. Some may see it, and the cyclical night of imprisonment, as an "unreal" or "magical" time. I read it as a dimension of consciousness.

Tortuous dream, chimerical self-delusion, metaphysical phantasy, mystical ecstasy—all apply to Tzinacán's abysmal ordeal. But one should stress that the prisoner has obeyed an inner compulsion, a commitment of self, that brings him, at its culmination, to a soul-shattering confrontation with an archetypal dimension of being. The act of transcendence implicit in the mystical vision of the wheel, or circle, annuls the force and value of his personal motives—hate, vengeance, worldly power—and his will to realize them.

The total exactitude of Borges' effects in "The Script," I suggest, arises from a number of equivalences of symmetries and antitheses, of which the most evident is the equivalence of the personal or individual dimension of being to the sequential sense of the disclosures, and the impersonal or archetypal dimension of being to their ultimate or instantaneous sense. An overall, exact displacement of the individual by the archetypal, or impersonal, is my explanation for its complete success. Once we look at the story in this fashion, we can detect the two sets of antitheses operative in a structure of hieratic symbols which seems impenetrable because the time dimension is actually a dimension of being, that is, of consciousness. I call it Borges' paradigmatic structure of consciousness because it conveys in symbolic form that tendency of his intellect and imagination to construe the ultimate value of an individual life as an emanation of a single, all-inclusive universal archetype. But the confrontation is a conflict, and for individual consciousness its outcome equivalent to death. These remarks, purposely exploratory, anticipate the theme of "The Immortal," perhaps the most hermetic of Borges' fictions.

The compressed contents of "The Script" can be expanded, evidently, to a critique on man in his world, a critique fusing metaphysics, theology, and occultism, anthropology, semantics, and literary symbolism along a narrow, tenuous band. In the other direction, in the sense of a parable, the story is susceptible to various readings; a parable of modern, existential man; of the scientific intellect obsessed by dreams of power; of the writer in Spanish America inured to the degrading tyranny of dictatorships. Perhaps this last possibility is a link between the impersonality of the story and Borges' personal existence in the Argentina of the 1940's.

RONALD J. CHRIST

"The Immortal"

The universal literary figure, the relationship to De Quincey, and the symbol of the labyrinth all come together in Borges' story "The Immortal" which is the perfection of his allusive method in a work that is more than ever a literature of literature. Beyond that, "The Immortal" is Borges' statement of themes which have preoccupied so many twentieth-century writers in a form which is comparable to that of Conrad, that of Joyce, that of Eliot, but is still personal, authentic. "The Immortal" is the culmination of Borges' art.

THE UNIVERSAL LITERARY FIGURE

The epigraph to "The Immortal" establishes the familiar theme in Borges' work and introduces the singleness of authorial mind which is the story's subject:

> Salomon saith. *There is no new thing upon the earth.* So that as Plato had an imagination, *that all knowledge was but remembrance*; so Salomon giveth his sentence, *that all novelty is but oblivion.*
> Francis Bacon: *Essays* LVIII

Four authors—Plato, Solomon, Bacon, and Borges himself—are here made to collaborate in expressing the Eternal Return in an intellectual or mental sense. This apparent plurality of minds and demonstrable unity of statement in an allusive tissue is at once the theme and the technique of the story, which uses the literary figure to reformulate definitively the principles of personality

From *The Narrow Act: Borges' Art of Illusion.* © 1984 by Ronald J. Christ. New York University Press, 1969.

49

and time found throughout Borges. It is the same theme he treats in "Everything and Nothing," but that is a commentary and a summary; "The Immortal" is a presentation and a demonstration.

In "Everything and Nothing" Borges writes of Shakespeare: "No one was so many men as that man, who, like the Egyptian Proteus, could exhaust all the appearances of being." The pun on "no one" divulges the removed, all-knowing approach Borges is taking in order to distill the essence of his subject. The distillation, however, is a little lifeless, droning; and the monotone is relieved only by the octave shift in the last sentences when God speaks. "Everything and Nothing," like so much in *El hacedor* [*Dreamtigers*], is a summation of previous work, but sapped of almost all energy, subdued by nostalgia. More varied, more complex is "The Immortal," which treats the same subject but from the inside so that the reader's understanding develops gradually and dramatically, along with that of the character. Furthermore, at the end of "Everything and Nothing," all is solved, resolved, while at the conclusion of "The Immortal" the sense of mystery, and complex mystery at that, still lingers. The one is a rapid disclosure, the other an intricate unfolding; and the intricacy comes not from the treatment alone but from the conception, because in "The Immortal" Borges takes the possibilities of both *everything* and *nothing* more seriously. The story shows that Homer's work is nothing—nothing extra-ordinary, that is—and that Homer is literally everything, *everyone* in the story.

The paradoxical everything and nothingness of Homer is indicated elsewhere by the expressly generic title of "El hacedor," "The Maker," which Borges bestows upon him; but in "The Immortal" the two exhaustive attributes are simultaneous modes of his work and personality. The story itself is a little Odyssey, and that, of course, is tribute to the universal, mythic proportions of Homer's work which nourishes subsequent writings, but the story in no way proposes the greatness or superiority of the Homeric epic, instead showing its mere inevitability in the scheme of things:

> Homer composed the *Odyssey*; given an infinite period of time, with infinite circumstances and changes, the impossible thing is not to compose the *Odyssey*, at least once. No one is anyone; a single immortal is all men.

The *Odyssey* belongs not to Homer but to History; it is nothing more or less than the story of the world. But it belongs to Language as well, for as Borges argues in "Versions of Homer," it is impossible "to know what belongs to the poet and what pertains to the idiom," and therefore the only certainty about Homer's style, his literary personality, "is the impossibility of separating what pertains to the writer from what pertains to the idiom." The logical deduction from this is that not Homer but everyone has written, continues to write the *Odyssey*, and that, in the end, as Cartaphilus writes, *"only words remain."* The most exact indication of the universal composition of Homer is the phrase "Pope's *Iliad*" on the first page of "The Immortal," an indication supported by a reference to "Pope's Odyssey" which Emerson makes in the course of arguing that all literature has been written by one person. The logic is clear: if "a single man is all men," then a single author is all authors, all men ("The genius is all," says Emerson), and all men are immortal because Homer is immortal. We are all Homer. Thus this story which gives what we have always lacked and so often desired—a biography of Homer—takes away far more than it gives:

> Like Cornelius Agrippa, I am god, I am hero, I am philosopher,
> I am demon and I am world, which is a wearisome way of saying
> that I am not.

Amplitude is a trait of the cipher.

As so often in Borges, the confirmation of being is an obliteration. But notice the peculiar absence of definite and indefinite articles in the series quoted above, and also notice the constant present tense. The added complexity in "The Immortal," one characteristically indicated by a suppression, is that character is not only multiple and sequential as it is presented in "Theme of the Traitor and Hero," in "The Circular Ruins," and even in section V of "The Immortal"; character is single and simultaneous as well: the apparent multiplicity of Types or Ideas exists in the present tense. Homer is all men *now*. That bloody horseman who dies at Rufus' feet in Part I is the same Rufus who undertakes an identical journey and dies in similar circumstances at the end of Part I; the Rufus speaking to Argos is Homer, who has forgotten that he is Homer, speaking to Homer, who has nearly forgotten the *Odyssey* he composed 1,000 years ago. The Princess of Lucinge reads Homer; Pope and his employees write Homer; Joseph Cartaphilus sells Homer; Nahum Cordovero comments on Homer. All these are aspects of Homer in a literary, mental sense.

This simultaneous multiplicity is revealed by personal pronouns in "The Immortal." The story begins, unusually for Borges, not with "I" but with "we" ("ofrecemos"), shifts to Homer's first person ("Que yo recuerde"), moves naturally between the first person plural ("Partimos") and first person singular ("devisé") in the course of narration, and then in Part IV shifts subtly to another "we," one which includes the Immortals:

> Neither was his own destiny interesting. His body was a submissive
> domestic animal, and each month the alms of a few hours of sleep,
> a little water and a scrap of meat were enough for him. Let nobody

wish to reduce us to ascetics. There is no more complex pleasure
than thought and we gave ourselves over to it.

Finally the story ends with the first person ("A mi entender"). The confusion
or expansion and contraction is partially clarified by Homer's statement: "The
story I have narrated seems unreal because in it are mixed the incidents of
two distinct men." But "distinct" is itself ambiguous and applies more to the
grammar than to the psychology or history of the character. An analogous
situation in Emerson is more illuminating. The same kind of shifts in person
have been noted by Richard Poirier in Emerson's "Nature," and they show
us, says Poirier, "the speaker's capacity to relinquish his particular identity and
assume an ever more inclusively general one." In Borges, the grammatical shift
re-enacts the myth of the Simurg, which begins with discrete "I's" and culminates
in a "We," and in fact that myth, found at the end of "The Approach," with its
difficult journey, its pilgrims falling by the wayside, its passage through Vertigo
and Annihilation, its final revelation that all are one (The Immortal Simurg)
informs Borges' later as well as his early story. The events in "The Immortal"
are thus to be read in two ways: first, as the apparent particulars they are,
of person, place, thing, and time: and second, as the manifestation of a single
character, who writes the *entire* fiction (including preface, narrative, and
postscript), but who is absent from the story as himself, except in so far as
he is all and everywhere. Without giving his readers the benefit of an explanatory
note, Borges has employed the same device Strindberg said he used in *Dream
Play*:

> In this dream play, . . . the Author has sought to reproduce the
> disconnected but apparently logical form of a dream. Anything can
> happen; everything is possible and probable. Time and space do
> not exist; on a slight groundwork of reality, imagination spins and
> weaves new patterns made up of memories, experiences, unfettered
> fancies, absurdities, and improvisations.
>
> The characters are split, double and multiply; they evaporate,
> crystallise, scatter and converge. But a single consciousness holds
> sway over them all—that of the dreamer. For him there are no
> secrets, no incongruities, no scruples and no law. He neither
> condemns nor acquits, but only relates, and since on the whole,
> there is more pain than pleasure in the dream, a tone of melancholy,
> and of compassion for all living things, runs through the swaying
> narrative.

In what it says both about characterization and about narrative procedure,
Strindberg's note is the best description of the story. There is one immortal

who is all the rest: the story's title is pointedly singular; Homer is the universal author.

Men are immortal then, like the rest of the universe: "To be immortal matters very little; except for man, all creatures are immortal since they do not know about death." As Sir Thomas Browne writes in "Religio Medici":

> For as though there were a Metempsuchosis, and the soul of one man passed into another, Opinions do find, after certain Revolutions, men and minds like those that first begat them. To see our selves again, we need not look for Plato's year: every man is not only himself; there hath been many Diogenes, and as many Timons, though but few of that name: men are liv'd over again, the world is now as it was in Ages past; there was none then, but there hath been some one since that parallels him, and is, as it were, his revived self.

Emerson recognized that immortality and also stressed our suppression of it: "We hide this universality if we can, but it appears at all points." Man has repressed his immortality or he is moved to forget it, a wish Emerson also understood:

> But it is not the intention of Nature that we should live by general views. We fetch fire and water, run about all day among the shops and markets, and get our clothes and shoes made and mended, and are the victims of these details; and once in a fortnight we arrive perhaps at a rational moment. If we were not thus infatuated, if we saw the real from hour to hour, we should not be here to write and to read, but should have been burned or frozen long ago. She would never get anything done, if she suffered Admirable Crichtons and universal geniuses.

Our principal antidotes to universality and immortality are death and forgetting. Because they confirm our mortality and our individual identity, death and forgetting are what make the universe bearable, real for us. On this point of forgetting I have already noted [elsewhere] Borges' story "Funes the Memorious" and I would also want to point to De Quincey, who, like Borges, feels assured "that there is no such thing as ultimate *forgetting*," but who nevertheless describes forgetting as a gift and an art:

> that art which the great Athenian Themistocles noticed as amongst the *desiderata* of human life—that gift which, if in some rare cases it belongs only to the regal prerogatives of the grave, fortunately in many thousands of other cases is accorded by the treachery of

the human brain. Heavens! what a curse it were, if every chaos, which is stamped upon the mind by fairs such as that London fair of St. Bartholomew in years long past, or by the records of battles and skirmishes through the monotonous pages of history, or by the catalogues of libraries stretching over a dozen measured miles, could not be erased, but arrayed itself in endless files incapable of obliteration, as often as the eyes of our human memory happened to throw back their gaze in that direction! Heaven be praised, I have forgotten everything.

Man lives by dying, that is, by forgetting; only God or an Immortal lives by remembering all. Thus "The Immortal" proceeds by a series of deaths or equivalent lapses of memory which give to the story its seemingly disjunctive form, the "disconnected but apparently logical form of a dream," as Strindberg says. On the other hand, these deaths and forgettings, as we shall see, are shams and illusions, and the inner reality, captured by the procedure of the story and described in the career of Homer, is one of eternal life and all encompassing memory.

Death makes men "precious and pathetic"; remove it or the knowledge of it and they are no longer precious *or* pathetic. Hence the curious description of "The Immortal" in the epilogue of *El Aleph* [*The Aleph*] as an "outline of an ethic for immortals." The story proposes a system of values, indeed a way of living or reading, which are much the same thing in Borges; an ethic of supreme equality in life (notice the phrase "The republic of immortal men" in Part IV), of sublime impersonality in literature. All claims to originality or invention—of experience or writing—as well as all accusations of plagiarism and influence are destroyed: "There is no new thing upon the earth." Books, like men, are no longer to be valued as either precious or pathetic: there is all eternity in which to write the Homeric epics, and it was inevitable that they should be written; there is all eternity to complete the ongoing work described in "The Dream of Coleridge," and a sentiment of loss about the missing lines of "Kubla Khan" is simply misguided and misplaced in time. Freed from the values death imposes, literature can at last be seen for what it is: "in the beginning of literature was myth, and also in the end." The ascendency of myth, of a literary collective consciousness, in "The Immortal" may be guessed when we realize how, in contrast to other stories about literary figures like Pierre Menard or Herbert Quain, how little there is about writing or planning of a book in "The Immortal"; how little, even of criticism, for this is a story whose intention is to question the basis of most criticism and appreciation of literature which develops from a notion of limits to man's life, from limits, which, the story argues, do not exist. It is the responsibility of literature, then, to deny mortality, to deny oblivion by ignoring the sleep of death and the sleep of forgetting and by emphasizing in their place the eternal dream of life and memory. Literature must be timeless memory: to be true, to be archetypally real, literature based on such a belief must deny its own novelty, and the position of the author must be that of grand remembrancer. Ironically, then, Cordovero's attack in the Postscript on the integrity of Homer's text is our assurance of its universal validity. The more it is nothing in itself, the more the story is everything.

"The Immortal" thus realizes a great victory over time and space and personality, but it is finally despondent and futilitarian. As "A New Refutation of Time" ended with "*And yet, and yet...*," "The Immortal" leaves us with a feeling of loss rather than of gain. The implicit morality and political ethic of the story are at first noble, but then dispiriting: the "perfection of tolerance" which the Immortals have achieved leads inevitably to a perfection of disdain and inactivity. And while we can accept the eternity of literature, the necessity for seeing people as eternal shades instead of flitting realities is too much for us. We want to believe that we are, which is to say that we shall die. Therefore the story leaves us with the fundamental antinomy of Borges' work: the achievement of metaphysical vision antagonistic to our very selves. Even Homer cannot bear the strain of his discovery and he lapses into forgetfulness and apparent death: "Again I am mortal, I repeated, again I am like all men. That night I slept until dawn." Of course he is not mortal; all the signs contradict it: "I repeated" and the twice-repeated "Again" call upon the Eternal Return, and the ellipsis with which the succeeding paragraph begins as well as the sleep into which Homer falls signal a new beginning based on forgetting. "The Immortal," Borges' incarnation of the universal writer, ends by dissipating that same literary figure. And so Borges joins that great train of writers who confer immortality only to deride it and lament it, that train which includes Petronius, Swift, De Quincey, Tennyson, and Eliot.

DE QUINCEYAN IMAGERY

De Quincey is called upon to supply the scene-meaning at the very center of "The Immortal," and as we might guess, it is a picture of disorder and meaningless reiteration. But so that we shall not miss the point, the Postscript refers us directly to De Quincey's *Writings* where we read a recollection of some Piranesi etchings Coleridge once described:

> Many years ago, when I was looking over Piranesi's "Antiquities of Rome," Coleridge, then standing by, described to me a set of plates from that artist, called his "Dreams," and which record the

scenery of his own visions during the delirium of a fever. Some of these (I describe only from memory of Coleridge's account) represented vast Gothic halls; on the floor of which stood mighty engines and machinery, wheels, cables, catapults, &c., expressive of enormous power put forth, or resistance overcome. Creeping along the sides of the walls, you perceived a staircase; and upon this, groping his way upwards, was Piranesi himself. Follow the stairs a little farther, and you perceive them reaching an abrupt termination, without any balustrade, and allowing no step onwards to him who should reach the extremity, except into the depths below. Whatever is to become of poor Piranesi, at least you suppose that his labours must now in some way terminate. But raise your eyes, and behold a second flight of stairs still higher, on which again Piranesi is perceived, by this time standing on the very brink of the abyss. Once again elevate your eye, and a still more aerial flight of stairs is descried; and there, again, is the delirious Piranesi, busy on his aspiring labours: and so on, until the unfinished stairs and the hopeless Piranesi both are lost in the upper gloom of the hall. With the same power of endless growth and self-reproduction did my architecture proceed in dreams.

This passage is definitive of what J. Hillis Miller calls "the Piranesi effect" in De Quincey, an effect we have all experienced apparently, but with less frightening overtones, in discovering a disquieting infinity on the label of a box of salt or can of cocoa. Borges' picture of the City of the Immortals is closely patterned on this passage, from the general impression of purposeless repetition to the details of the staircases which "died without reaching anywhere," and even to the conditional quality imposed because the scene is only recalled, and recalled from another's description, not actually witnessed. On this point, the reference is furtively expressive since no such Piranesi etching exists, and we do not even know who invented—De Quincey or Coleridge—the one described by De Quincey. The Postscript thus accuses the narrative of being false for plagiarizing De Quincey, who in turn is equally false. But more significantly De Quincey's image specifies the abomination at the core of life's labyrinth for Borges: at the center, or "cell" as De Quincey calls it there is no resting place, not even a destructive monster, but instead another labyrinth without plan or end. In effect, there is no center, but only "the Piranesi effect" of labyrinth within labyrinth, and "What we all dread most," Father Brown says, "is a maze with no centre." Both De Quincey and Borges collaborate in describing such a maze. The labyrinth of the Immortals should lead to death, to a termination, to eternal rest; instead it turns upon itself and centrifugally flings the searchers out into newer and newer existences. De Quincey's visual "Piranesi effect" is here made to serve the office of a horrifying, distempered "Vision of Er."

The City of the Immortals is the symbolic center of Borges' universe, and from it emanates all the anxiety undermining that world. As in "The Approach [to Al-Mu'tasim]," Borges usually withholds the final vision and concentrates on the way to the center, leaving the character on the very door sill of revelation, but in "The Immortal" we are conducted to this center and enter into the absolute mythic reality which Eliade tells us is associated with such places:

> The center, then, is pre-eminently the zone of the sacred, the zone of absolute reality . . . . The road leading to the center is a "difficult road" . . ., and this is verified at every level of reality: difficult convolutions of a temple (as at Borobudur); pilgrimage to sacred places (Mecca, Hardwar, Jerusalem); danger-ridden voyages of the heroic expeditions in search of the Golden Fleece, the Golden Apples, the Herb of Life; wandering in labyrinths; difficulties of the seeker for the road to the self, to the "center" of his being, and so on. The road is arduous, fraught with perils, because it is, in fact, a rite of the passage from the profane to the sacred, from the ephemeral and illusory to reality and eternity, from death to life, from man to divinity.

The Library of Babel is one representation of this reality, and the City of the Immortals is a more terrifying one still. Of its sacred nature there can be no doubt—we are told that the gods have built it, and the Immortals do live there—but instead of giving rise "to a life that is real, enduring and effective," this perverse heaven gives rise to an existence that is nightmarish, eternal, and futile, for *"The gods who built it were mad."* This city

> *is so horrible that its mere existence and perpetuation, even in the center of a hidden desert, contaminates the past and the future and in some way compromises the heavenly bodies. While it lasts, no one in the world can be valiant or happy.*

The description goes beyond De Quincey's personal nightmares, and the word "horrible" can serve as our introduction to this loathsome realm, the Conradian heart of darkness. The odyssey of "The Immortal" is a Conradian journey to the center of the world, another journey to the center of Africa, where Rufus encounters the same reality as Mr. Kurtz: "The horror! The horror!" Once there, there is nothing for either Homer-Rufus or Marlow to do but to turn around and rethread the windings of their approach. The mythic structure of "The Immortal" is thus supported by the mythological universe of Conrad, where to seek is to wander in a labyrinth—of adventure for the characters, of Marlow's style for the reader—and to find is to discover the abyss—Marlow says of Kurtz: "True, he had made that last stride, he had stepped over the edge, while I had been permitted to draw back my hesitating foot." Conrad is actually worked into "The Immortal" by having Homer ship on the *Patna*, Jim's boat in *Lord Jim*, and the importance of Conrad to Eliot as well as to Borges serves to unite the three in their depiction of a world where, if all is not exactly desert, as in "The Immortal" and *The Waste Land*, everything wears "a vast and dismal aspect of disorder," a world where there is no meaning and no utterance beyond the cry for death.

The meeting of De Quincey, Chesterton, Conrad, and Borges in a common image is striking because they illuminate each other's thought. Chesterton, for example, serves to remind us that the labyrinth was originally a burying place. Looking at "a vast black bulk of the cyclopean building" in "The Point of a Pin," Father Brown says:

> It reminds one of Coppée's poem about the Pharaoh and the Pyramid. The house is supposed to be a hundred houses; and yet the whole mountain of buildings is only one man's tomb.

And Flambeau describes another labyrinth which also connects that structure with the grave:

> "Died," repeated Flambeau, "and that's about as much as we can say. You must understand that towards the end of his life he began to have those tricks of the nerves not uncommon with tyrants. He multiplied the ordinary daily and nightly guard around his castle till there seemed to more sentry-boxes than houses in the town, and doubtful characters were shot without mercy. He lived almost entirely in a little room that was in the very centre of the enormous labyrinth of all the other rooms, and even in this he erected another sort of central cabin or cupboard, lined with steel, like a safe or battleship. Some say that under the floor of this again was a secret hole in the earth, no more than large enough to hold him, so that, in his anxiety to avoid the grave he was willing to go into a place pretty much like it."

In fact we should have guessed, on the basis of "The Cult of the Phoenix," that the City of Immortals would be a vast graveyard, a universal mausoleum. But if we did not guess, Borges puts the information in our way:

On finally disentangling myself from that nightmare, I found myself manacled and thrown into an oblong niche, no bigger than an ordinary sepulcher, shallowly excavated in the sharp slope of a mountain. . . . About a hundred irregular niches, like mine, furrowed the mountain and the valley.

The nightmare is one labyrinth ("desen*red*arme") and the city is another. Between them lies the grave and rebirth. We might even have known from the beginning that the labyrinth, in its oldest, Egyptian form (the form invoked by the setting of "The Immortal") is precisely a symbol of life through death, as C. N. Deedes tells us:

Above all, the Labyrinth was the centre of activities concerned with those greatest of mysteries, Life and Death. There men tried by every means known to them to overcome death and to renew life. The Labyrinth protected and concealed the dead king-god in order that his life in the after-world might be preserved. . . The Labyrinth, as tomb and temple, fostered the development of all art and literature, activities which in those days possessed a religious and life-giving significance.

It is the peculiar virtue of Borges' story, however, to have seen the potential horror in such a resurrection symbol and to have put De Quincey's famous passage so dramatically to work. Nevertheless, we might remind ourselves that Borges did not have to rely on De Quincey's Gothic nightmare, except as the singularly fine example it is. He could have drawn, and in some ultimate way does, on Chesterton's equally fantastic architecture:

Immediately beneath and about them the lines of the Gothic building plunged outwards into the void with a sickening swiftness akin to suicide. There is that element of Titan energy in the architecture of the Middle Ages that, from whatever aspect it be seen, it always seems to be rushing away, like the strong back of some maddened horse. This church was hewn out of ancient and silent stone, bearded with old fungoids and stained with the nests of birds. And yet, when they saw it from below, it sprang like a fountain at the stars; and when they saw it, as now, from above, it poured like a cataract into a voiceless pit. For these two men on the tower were left alone with the most terrible aspect of the Gothic: the monstrous foreshortening and disproportion, the dizzy perspectives, the glimpses of great things small and small things great; a topsy-turvydom of stone in the mid-air. Details of stone, enormous by their proximity, were relieved against a pattern of fields and farms, pygmy in their distance. A carved bird or beast at a corner seemed like some vast walking or flying dragon wasting the pastures and villages below. The whole atmosphere was dizzy and dangerous, as if men were upheld in air amid the gyrating wings of colossal genii; and the whole of that old church, as tall and rich as a cathedral, seemed to sit upon the sunlit country like a cloudburst.

"Dizzy and dangerous" (Chesterton is always more jovial and buoyant, even when detailing the hideous): the phrase applies to Piranesi climbing the fantastic staircase in De Quincey's memory, and it applies to the City of the Immortals as well. That it comes from Chesterton may serve to remind us that Borges' allusions, by putting us into a universal vein of imagery, direct us to vaster land than the legend on the sign indicates.

What the reference in Borges' Postscript does not tell us is that much background information for "The Immortal" can be found in another of De Quincey's essays, "Homer and the Homeridae," and that while this essay, in relation to Borges' story, fits into the category I call congenerous, it does present another image which is perhaps even more basic to this story than the labyrinth itself.

In "The Immortal" we read of the multitudinous survival of Homer down to our present time when he is discovered to be, in a typical Borges' pun, an "antiquarian," whose form is understandably exhausted: "He was. . . a worn out and earthen man, with grey eyes and gray beard and singularly vague features." This is a comedown from the colorful existence he had even as a Roman whose name was brightly, perhaps doubly tinted: Marcus Flaminius Rufus. (*Rufus* is Latin for red and while *Flaminius* may evoke flame or red for us, it comes from the Latin *flamen*, meaning priest, in which case it may call to mind the grey priest in "The Circular Ruins," so notably associated with fire.) The waning of primordial fires into ash is a recurring pattern in Borges, who, adopting the everpresent of the Eternal Return, nevertheless describes life as if it were gradually burning out in each repetition, getting paler as it moves from the crimson life-blood of myth—"The Red Adam of Paradise"— to the paler rose color of the historical past—the wall in "Feeling in Death" belonging to the 1890's—to the pale greyness of the contemporaneous. The pattern is pinpointed by one of the metaphysical schools of Tlön:

> Another school declares that *all time* has already transpired and that our life is scarcely the memory or twilight reflection, now undoubtedly falsified and mutilated, of an irrecoverable process.

The diminishing intensity of life veins Borges' work with melancholy and explains the backward urge of his mind, first to the time of childhood, and then to the mythic past. De Quincey felt such an urge too, and in a sense both writers are "escapists," but in particular, De Quincey's application of the aging, diminishing quality of the world to Homer, as he expressed it in "Homer and the Homeridae" seems to have caught Borges' fancy.

In that essay Borges could have read of a Homer who is "the general patriarch of Occidental Literature"; of a Homer who could not write, like the Argos who composed the Odyssey but cannot make intelligible signs in the sand; of a Homer born in Smyrna like "the antiquarian Joseph of Smyrna"; of a Homer who "at the islands of Ios, of Chios, and of Crete. . .had a standing invitation" like that same Cartaphilus who is buried at Ios, one of the traditionally ascribed burial places of Homer; of a Homer who never existed and whose poems were composed by many different men; and even of a Homer who was himself one and yet many like the Homer in Section V of Borges' story:

> Others, like our Jacob Bryant, have fancied that he was not merely coeval with those heroes, but actually was one of those heroes— viz. Ulysses; and that the "Odyssey," therefore, rehearses the personal adventures, the voyages, the calamities of Homer himself. It is our old friend the poet, but with a new face; he is now a soldier, a sailor, a king, and, in case of necessity, a very fair boxer.

Such correspondences, and the others like them, are curious, and it is quite possible that Borges first encountered them in De Quincey; but what is really striking in the De Quincey essay is a metaphysical equation of the survival of Homer's text to the survival of his body, and a consequent description of Homer as a monstrous ancient.

> Homer, they say, is an old—old—very old man, whose trembling limbs have borne him to your door; and, therefore—what? Why, he ought to look very old indeed. Well, good man, he *does* look very old indeed. He ought, they say, to be covered with lichens and ivy. Well, he *is* covered with lichens and ivy. And sure I am that few people will undertake to know how a man looks when he is five hundred years old by comparison with himself at four hundred. Suffice it here to say, for the benefit of the unlearned, that not one of our own earliest writers, hardly Tomas of Ercildoune, has more of the peculiar antique words in his vocabulary than Homer.

Here, as throughout De Quincey's essay, Homer is his poems, so that archaic words in an already ancient text becomes lichens on the old man's body—an astonishing image, one that would please Borges and perhaps lead him to join it with another of De Quincey's favorite figures, appropriate to this picture of Homer but not actually invoked in "Homer and the Homeridae."

The figure of Swift's Struldbrugg comes to De Quincey's mind whenever he wants to image the decrepit survival of the ancient world into the modern. Of course he does not think of Homer as decrepit (even though his imagination leads him to picture Homer that way), so that Struldbruggs are not found in "Homer and the Homeridae"; but the following passage shows De Quincey's typical use of the image:

> The Romans were essentially the leaders in civilisation, according to the possibilities then existing; for their earliest usages and social forms involved a high civilisation, whilst promising a higher: whereas all Moslem nations have described a petty arch of national civility— soon reaching its apex, and rapidly barbarising backwards. This fatal gravitation towards decay and decomposition in Mahometan institutions, which at this day exhibit to the gaze of mankind one uniform spectacle of Mahometan ruins,—all the great Moslem nations being already in the *Struldbrug** state, and held erect only by the colossal support of Christian powers,—could not . . . have been healed by the Arabian prophet.
>
> *(To any reader who happens to be illiterate, or not extensively informed, it may be proper to explain that *Struldbrugs* were a creation of Dean Swift. They were people in an imaginary world, who were afraid of dying, and who had the privilege of lingering on through centuries when they ought to have been dead and buried, but suffering all the evils of utter superannuation and decay; having a bare glimmering of semi-consciousness, but otherwise in the condition of mere vegetables.)

Those Mahometan institutions now in ruins cast good light on the horrendous city of the Immortals in Borges' story, and Homer in that story certainly qualifies as a Struldbrugg. The allusion, as De Quincey's charming condescension makes clear, is to Swift, and to the only part of Swift which has any meaningful connection with Borges—the Third Book of *Gulliver's Travels*. But just as quickly, it calls to mind Petronius' Sibyl, invoked by Eliot in the epigraph to *The Waste Land*, and Tennyson's "Tithonus" to name only two versions of the myth which probably has its widest currency in English through Coleridge's "Ancient Mariner." As the "Everlasting Jew" the myth is noted by De Quincey:

> *"The Everlasting Jew"*: — The German name for what we English call the Wandering Jew. The German imagination has been most struck by the duration of the man's life, and his unhappy sanctity from death: the English by the unrestingness of the man's life, his incapacity of repose.

Borges' story is another version of this myth; one which significantly differs from De Quincey's interpretation of Homer, but could, nonetheless, have been suggested by it:

> When you describe Homer, or when you hear him described, as a lively picturesque old boy (by the way, why does everybody speak of Homer as old?), full of life, and animation, and movement, then you say (or you hear say) what is true, and not much more than what is true.

De Quincey insists on Homer's liveliness, but he gives no images to that liveliness; Petronius, Swift, Tennyson, Eliot, and Borges all envision a weary immortal with a single desire: to die.

What Borges has done is apply the myth of the Everlasting Jew to literature, making the eternal figure the author himself. In doing so, Borges writes another entry in an old controversy and establishes himself with those who believe that *we* are the ancients. He mentions this argument in his preface to Ray Bradbury's *Martian Chronicles*: "The Renaissance had already observed, through the words of Giordano Bruno and Bacon, that we are the true ancients and not the Men of Genesis or of Homer." Bradbury looks to the future of 2004, and we feel, Borges notes, "the gravitation, the vast and vague accumulation of the past." Borges looks to the past, of course, but we feel the same thing. What distinguishes Borges in the Quarrel of the Ancients and Moderns is that he sees no final superiority on either side — all the fight has been taken out of the Battle of the Books. The human brain for him, as for De Quincey, is a palimpsest, "A membrane or roll cleansed of its manuscript by reiterated successions." Patches of writing from various ages and in various languages show through, but he sees the writing getting ever weaker, ever vaguer as initial rubrics are gradually faded by consecutive forgettings and rewritings. Ancient or Modern, all is a reflection of an archetype, and therefore less than real.

ALLUSION

The truest thing about "The Approach" was myth, and one of the most nearly real things in "The Immortal" is a made-up book. "Real," that is, in that

it tells a kind of truth about the story and provides a thread for the labyrinth
Borges has carefully built, so that reader, unlike character, will not be left with
meaningless confusions at the core. This thread is given in the Postscript, which
is a manifest rationale for the story, but one which is integral and dramatic,
for unlike the notes to *The Waste Land*, in "The Immortal" there is no change
of authorial voice from introductory section to postscript which frame the narrative. What Eliot tells us in his notes is demonstrably, authoritatively factual;
what the narrator of "The Immortal" tells us is pure fiction; that is, invention
based on fact. In this respect, Borges has gone a step beyond either Joyce or
Eliot in his relation to both text and reader, following a tendency which has
been exploited by Nabokov, as I indicated [elsewhere], in *Pale Fire* and apparently in his projected novel *The Texture of Time*. The device arises from one of
the oldest conventions of fiction and is common to the novel from the time of
Cervantes, but the reflecting diptych of critical fiction and fictional criticism in
a peculiarly compact, intellectual, literary format is characteristically Borgesean.
Before him, no one could astound or please in quite that way.

The thread, or solution to the story's form and meaning, is put into a
summary of an imaginary book entitled *A Coat of Many Colours*. As a whole
the story follows the usual pattern of *presentation* (introduction, Parts I, II, III),
discussion (Parts IV, V), and *solution* (Postscript); and the Postscript itself conforms
to the fundamental procedure of *proposition* (summary of *A Coat of Many Colours*)
and *rejection* (concluding paragraph), which we have seen at the end of "A New
Refutation of Time" and the beginning of "The Approach," the same pattern
described in an item from the bibliography of Pierre Menard's works:

> (e) a technical article on the possibility of enriching chess by
> eliminating one of the rook's pawns. Menard proposes, recommends,
> discusses and concludes by rejecting such an innovation.

This pattern indicates the degree to which Borges' work and his system are
hypothetical projections or constructions of the intellect; they are "pure" in
this respect, not valid philosophical schemes, not "true" for Borges in the sense
that Schopenhauer's metaphysic, say, was true for Schopenhauer, but rather
lucid improbabilities. The pattern is also a measure of the degree to which
Borges' work is intellectual *play*, resting frequently on a jest. Few words in
his vocabulary are more repeated than "game" or "play" ("juego"), and there
is no better word to describe the effect his work has on readers. Certainly
there is a strong element of play in his summary of the nonexistent critical
study, *A Coat of Many Colours*, a summary which is nothing more or less than
a meaningful joke.

A Coat of Many Colours, like a Borges' essay, classifies "The Immortal" and places it in a literary tradition. The class is that of the cento and the tradition includes the centos of classical antiquity as well as works by Ben Jonson, Alexander Ross, George Moore, and T. S. Eliot, each of whom created works comprised of "retazos" or remnants of other works. Both the title, *A Coat of Many Colours*, and the author's name, Nahum Cordovero, however, disclose an artifice within artifice which is the hallmark of Borges. *A Coat of Many Colours* is an appropriate name for the book because it recalls the Biblical Joseph and his famous garment and thus invokes *Joseph* Cartaphilus, but also because *cento* is simply Latin for rag cushion or patchwork quilt, an etymological definition which gives new meaning to the word "retazo." The book's title is equally appropriate to the story; in fact, the briefly imagined book stands in exact relationship to the produced story as a picture within a picture: the one is the compressed, analytic reflection of the other, almost to the point of a one-to-one correspondence. For if Homer, that imaginary author, wrote "The Immortal," compiled the Postscript in fact, then a no less imaginary author, Nahum Cordovero, wrote the study. But once again, as with the title, we must read hieroglyphically. *Nahum*, the first name of this writer who provides a key to our perplexities about the text, means "comforter" or "source of comfort" in Hebrew, while *Cordovero* is similarly, Kabbalistically prophetic: Moses Cordovero is the name of a famous Kabbalist writer whom Scholem calls the greatest theoretician of Jewish mysticism. The word *cordovero* itself can be broken down into *string* (the Latin *chorda*, meaning catgut, derives from the Greek *khorde*, meaning yarn) and *true*: Nahum Cordovero is literally a latter-day Ariadne! The typically Borgesean twist in this word game is that the utterly false and fantastic source provides accurate information, pointing to the inner structure and outer reality of the story, for Cordovero concludes that "the whole document is apocryphal." The apocryphal naming the apocryphal: that is "the Piranesi effect," that is the true Borges. Also Borgesean is the sense of humor. There is only grim humor in *The Waste Land* and there is no deep laughter in "The Immortal," but Borges is seldom — *El hacedor* is a notable exception — without sly wit. We saw the beginnings of that wit in feebler form in *Universal History of Infamy*; now we see it as subordinated effect and still another way in which Borges' writing may properly be described as *juego* or "game."

The main body of the Postscript is a list, another of Borges' connective series, ranging from classical antiquity to the times of Bernard Shaw. The books alluded to fall into two fundamental categories — naturally overlapping — which are the paradigmatic of form and the paradigmatic of content. There are no artless referential allusions here — each item is expressive; in sum they are substantive. The first group needs little explanation: it establishes the precedent for creating literature from literature, and it is made up of works based on other works, like Alexander Ross' *Virgilius Evangelizans*, a poem in Vergilian Latin dealing with the life of Christ, and George Moore's *The Brook Kerith*, an incredibly turgid historical novel about Christ in deliberately anachronistic Biblical language. In both cases, what Borges is getting at, clearly, is a tendency of literature to recapture old subjects in old language based on previous writing. It is a tendency we have marked in Borges' own writing, and it is one the narrator of "The Immortal" calls to our attention in the introduction: "The original is written in English and abounds in Latinisms" ("El original está redactado en inglés y abunda en latinismo"). The word *redactado* (rather than *escrito*) is especially important here, implying as it does that the manuscript is not so much written as rewritten, a fact substantiated by the Latinisms. But what is equally important is that each of the writers specifically referred to has a direct bearing on the theme of the Immortal as Borges develops it.

Christ is literally the everlasting Jew, and therefore Ross's poem celebrates the Immortal in still another guise, while Moore's novel, like Lawrence's *The Man Who Died*, shows that the Crucifixion was not fatal to Jesus, who merely underwent the imitative death of coma and revived to live another life in his own lifetime. (An appropriate subtitle for Moore's nearly forgotten novel could be taken from his completely forgotten play *The Making of an Immortal*, which deals with a writer.) Jonson, too, in his poem on Shakespeare contributes to the theme. The Postscript cites "Ben Jonson, who defined his contemporaries with remnants from Seneca," and Borges obviously has in mind, as a corollary to Homer's universal immortality, the everything and nothingness of Jonson's contemporary Shakespeare. Otherwise, Shakespeare, so appropriate to Borges' theme, would be conspicuously absent from "The Immortal." Turning to the text of Jonson's poem, memorializing Shakespeare, we see that a particular passage even further reinforces the theme and technique of Borges' story:

> And though thou hadst small *Latine*, and lesse *Greeke*,
>   From thence to honour thee, I would not seeke
> For names; but call forth thund'ring *Aeschilus*,
>   *Euripides*, and *Sophocles* to us,
> *Paccuvius*, *Accius*, him of *Cordova* dead
>   To life againe. . . .

The method of involving other authors is Borges', and the resurrection of Seneca, "him of *Cordova* dead," is a re-enactment of "The Immortal." The procedure hinges on "contemporaries"—literature can make contemporaries of Vergil and Alexander Ross; it can raise from the dead, as in the case of Jonson and Seneca. The Immortal is Author; his immortality is Literature.

The last precedent cited by Cordovero is the most important: *The Waste*

Land provides not only an analogous form but parallel content as well. In a word, both *The Waste Land* and "The Immortal" are centos which come to pretty much the same conclusion:

These fragments I have shored against my ruins.

When the end approaches, wrote Cartaphilus, *images of what is remembered no longer remain: only words remain*. Words, mutilated and displaced words, words of others, were the poor dole left him by the hours and the centuries.

The Tithonus-like weariness of Borges' Homer is reflected in Eliot's Tiresias, who, like De Quincey's Homer, is ancient in other than a personal sense. Moreover, both works are world visions, moving between the ancient and modern, the East and the West, presenting the world as a desert ruin; both employ the device of the narrator who is all the characters and whose memory is their medium of existence; both are self-consciously mythic and rely on the quest or search for their central action and employ the metaphor of thirst as the fundamental yearning, a thirst which is both for the River of Life and the River of Death; both are ostentatiously learned and employ literary allusion as matter and method. If there is a striking difference, it is the characterizing one that Eliot's poem is social, religious, irrationalistic, and concerned with the kinds of love, while Borges' story is abstracted from society, fantastic, intellectual, cogent, and unconcerned with human relations. Both works are modified monologues, though it is worthwhile noting that in Eliot's we sometimes (as in parts of "The Game of Chess") lose sight of the central figure, while in Borges' story the central figure is an almost constant focus. (In Borges there is a general tendency to limit narrative to one figure, and to one figure who is not in vital, emotional contact with others, to whom other people figure largely as ideas or stimuli to action. This is a condition of Borges' lonely world, and it is a severe limitation upon the possibilities of his fiction; but on the other hand it is the condition which enables him to operate in an atmosphere that is almost purely speculative and imaginary. Then too, there is often a suggestion, never developed, sometimes censured, of political and moral implications in Borges. I have noted one example in "The Immortal" and I do not think it would be hard to derive a fairly cogent, if not satisfactory, ethic from his writings. But such an effort, so essential to an understanding of parts of Eliot, is foreign to Borges' writing, which presents morality, like murder, as one of the fine arts.) But how can two men who have such a similar vision, and a similar imagery, who rely on the same schemes, as of the Eternal Return (embodied in Eliot in the Tarot cards and the chess game, which symbols are among Borges' favorites), how can two such men create such formally different works? The answer lies, again, in the vantage point. Eliot, at least in *The Waste Land*, is on the order of De Quincey, and Borges works more in the vein of Joyce, whose writings also function on the principle of the Eternal Return. I am speaking, of course, of esthetic dispositions which tend toward the open, aspiring, inevitably inconclusive and those which tend toward the closed, formulated, finished work. Specifically, Eliot's view in *The Waste Land*, as we can gather from the related "Gerontion," is from within the labyrinth:

> Think now
> History has many cunning passages, contrived corridors
> And issues. . . ,

and he shows a character, who like De Quincey, "can connect/Nothing with nothing," even though he does exist in a work which, like De Quincey's, is busy making parallels. Borges, in contrast, leads his character to the moment of awareness: "Everything became clear to me that day." Joyce, Eliot, Borges are all labyrinthine; all employ the image and symbol of the labyrinth; but only Joyce and Borges, by their use of "magic" correlation, which is an ordering expression of the Eternal Return, create labyrinths which are complete and decipherable; all three aim at mystification, but Eliot chooses that mystification as a final intention. One advantage which emerges from such a comparison is the possibility of uniting our views of Borges, Joyce, Eliot (and Yeats too, of whom Borges writes: "like so many others, he conceived a cyclical doctrine of history") in the study of a common theme—the Eternal Return. Such a comparison is beyond the scope of my present interest, but it indicates once again the synthesizing quality of Borges' work, and, by association, implies its value.

The second group of allusions in the Postscript has less to do with the cento-technique and more with the substance of the story. In each instance something has been borrowed from the acknowledged source and interpolated into "The Immortal." But it is no case of literal theft or simple annexation. Pliny is a good example. On the surface it would seem that the allusion to *Natural History* is referential, an allusion to informative writing which is the source of the passage in question. In fact "source" seems to be the right word here, for Borges does take a description from Pliny and filter it into his own text. In Part I of "The Immortal," where Cordovero finds an interpolation from Pliny, we read:

> We left from Arisnoë and entered the scorched desert. We crossed
> the land of the troglodytes, who devour snakes and lack all verbal

communication; that of the garamantes, who keep their females
in common and nourish themselves on lions; that of the augyls,
who worship only Tartarus. We wearied other deserts, where the
sand is black, where the traveler must usurp the hours of night
because the fervor of day is intolerable. From far off I caught sight
of the mountain that gave its name to the Ocean: on its slopes grows
spurge, which neutralizes poisons; on its summit live the satyrs,
a nation of cruel, savage men, given to lust. That those barbarous
regions, where the earth is mother of monsters, could shelter in
their bosom a famous city, seemed inconceivable to all of us. We
continued our journey since it would have been a dishonor to retreat.
A few rash men slept with their faces exposed to the moon; fever
burned them; in the depraved water of the cisterns others drank
madness and death.

And in the section of Pliny Cordovero precisely directs us to we do find the
framework for the description in Borges:

In the middle of the desert some place the Atlas tribe, and next
to them the half-animal Goat-Pans and the Blemmyae and
Gamphasantes and Satyrs and Strapfoots.

The Atlas tribe have fallen below the level of human civilization,
if we can believe what is said; for they do not address one another
by any names, and when they behold the rising and setting sun,
they utter awful curses against it as the cause of disaster to themselves
and their fields, and when they are asleep they do not have dreams
like the rest of mankind. The Cave-dwellers hollow out caverns,
which are their dwellings, they live on the flesh of snakes, and they
have no voice, but only make squeaking noises, being entirely devoid
of intercourse by speech. The Garamates do not practice marriage
but live with their women promiscuously. The Augilae only worship
the powers of the lower world. The Gamphasantes go naked, do
not engage in battle, and hold no intercourse with any foreigner.
The Blemmyae are reported to have no heads, their mouth and
eyes being attached to their chests. The satyrs have nothing of
ordinary humanity about them except human shape. The form of
the Goat-Pans is that which is commonly shown in pictures of them.
The Strapfoots are people with feet like leather thongs, whose nature
it is to crawl instead of walking. The Pharusi, originally a Persian

people, are said to have accompanied Hercules on his journey to the Ladies of the West. Nothing more occurs to us to record about Africa.

The borrowing, however, is neither exact nor artless. Of course Borges has condensed Pliny, but then he has also blended his sources, creating a pastiche of pastiches, as in the fragment about men being burned to death by the moon, which is not found in that part of Pliny and which may have come to Borges through De Quincey:

> In p. 50 of the "Annotations" upon Glanvill's *Lux Orientalis* the author . . . having occasion to quote from the Psalms "The sun shall not burn thee by day, neither the moon by night" in order to illustrate that class of cases where an ellipsis is to be suggested by the sense rather than directly indicated, says "The word *burn* cannot be repeated, but some other more suitable verb is to be supplied." A gentleman, however, who has lately returned from Upper Egypt, &c., assures me that the moon *does* produce an effect on the skin which may as accurately be expressed by the word "burn" as any solar effect.

Finally the most meaningful thing about the passage in Pliny is that fact, first, that the description of these monstrous peoples is fitted into a geographical sequence which suggests a journey and, second, that Homer himself is cited as an authority for the information:

> Eastward of all of these there are vast uninhabited regions spreading as far as the Garamantes and Augilae and the Cave-dweller—the most reliable opinion being that of those who place two Ethiopias beyond the African desert, and especially Homer, who tells us that the Ethiopians are divided into two sections, the eastward and the westward.

The clear implication is that Homer has made the trip, knows the land firsthand, an implication which reinforces Borges' identification of Homer as Rufus, the man who makes the trip to the City of the Immortals. The relationship between Borges and Pliny is active: if Borges borrows from Pliny, he enriches the Pliny text by eliciting a new meaning.

The other sources are used similarly. The actual reference is not exhaustive, and if we take the trouble to consult the passage in question, we find something new in the story and often in the source as well. Skipping over the De Quincey passage, which I have already discussed, we can compare "A letter from Descartes to the ambassador Pierre Chanut" with Borges' version:

if I had been only as wise as they say savages persuade themselves monkeys are, I should never have been known by anyone as a maker of books: for it is said that they imagine that the monkeys would be able to speak if they wished, but that they refrain from doing it so that they will not be forced to work.

I recalled that it is famous among the Ethiopians that the monkeys deliberately do not speak so that they will not be forced to work and I attributed Argus' silence to suspicion or fear.

This is the direct correspondence, but more interesting to the motto Descartes takes from Seneca's *Thyestes* at the end of the same letter:

And so I think the best thing I can do from now on is to abstain from writing books; and having taken for my motto:

Death lies heavy upon that man who,
unusually well known to others, dies
unknown to himself.

In Descartes' allusion to antiquity, and to the same figure Jonson employs and Cordovero mentions, Borges shows the centrifugal force of literature; and by noting the sense of Seneca's lines we are directed to the pathos of the conversation between Rufus and Homer who has become a dog-like creature and forgotten his own nature: there is a worse death: to be famous to all, and to die unknown to oneself. Notice, however, that neither the allusion in the Postscript nor the passage about the monkeys in the narrative directly evokes this motto. The evocative quality of this allusion is only remotely present, almost silent, as is customary in Borges. Nevertheless, if the motto serves for Descartes, it likewise can serve for Borges' story, for each of us, having forgotten that we are Homer, dies famous throughout the world but unrecognized by ourselves.

As with the first group of allusions I considered from the Postscript, the last in the second group is the most important: Cordovero directs us to *Back to Methuselah*, Act V, but once again while he points in the right direction, his scope is not nearly broad enough. The parallels between the Shaw play and Borges' story are close and pervasive, even though the attitude taken toward immortality in each is different. Shaw's theme, as described by Borges, is optimistic, corrective, while the one we have seen in Borges is dejected and dispiriting:

In *Man and Superman* he declares that heaven and hell are not places but conditions of the human spirit; in *Back to Methuselah* that man

ought to resolve to live 300 years so as not to die at 80 in full
immaturity with a golf club in his hand, and that the physical
universe began by Spirit and shall return to Spirit.

Here then is another ethic for immortals and one that brings the world back
to its originating spirit as well, but Borges' story is far from the joking argument
for creative evolution that Shaw's play is. Nevertheless Borges found much
to his use and liking in Shaw's "cerebral capers."

Shaw's play, as his preface states, shows that "human life is continuous
and immortal," and it uses the mythic image of the Wandering Jew as well
as the literary unity Borges hypothesizes: "An ancient writer whose name has
come down to us in several forms, such as Shakespeare, Shelley, Sheridan,
and Shoddy," and it even voices the fundamental notion of art as dream when
Eve tells Adam of certain of their sons who

> borrow and never pay; but one gives them what they want, because
> they tell beautiful lies in beautiful words. They can remember their
> dreams. They can dream without sleeping. They have not will
> enough to create instead of dreaming; but the serpent said that every
> dream could be willed into creation by those strong enough to
> believe in it.

In the last act, which is commended to our attention by Cordovero, the time
is A.D. 31,920, yet the matter is the same as that of Borges' antiquity, and
the point is made that tomorrow is "The day that never comes." In this world
beyond Bradbury, the most specific locus of comparison between the two texts
is the Swiftian notion, complicated by the Emersonian doctrine of compensation,
that the Immortals have grown completely indifferent because in the end all
things balance out. In Borges we read:

> Instructed by centuries of practice, the republic of immortal men
> had achieved the perfection of tolerance and almost of disdain. It
> knew that in an infinite term all things happen to every man. On
> account of his past or future virtues, every man deserves all goodness,
> but also deserves all treachery because of his past or future infamies.

This is the intolerable ethic Borges extracts with all the irony of the defeated
victor, while in *Back to Methuselah* we find that Shaw's immortals, like Borges',
are indifferent to discomfort and pleasure, for, as they recognize: "Everything
happens to everybody sooner or later if there is time enough. And with us
there is eternity." But the passage we remember from Shaw's play as being
most Borgesean of all is one in a completely different vein; one, nevertheless,
where eras, texts, authors coalesce into one unified cultural senility:

There is a prehistoric saying that has come down to us from a famous woman teacher. She said: "Leave women; and study mathematics." It is the only remaining fragment of a lost scripture called The Confessions of St. Augustin, the English Opium Eater. That primitive savage must have been a great woman, to say a thing that still lives after three hundred centuries.

Like the other allusions, the one to *Back to Methuselah* has its secret aspect too. In the third act, not the fifth, which Cordovero directs us to, we can find a solution for the apparent death of Homer which is related in the introduction of "The Immortal": "In October the princess heard from a passenger on the *Zeus* that Cartaphilus had died at sea on returning to Smyrna and that they had buried him on the island of Ios." Nowhere in the text does Borges offer an explanation for this apparent death, but if we turn to the third act of Shaw's play we find a character quoting a report which "points out that an extraordinary number of first-rate persons . . . have died by drowning during the last two centuries." The explanation for these drownings, which surely includes the death of Cartaphilus at sea, is given by a near-immortal archbishop who ran into bureaucratic problems trying to collect his pension at the age of ninety-seven because he looked so young. His solution was simple—pretend to die and start life all over again.

> I did kill myself. It was quite easy. I left a suit of clothes by the seashore during the bathing season, with documents in the pocket to identify me. I then turned up in a strange place, pretending that I had lost my memory, and did not know my name or my age or anything about myself. Under treatment I recovered my health, but not my memory. I have had several careers since I began this routine of life and death. I have been an archbishop three times. When I persuaded the authorities to knock down all our towns and rebuild them from the foundations, or move them, I went into the artillery, and became a general. I have been a President.

Even the question of Homer's burial is solved by this Archbishop, who, in his architectural plans, may even remind us of Borges' Homer. When asked how he can have been President Dickenson, whose body was cremated and whose ashes lie in St. Paul's, the Archbishop replies:

> They almost always found the body. During the bathing season there are plenty of bodies. I have been cremated again and again. At first I used to attend my own funeral in disguise, because I had read about a man doing that in an old romance by an author named

Bennett, from whom I remember borrowing five pounds in 1912.
But I got tired of that. I would not cross the street now to read
my last epitaph.

Here then is the sham death practiced by the Immortals so as not to arouse
suspicion, and here too is the necessary loss of memory to permit the renewal
of life. This death-by-water motif is further suggested by Homer's explanation
that "On the fourth of October, 1921, the *Patna*, which was carrying me to
Bombay, had to cast anchor in a port on the Eritrean coast." The *Patna*, "a
local steamer as old as the hills," carrying "eight hundred pilgrims (more or
less)," is Jim's boat in Conrad's *Lord Jim*, and we read there of a Captain Brierly
who commits suicide by jumping overboard. Jim, on the other hand, also jumps
ship in the crucial moment of his life, and Conrad has him explain: "It was
as if I jumped into a well—into an everlasting deep hole." In light of Borges
we read this passage somewhat differently, and are not surprised to find another
character urging the following plan for Jim: "Let him creep twenty feet
underground and stay there," and still another remarking, "Bury him in some
sort." Of course this is what in effect happens and Jim, "the youngest human
being now in existence," revives to lead a new life.

This last allusion to Conrad demands our recognition that "The Immortal"
is immensely more allusive than Borges admits. The *Lord Jim* allusion really
tells us nothing about "The Immortal" but it invokes the same theme from
other writings, and thus establishes the mirror relationship in literature which
the Immortals recognize in life:

> Among the Immortals . . . each act (and each thought) is the echo
> of others which preceded it in the past, without apparent principle,
> or the faithful omen of others which will repeat it, to the point
> of vertigo, in the future. There is no thing that is not lost, as it
> were, amidst indefatigable mirrors. Nothing can occur only once,
> nothing is preciously precarious.

Allusion is thus the device which reflects one work in another; and despite
the lack of apparent principle in repetition which the Immortals describe, allusion
repeats meaningfully, ordering the chaos which is at once literature and life.
Thus we have in the story major themes alluded to, as in the case of "the
nightingale of the Caesars," which invokes Keats'

> The voice I hear this passing night was heard
> In ancient days by emperor and clown.

And we have minor works, like the reference to a novel by Ellis Cornelia Knight which Borges probably read of in De Quincey's review of another book. The novel's title tells us about all we need to know of it: *Marcus Flaminius; or a view of the military, political and social life of the Romans: in a series of letters from a patrician to his friend; in the year DCC.LXII. from the foundation of Rome to year DCC.LXIX.* There are no significant parallels in the novel to Borges' story, except perhaps for one lamenting letter which reads in part: "death flies from the cavern of despair and only delights to overthrow the pompous fabrics of hope: your friend still lives; his youth and the strength of his constitution have once more snatched him from the arms of freedom." This last-minute reference, gathered magpie fashion by Borges in the course of his reading, establishes a pole, and an end, to the range of allusion I have been noting in "The Immortal." From the basic outline of Eliot's *The Waste Land*, which supplies the form of Borges' story, and the specific material of Shaw's *Back to Methuselah*, which supplies much of the content, to Miss Knight's *Marcus Flaminius*, which supplies at least a single item, we have the entire rank of allusion. One could spend more time filling in the degrees and undoubtedly Borges will give rise to his own academic "industry" just as Eliot and Joyce have, but what is more important, what concerns all readers of Borges and not just the detectives, is the purpose and meaning of these allusions.

Borges has taken care to see that all readers will know the allusive nature of "The Immortal" even if they do not grasp the extent of that allusiveness. Hence all readers are aware of the substantive as well as the secret quality in this work. Like *Ulysses*, like *The Waste Land*, "The Immortal" uses allusion not only as a means to an end but as an end itself. Each of the allusions contributes to our awareness of literature as universal memory, which, in not seeming to lose sight of anything, guarantees the survival of all, is, in a word, immortality. To break down the story into its constituent allusions is an inevitable desire of the inquiring mind, but to do so takes one no closer to the monistic meaning of the narrative which has as its purpose the fictional embodiment of the philosophy Borges reads in Emerson: "a faith which eliminates circumstances, and which declares that every man is all men and that there is no one who is not the universe." On the other hand to be at least aware of these borrowings is to be in touch with the secret meaning of the story, is to read it Kabbalistically, hieroglyphically, to solve its puzzle with the clues given.

In the use of allusion Borges has never pushed farther than "The Immortal." Nor has he ever written another story which so completely embodies his metaphysical and literary theories, for in this one narrative he actually creates a character of extraordinary implication and presents him a situation where we perceive a phase of his emergence and disintegration. The character, the only character, I think, in all of Borges, is the literary Over-Soul. Emerson, in his notes to an essay on the Over-Soul, had jotted down the following observations:

> There is one soul.
> It is related to the world.
> Art is its action thereon.
> Science finds its methods.
> Literature is its record.

Borges takes the first of these jottings as his premise and the last as his method. Emerson said he liked to read "for the lustres, as if one should use a fine picture in a chromatic experiment, for its rich colours." Borges seems to read that way in preparation for his stories, and in reading him we do the same, noting the allusions — some of them — for the originals they are, and in this way we discover, with Emerson, that "It is a greater joy to see the author's author, than himself."

The author's author is first of all Borges, because of the involutions of his fictional worlds; but then the author's author is the figure Borges' essays define with tireless precision, whose spirit moves in and above Borges' work to bring it into line with all other works. It is toward an intimation of this spirit that all his works move, asking the same fantastic question we ask when, in different terms, we consider literary history and tradition:

> The player is also prisoner
> (the phrase is Omar's) of another table
> of black nights and white days.
>
> God moves the player, and he the piece.
> What god behind God begins the plot
> of dust and time and dream and agony?

Borges began by introducing his own imaginary passages into already existing books, then progressed to the fabrication of imaginary books with bits of real ones worked in, and finally created a single character who not only is responsible for this story, but for all literature: the author of authors: The Immortal. That creation represents a mastery by order and reason of infinite chaos; that it is, ironically, a destruction of all that is personal and real is only the character of his achievement and the dilemma of our irrational existence.

Borges' is the hand that points: his essence is a direction away from his own substance. To see beyond his work — really, to see through it to other writings — is the greatest necessity, and achievement, of his labor. He stands midway between the cataphysical characters of his stories and the metaphysical spirit of literature, reflecting primary light onto tertiary beings. He does this with intricate allusion, and if we are tempted to undervalue his genius because he seems to borrow all that is his, let us remember what De Quincey wrote of Coleridge with generosity and accuracy, a statement which applies to each of these three men—Coleridge, De Quincey, Borges—in different ways, but which, in that minor variation of a perpetual gesture, constitutes their literary identity. De Quincey writes: "if he took—he gave. Constantly he fancied other men's thoughts his own; but such were the confusions of his memory that continually, and with even greater liberality, he ascribed his own thoughts to others."

JAIME ALAZRAKI

Kabbalistic Traits in Borges' Narration

The reader well acquainted with the short stories of Jorge Luis Borges knows that his texts do not exhaust themselves at the level of literal meaning. Like most of his narratives in which one easily distinguishes a denotative plot and a connotative symbol or allegory, his prose too offers an immediate and manifest layer and a more oblique and allusive one. Even the casual reader perceives in his stories an obverse-*fabula* and a reverse-symbol, although he may fail to define the bounds of the former with respect to the latter. On the other hand, in the realm of language, even the alert reader tends to accept the text in its externality, dismissing that interior and elusive side, which may be invisible at first glance but which is no less present and functional than its visible counterpart. One of the wonders of Borges' art is precisely that Kabbalistic feature apparent in many of his narrative texts. This art is Kabbalistic in a sense defined by Borges himself in his essay "A Vindication of the Kabbalah," where he explains that his purpose is to vindicate not the doctrine but "the hermeneutic or cryptographic procedures which lead to it." To further elaborate: "These procedures are the vertical reading of the holy text, the reading called *bouestrophedon* (from right to left, one line, from left to right the following one), the methodical substitution of some letters of the alphabet for others, the sum of the numerical value of the letters...." Borges refers here to "certain techniques of mystical speculation which are popularly supposed to represent the heart and core of Kabbalism," yet, according to Gershom Scholem, "none of these techniques of mystical exegesis can be called Kabbalistic in the strict sense of the word.... What really deserves to be called Kabbalism has very

From *Studies in Short Fiction* 8, no. 1 (Winter 1971). © 1971 by Newberry College.

little to do with the 'Kabbalistic' practices." However, it is this technical side
of Kabbalism that interests us. In essence what is involved are the possible
alternatives to the reading of a text. The Kabbalists differentiate between an
exoteric interpretation of the Scripture and an esoteric one. In the first case
the meaning of the text is literal, but in the second "the Holy Scriptures" —
explains a Talmudic mystic — "are like a large house with many, many rooms,
and outside each door lies a key — but it is not the right one. To find the right
keys that will open the doors — that is the great and arduous task." The Kabbalists
found that each word of the Torah (Pentateuch) "has six hundred thousand
'faces,' that is, layers of meaning or entrances," and that "it is made up not
only of the names of God but is as a whole the one great Name of God."
According to an early Midrash, God "looked into the Torah and created the
world, since the cosmos and all nature was already prefigured in the Torah,
so that God, looking into the Torah, could see it, although to us this aspect
of the Torah remains concealed." For Joseph Gikatila, a leading Spanish Kabbalist
of the thirteenth century, "the Torah is not itself the name of God but the
explication of the Name of God, and the letters are the mystical body of God,
while God is the soul of the letters." In order to penetrate to recondite strata
of the Holy text, the Kabbalists developed four levels of interpretation: *peshat*
or literal meaning, *remez* or allegorical meaning, *derasha* or Talmudic and Aggadic
interpretation, and *sod* or anagogic meaning. In addition to these levels of
interpretation, they used several techniques of speculation such as *Gematria*
or calculation of the numerical value of Hebrew words and the search for
connections with other words or phrases of equal value, *Notarikon* or
interpretation of the letters of a word as abbreviations of whole sentences,
Temurah or interchange of letters according to certain systematic rules. Applying
each of these techniques, the possibilities are almost infinite.

To the question "Have you tried to make your own stories Kabbalistic?"
Borges replied, "Yes, sometimes I have." The question as well as the answer
are broad and ambiguous enough to encourage speculation. Borges' availability
as a reader of his own work (through the innumerable interviews he has given)
has provided rich and valuable information that no student of his work can
afford to ignore. In some instances he has furnished possible and alternative
clues for the reading of his stories; in others he has suggested new and refreshing
interpretations of narratives whose trite understanding was becoming more
and more rigid and stereotyped. He has compiled his own anthologies, a
conventional undertaking that he has turned into a Kabbalistic reading of his
work, not so much because he claims that he would like "to be judged by
it (his *Personal Anthology*), and justified or reproved by it," but rather because
the preferences change from edition to edition as if Borges were reminding

the reader that an author must be judged by his work and not by his opinions of it. So, an author who usually is the absolute creator of his book, cannot be the absolute reader of it. The degree of lucidity varies from author to author, but whatever the acuteness may be "there are many things in an author's work not intended and only partially understood by him." When Borges was asked about the Kabbalistic quality of his writing, he may have thought of the fact that as the literature of the Kabbalah has been defined as "a narrative philosophy," so his tales have been characterized as "metaphysical fantasies." He may have thought about the idea that the whole world is for the Kabbalists a *corpus symbolicum*, and the definition of himself as "a man who interweaves these symbols." Or he may have simply referred to the belief that as the Torah has for the Kabbalists "seventy faces" (a number standing for infinite), so the symbols he has coined "are capable of many, perhaps incompatible values."

We are not suggesting an application of the method of the Kabbalah to Borges' writings. The Kabbalistic exegesis of the Scripture is motivated by the belief that "a work dictated by the Holy Spirit was an absolute text: a text where the collaboration of chance is calculable to zero." Thus, if the word *light* occurs five times in the story of the first day of Creation, the number is not, cannot, be accidental: it corresponds, as explained in the *Midrash Genesis Rabbah*, to the five books of the Torah. If the Torah begins with the letter Beth, whose numerical value is two, it is because, explains the *Zohar* (*The Book of Splendor*), "the process of creation has taken place in two planes, one above and one below. . . . The lower occurrence corresponds to the higher; one produced the upper world, and the other the nether world (of the visible creation)." It is absurd to think that in Borges' writings "every word is capable of becoming a symbol" as is the case of the Scripture for the Jewish mystic, but it is not preposterous at all to treat Borges' texts with a rigor similar to the zeal displayed by the Kabbalists in their reading of the Scripture. After all, the efforts of the Kabbalists to find new layers of meaning in the Biblical text are not essentially different from the endeavors of the critic to establish new possibilities or perspectives of interpretation of the literary text. There are two more reasons that reinforce our contention: first, the enthralling fascination that the Kabbalah has exerted on Borges' mind; second, the fantastic character of his stories induces us often to estimate some seemingly incoherent words and occurrences as whimsical displays of arbitrary fantasy, thus missing the true impact of those masterfully constructed whimsicalities. An example of this kind of word is the adjective *unanimous* to modify *night* in the first line of the story "The Circular Ruins;" the word is used for its etymological constituents (*unus animus*) rather than for its normative meaning in order subtly to anticipate what is literally disclosed in the last line of the story: the magician's condition of appearance dreamt by another. An example of the kind of occurrence that may seem to the reader a playful detour of the imagination just to stress the fantastic character of his tale occurs in the story "The Approach to Al-Mu'tasim." The protagonist, a law student in Bombay, finds himself in the center of a civil tumult between Moslems and Hindus; he joins the fray and kills a Hindu. When the police intervene, the student takes flight and makes for the farthest outskirts of town. "He scales the wall of an entangled garden, at the back of which rises a circular tower. . . . Once on the roof, where there is a blackish well in the center, he encounters a squalid man. . . [who] confides in him that his profession is to rob gold teeth from the white-shrouded cadavers which the Parsees leave in this tower." The encounter of the student with the despoiler of cadavers is an essential link in the sequence of the narrative; the presence, on the other hand, of white shrouded cadavers left in a tower is rather perplexing to the reader unfamiliar with the practices of the Parsees. In the context of Borges' story, though, the detail is far from being a whim meant to astonish. The tower where the student takes shelter is a *dakhma* or Tower of Silence and in those *dakhmas* Zoroastrians in Persia and India dispose of their dead. The Parsees (Indian Zoroastrians) believe that water, fire, and earth are pure and holy and must be protected and, thus, a corpse—the most impure and contaminating object—may not be buried in the earth or cast into a stream, a pool, or the sea, nor may it be destroyed by fire. Instead they place the corpse in towers built for that purpose where the flesh is consumed by vultures. The *dakhma* is a round tower, some twenty feet high, built of stone in the shape of an open cone, with one door near the base, through which the body is carried in. In the center of the tower there is a pit about six feet deep lined with concentric shelves and paved with stones. Once the flesh has been stripped away by vultures, the bones are cast into the central well where they lie until air, rain, and sun change them into dust, thereby making them pure again. There are seven Towers of Silence in the vicinity of Bombay.

In the light of this brief description of a *dakhma*, Borges' enigmatic detail gains a completely unexpected function within the narrative. It is no longer a fantastic oddity as the outward appearance seems to imply, but rather a necessary element that fully integrates with the story as a whole. Borges uses all the materials at his disposal to recreate the setting of his tale; he himself has disclosed certain analogies in the first scene of the story with elements from Kipling's "On the City Wall." Yet, the last thing Borges is willing to do is to produce an effect of local color. He has elaborated on this subject in his essay "The Argentine Writer and Tradition"; there he wrote:

Gibbon observes that in the Arabian book *par excellence*, in the

Koran, there are no camels; I believe if there were any doubt as to the authenticity of the Koran, this absence of camels would be sufficient to prove it is an Arabian work. It was written by Mohammed, and Mohammed, as an Arab, had no reason to know that camels were especially Arabian; for him they were a part of reality, he had no reason to emphasize them; on the other hand, the first thing a falsifier, a tourist, an Arab nationalist would do is have a surfeit of camels, caravans of camels, on every page; but Mohammed, as Arab, was unconcerned: he knew he could be an Arab without camels. I think we Argentines can emulate Mohammed, can believe in the possibility of being Argentine without abounding in local color.

One should remember that Borges' story is written as a summary of the novel *The Approach to Al-Mu'tasim* by the Bombay lawyer Mir Bahadur Ali. As such, he rightly assumes that by just describing the facts as they are, his readers will understand that the encounter of the student with the robber takes place in one of seven *dakhmas* found in the vicinity of Bombay, since—paraphrasing Borges—Bahadur Ali, as a native of Bombay, had no reason to know that *dakhmas* were especially Indian; for him they were part of reality, he had no reason to emphasize them. We know, though, that the summary of the hypothetical novel is an artifice of Borges, but precisely because it is so, Borges has given enough and accurate information—and his description is a true model of minute accuracy—to enable the perceptive reader to realize that he is referring to a *dakhma*; and, at the same time, he has subtly avoided excessive explanation so as not to destroy the magic of the illusion.

In some instances Borges himself provides the clue to the Kabbalistic construction of his narrative. Towards the end of the same story—"The Approach to Al-Mu'tasim"—, he suggests an allegorical reading of the "detective novel:" "Al-Mu'tasim is the emblem of God, and the punctual itinerary of the hero is in some manner the forward progress of the soul in its mystic ascent." The search of the student becomes, thus, a mystical experience no different from the one revealed in the Sufistic poem *Mantiq ut-Tair*, which Borges fully describes in a footnote as the solution to the enigmatic ending of the apocryphal novel. Since its author and its protagonist are Muslim, Sufism is the Islamic form of mysticism that best befits the mystical reverse of the story. Yet other possibilities are suggested as probable sources or clues. Borges mentions among those distant and possible predecessors of Bahadur Ali, the Jerusalem Kabbalist Isaac Luria, "who in the sixteenth century proclaimed that the soul of an ancestor or that of a master might enter the soul of an unfortunate to comfort or instruct him." But if we accept Borges' *locus classicus* according to which "each writer creates his own precursor," other predecessors could be added to his list. The story may be read as a Sufistic experience, as an expression of Kabbalistic *Ibbur*, and also as a narrative translation of Hindu *Ātman*. As in Ferid ed-Din Attar's poem where the Simurg is God and all men are the Simurg, in *Mundaka* Upanishad "all things proceed from Brahman as sparks from a fire, and all things return to him as rivers to the sea—*Ātman* (the eternal soul) is the means by which one obtains Brahman"; thus, Brahman is *Ātman* and *Ātman* is Brahman. It could be argued that once one mystic system is presented, the others are essentially implied in it. In our case Hindu *Ātman*, Sufism (a form of mysticism that has been defined as "Vedanta in Muslim dress") and the *Ibbur* of the Kabbalah are different manifestations of a same attempt: to feel the presence of the Godhead in such a way that God becomes the center and the circumference or, as the *Brihad-aranyaka* Upanishad puts it, "the hub and felly of the wheel of which the individual souls are the spokes."

Yet, it is this well-wrought ambiguity in Borges' stories that often generates their density of meaning. The apparent ambiguity is produced by the conjunction of several intuitions, by the overlapping of several motivations and sources that, like thin layers, were masterfully pressed into one tight and limpid fabric. One can simply enjoy the product in its outward result, or one can attempt to strip off those layers in order to comprehend fully the hidden richness embedded in the whole. When the reader recognizes in the wanderings of the Bombay student a form of the mystic ascent of the soul, the detective novel gains in breadth; when, later in the story, Borges discloses that his tale can be read as an echo of the Sufistic poem, one can sense that a new dimension has been added to the narrative. By providing new perspectives for reading the story, Borges has become—without leaving the bounds of the narration— his own critic: he offers to the reader new ways of understanding the story and additional clues for further enjoying it. Yet Borges is far from having singled out all the strands braided in his tale. We have seen that the Hindu notion of *Ātman* may as well be implied in the Bombay student's search, to be more precise, in the moment when the student finally "arrives at a gallery at the rear of which there is a door hung with a cheap and copiously beaded mat curtain, behind which a great radiance emanates. The student claps his hands once, twice, and asks for Al-Mu'tasim. A man's voice—the incredible voice of Al-Mu'tasim—urges him to come in. The student draws back the curtain and steps forward. The novel ends." The previous adventures throughout India become, thus, only steps leading towards this Atmanic fulfillment. Borges has also anticipated the critic by disclosing "certain analogies" in the first part scene of the novel with elements from Kipling's story "On the City Wall," but he had said nothing about the "possible" analogies with the motif of the searcher knocking at the door of a house where the mystic union is about to occur. The motif, notwithstanding, as presented by Borges in the passage we have troubled to quote in its entirety, is found in the first part of the Sufi collection of mystical parables, *Masnawi*, of the Persian poet Jalal-ud-din Rumi. Here, a man knocks on the door of his friend. The latter asks, "Who is it?" He answers, "I." The friend sends him away. For a whole year the sorrow of separation burns in him; then he comes again and knocks once more. To the question of his friend, "Who it is?" he replies, "Thou." And at once the room is opened to him in which there is not room for two "I's," that of God and that of man. Martin Buber has found a parallel to this motif in a Hasidic tale that obviously shows traces of Sufi influence. In the Jewish version, the element of a man (a fellow friend of Rabbi Aaron of Karlin) knocking at his friend's door is also present. "Who are you?" asked a voice from within, and, certain that his friend would recognize him by his voice, he answered, "I." No reply came, and the door did not open even though he knocked again and again. Finally he cried, "Aaron, why do you not open for me?" Then he heard from within, "Who is it who presumes to say 'I', as it is fitting for God alone to do!" He said in his heart, "I see then that I have not yet finished learning."

In the context of this old mystic motif, Borges' rather vague and mysterious passage regains the quasi-geometric cohesiveness characteristic of most of his narratives. The detailed explanation supplied by Borges as a footnote at the end of the story only confirms what is subtly alluded to at the conclusion of the student's peregrination. The full description of Ferid ed-Din Attar's poem operates at an outward level: it tells the reader, in a literal manner, that at the moment the student is confronted with the "splendor" coming from the inside, he realizes that he, too—as the birds of the poem with respect to the Simurg—is Al-Mu'tasim. The variation of the motif of Jalal-ud-din Rumi's parable implied in the last ambiguous link of the narration tells the same, but with the Borgesian finesse that converts an apparently insignificant detail into the magic key of the story. The exoteric and esoteric levels of meaning thus coalesce in a text that has the texture of a Kabbalistic cryptogram.

Although one can find these Kabbalistic traits throughout most of his narratives, it is only natural that they are particularly stressed in stories with some degree of mystic coloring. "The Zahir," "The Aleph," and "The God's Script" are in the same line with "The Approach to Al-Mu'tasim." In three of them, Borges intends, as it were, to show that "there is no fact, however insignificant, that does not involve universal history and the infinite concatenation of cause and effect . . . , the visible world is implicit in every phenomenon." To achieve this, Borges coins three symbols and presents them as depositories of a microcosmic totality that as such is no different from the

Godhead that holds in Himself all that is, was, and will be. The three symbols have deep roots in three different religions. At the outset of the first story, the Zahir is presented as "an ordinary coin" whose worth is twenty centavos. By the middle, Borges explains, "Zahir in Arabic means 'notorious,' 'visible'; in this sense it is one of the ninety-nine names of God." The information comes from the *Koran*, where (Surah, LV, 3) it is written that Zahir—the evident, the manifest—"is one of the ninety-nine attributes of God; He is the First and the Last, the Visible and the Occult." The coin is no longer a fortuitous object and becomes a form of mystic illumination. At the end of the tale, the narrator concludes: "In order to lose themselves in God, the Sufis recite their own names, or the ninety-nine divine names, until they become meaningless. I long to travel that path. Perhaps I shall conclude by wearing away the Zahir simply through thinking of it again and again. Perhaps behind the coin I shall find God."

What in "The Zahir" is presented only as a possibility, takes place in "The God's Script": "There occurred the union with the divinity, with the universe (I do not know whether these two words differ in meaning)." A magician, secluded in the darkness of a prison (it goes without saying that for the mystic the body is a dark prison that he strives to transcend), searches for the magical sentence that the god wrote on the first day of Creation "with the power to ward off" the devastation and ruin bound to happen at the end of time. In the prison, he devotes himself to the task of deciphering that secret sentence. Here it should be recalled that for the Kabbalists the Creation is but the result of multiple combinations of the twenty-two letters of the Hebrew alphabet. In the *Sefer Yetsirah* (*Book of Creation*), we read: "Twenty-two letter-elements: He outlined them, hewed them out, weighed them, combined them, and exchanged them, and through them created the soul of all creation and everything else that was ever created" (II, 2). The combination of the letters from which the Creation sprang was put into the Torah (the Pentateuch) but, explains a Midrash on Job 28:13, "No one knows its right order, for the sections of the Torah are not given in the right arrangement. If they were, everyone who reads in it might create a world, raise the dead, and perform miracles. Therefore the order of the Torah was hidden and is known to God alone." The tradition of a magical and divine script that Borges recreates in his tale is also a Christian motif: in the Gospel it is said that Christ is the word that will save men from the horrors of the end of all times.

The revelation of the god's script comes finally in a vision of "an exceedingly high Wheel, which was not before my eyes, nor behind me, nor to the sides, but every place at one time." Here, Borges resorts to a symbol from Hinduism, the *Bhavacakra* (*Wheel of Life*), which represents the different spheres of existence where the infinite concatenation of causes and effects operates. References to the Wheel and its explicit significance are found in two fundamental texts of Hinduism. In the *Bhagavad Gita* we read, "Thus was the Wheel (*cakram*) set in motion, and that man lives indeed in vain who in a sinful life of pleasures helps not in its revolutions," (III:16). In *Svetasvatara* Upanishad, the notion of the Wheel (of Brahman, of Creation, of Life, as it is often translated) is further developed:

> We understand him as a wheel with one fell, with a triple tyre, sixteen ends, fifty spokes, twenty counter-spokes, and six sets of eight. . . .
>
> (I:4)

> This is the great wheel (*cakram*) of Brahman, giving life and livelihood to all, subsists in all: in it the swan of the soul is hither and thither tossed.
>
> (I:6)

The vision of the Wheel, as seen by Tzinacán, is introduced in Borges' story with the following words, "That Wheel was made of water, but also of fire, and it was (although the edge could be seen) infinite. Interlinked, all things that are, were and shall be, formed it, and I was one of the fibers of that total fabric. . . . There lay the causes and the effects and it sufficed me to see that Wheel in order to understand it all, without end." This description seems to be an echo or paraphrase of Chapter XI of the *Bhagavad Gita*, a book that Borges familiarly quotes in his essay "Note on Walt Whitman." There he evinces an acquaintance with the *Gita* that goes beyond the casual reading of the book; on the contrary, he rather exhibits a close perusing of it. Even the image of "the infinite fibers of a total fabric" is from Vedantic lineage: "one rope of innumerable strands" says *Svetasvatara* Upanishad, referring to Hindu Wheel.

The *Gita* is the major devotional book of Hinduism. It is an episode of India's great epic, the *Mahābhārata*. Its main story is the war between two branches of the Kaurava family. The *Gita* consists of a long dialogue between Arjuna and Krishna, a local prince who volunteered to act as Arjuna's charioteer; but Krishna was not merely a prince—he was God incarnate, the great God Vishnu. Arjuna sees many of his kinsmen and friends in the ranks of the opposing army and refuses to fight, declaring that he would rather die than kill those he loves. To convince him that he must fight, Krishna is not content merely to use arguments already familiar to him, his caste-duty as a warrior, for instance. He sees fir rather to reveal to him the structure of the universe as it really is, and in which Arjuna is just a pawn moved by the hand of an all-powerful

God whose will no man or god can resist or thwart. "The ostensible purpose
of the *Gita* is to persuade Arjuna to fight; but the bulk of the poem is not
concerned with the respective merits of war and peace, but with the deepest
things of man and God."

Chapter XI constitutes the climax of the *Gita*. In it, Krishna reveals Himself
in all His terrifying majesty. Arjuna, not content with the account of Krishna's
powers of which he had heard, asks to see him. Krishna grants his request
and gives him "a celestial eye" with which he may behold his transfiguration.
The rest of the chapter is an account of the tremendous vision: we see the
universe in all its variety as Krishna's body, all its multiplicity converging onto
One. Arjuna then describes what he sees: the entire world is rushing headlong
into Krishna's mouths. It is at this point that Tzinacán's account of his vision
in "The God's Script" bears striking similarities to Arjuna's in the *Gita*. In both
cases a universal totality is presented within the unlimited limits of a microcosmic
image. Borges' text reads:

> I saw the universe and I saw the intimate designs of the universe.
> I saw the origins narrated in the Book of the Common. I saw the
> mountains that rose out of the water, I saw the first men of wood,
> the cisterns that turned against the men, the dogs that ravaged their
> faces. I saw the faceless god concealed behind the other gods. I saw
> infinite processes that formed one single felicity and, understanding
> all, I was able also to understand the script of the tiger.

In both, Borges' story and the *Gita*, the godhead and the universe are referred
to as synonyms. We have seen earlier that Tzinacán fails to distinguish between
the divinity and the universe, "I do not know if these words are different,"
he says. Krishna, before giving Arjuna the "celestial eye," tells him, "See now
the whole universe with all things that move and move not, and whatever
thy soul may yearn to see. See it all as One in me (XI:7)." As Tzinacán's vision
is not the result of mystical meditations and ecstasy but a kind of miraculous
apparition, so the union (or *yoga* as it is often called in the *Gita*) with the One
is not mystically reached by Arjuna—it is rather granted to him as a token
of Krishna's omnipotence.

Arjuna's vision is also described in terms similar to those that introduced
Tzinacán's vision. Borges presents the Wheel as "made of water but also of
fire." And in verse 28 Arjuna describes his vision, "As roaring torrents of *water*
rush forward into the ocean, so do these heroes of our mortal world rush into
thy *flaming* mouths." For the *Gita* the flames of Arjuna's mouths burning the
world up are a representation of Time, which at the end of a world-aeon will
devour all the worlds. We know that for Borges, too, Time is a consuming

fire and a sweeping river, but—as he adds—"I am the fire . . . , I am the river."
Likewise, in verse 32, Krishna reveals Himself as Time, "I am all-powerful Time
which destroys all things." The same imagery, though, conveys different
meanings: in the *Gita*, it underlines Krishna's condition of absolute master of
all; in Borges' text, it suggests that man is at the same time the master and
the victim of his fate.

Yet the closest parallel between the two texts occurs in the description
of the theophany itself. Neither the *Gita* nor Borges is willing to substitute
the fullness of the vision for an emblem or symbol as the mystic does in a
similar situation. Borges names some of the most memorable symbols in the
history of mysticism: a blazing light, a sword, a rose, a bird, a sphere, an angel,
and adds, "Perhaps the gods would not be against my finding an equivalent
image, but then this report would be contaminated with literature, with
falsehood." The challenge (for the writer) lies in confronting the reader with
the same shocking vision experienced by the seer, in reconstructing with words
an infinite diversity that transcends words. The alternative left to the poet is
the creation of a literary illusion, of a linguistic reality that becomes a reality
in itself. In the description of his vision, Arjuna uses—as Tzinacán—the same
anaphoric subject-verb that underscores the overwhelming feeling of perplexity.
It is also a way of reinforcing the illusion of a genuine translation: What I
am describing is indeed what I see—there seems to be the understated intention:

> I see in thee all the gods, O my God; and the infinity of the beings
> of thy creation. I see god Brahma on his throne of lotus, and all
> the seers and serpents of light . . . . I see the splendour of an infinite
> beauty which illumines the whole universe. It is thee! with thy crown
> and sceptre and circle. How difficult thou art to see! But I see thee:
> as fire, as the sun, blinding, incomprehensible . . . . I see thee without
> beginning, middle, or end . . . . I see thine eyes as the sun and the
> moon. And I see thy face as a sacred fire that gives light and life
> to the whole universe . . . . The Rudras of destruction, the Vasus
> of fire, the Sadhyas of prayers, the Adityas of the sun; the lesser
> gods Visve-Devas, the two Asvins charioteers of heaven, the Maruts
> of winds and storms, the Ushmapas spirits of ancestors; the celestial
> choirs of Gandharvas, the Yakshas keepers of wealth, the demons
> of hell and the Siddhas who on earth reached perfection: they all
> behold thee with awe and wonder.
>
> Gazing upon thy mighty form with its myriad mouths, eyes,
> arms, thighs, feet, bellies, and sharp, gruesome tusks, the worlds
> all shudder in affright,—how much more I!
>
> (*Gita*, XI)

The technique of chaotic enumeration is also evident in both accounts of the theophany. The most obvious difference between the two, though, is the secular character of Tzinacán's vision as compared to the divine nature of Krishna's transfiguration. In the *Gita*, the universe is described in terms of the tremendous sight of God; conversely, in Borges' text, God is described in terms of the infinite multiplicity of the universe, hence Borges' remark, ". . . the divinity, the universe, I do not know whether these two words differ in meaning."

Borges repeats the experience in "The Aleph." The seer now is Borges himself as the narrator of the story, and the mystic symbol is the Aleph, as before the Zahir and the Wheel. This time, he chose a letter, the first letter of the Hebrew alphabet, and we ask why. Borges' postscript is only half of the answer. For the Kabbalah the divine language is the very substance of reality: the Creation is just the result of the infinite combinations of these twenty-two letters. For the Spanish Kabbalist of the thirteenth century, Abraham Abulafia, "every letter represents a whole world to the mystic who abandons himself to its contemplation." It is the contemplation of a letter—the Aleph—that Borges describes in the last part of his story, a letter which soon becomes a vision of the whole world. A disciple of Abulafia describes a mystical experience in which he saw the letters of God's Name, permuted and combined, taking on the shape of great mountains, the form of a polished mirror shining, as it were, from inside. In the *Sefer Yetsirah* (Book of Creation) the letters *aleph*, *mem*, and *shin* are called mothers. They are not only the three mothers from which the other letters of the alphabet are formed, but they are also symbolical figures for the three primordial elements: the mute *mem* is the symbol of the water in which the mute fish live; the hissing *shin* (or *sin*) corresponds to the hissing fire; the airy *aleph* represents the air. The first emanation from God was the *ruach* (air) that produced fire, which, in its turn, formed the genesis of water (*Sefer Yetsirah*, III). So, the *aleph* constitutes for the Kabbalah the source of all articulate sound; it is regarded as the spiritual root of all other letters.

Borges describes the Aleph as "a small iridescent sphere, of almost intolerable brilliance. . . . Its diameter must have been about two or three centimeters, but Cosmic Space was in it, without diminution of size." Here too the vision is presented in the best tradition of the Kabbalah. An old Midrash of the thirteenth century refers to God as having concentrated His *Shekhinah*, his divine presence, at the place of the Cherubim, as though His whole power were concentrated and contracted in a single point. The sixteenth-century Kabbalist of the Safed School, Isaac Luria, developed this idea in the doctrine of the *Tsimtsum* (concentration or contraction). Luria explains that "sparks of the *Shekhinah* are scattered in all worlds and there is no sphere of existence, including organic and inorganic nature, that is not full of holy sparks which are mixed up with the *kelipoth* (material world) and need to be separated and lifted up." The Aleph is revealed in Borges' story in a cellar of a house that is about to be demolished so that a restaurant can be built there. Borges seems to be repeating Moses Cordovero's pantheistic formula: Where you stand, there stand all the worlds."

The description of the Aleph is a variation of the vision of the Wheel. Now the images are less apocalyptic and more personal because the narrator is not a magician of the pyramid of Qaholom, but Borges himself. In them, one can see, as through a kaleidoscope, the most essential fragments of the two Borges: the one of Androgué y Fray Bentos, and the other concerned with mirrors, tigers, and labyrinths.

These few examples are indicative of the pregnant quality of Borges' art. The Kabbalistic texture of his narrative adds to their manifold complexity and to their richness of meaning. Borges challenges the reader to activate all his resources, to become himself a Kabbalist. He seems to be saying: If man, powerless to solve the labyrinths of the gods, is left with the choice of weaving and deciphering his own, let us—at least—devise them as close as possible to the divine model, let us write a secular text in the manner that the Holy one was fashioned. A second understated motivation comes to our mind: If "universal history is the history of the diverse intonation of a few metaphors" and "true metaphors have always existed," the most a writer can do is to reinterpret them, to find new intonations of those few ones that have always existed. Borges' unhesitant use of old myths, motifs, *topoi*, and even metaphors in the literal sense, is perhaps a form of suggesting that the task of literature lies not in the hunt after the new, in being original (as conventionally understood) but rather in finding new forms of perceiving the old, in being creative with respect to the already created literature. What renders the old, new, the unoriginal, original is, thus, the ability to read the old texts afresh. Like the Kabbalah, which has generated a whole literature out of the Scripture, Borges implies—in praxis—that to write new literature is to read the old one anew. He has said it poignantly, "If I were able to read any contemporary page—this one, for example—as it would be read in the year 2000, I would know what literature would be like in the year 2000."

JAMES E. IRBY

Borges and the Idea of Utopia

> Il n'y a pas de hors-texte.
> —JACQUES DERRIDA, *De la grammatologie*

> . . .*ce lieu obscur qui ne songe interminablement
> qu'à se déchiffrer.*
> —JEAN RICARDOU, *Problèmes du nouveau roman*

Toward the end of 1938, under circumstances he has told in interviews and fictionalized in his story "El Sur" ["The South"], Borges nearly died of septicemia. This delirious ordeal, which also caused him to fear for his sanity, soon was revealed, however, as an incredible stroke of good fortune. Prompted by a desperate resolve to test his mental capacity, the convalescent Borges undertook to write something in a new genre, to write—as he said later—"something new and different for me, so that I could blame the novelty of the effort if I failed." This new work was the story "Pierre Menard, autor del Quijote" [Pierre Menard, author of the Quixote], the first of a rich and dazzling series of metaphysical tales with which, after some years of relatively scant and tentative writings, Borges did considerably more than just reaffirm his creative powers. In May 1939, "Pierre Menard, autor del Quijote" was published in Victoria Ocampo's review *Sur*. Exactly one year later, in the same journal, appeared the next such tale, "Tlön, Uqbar, Orbis Tertius," which subsequently opened the volumes *El jardín de senderos que se bifurcan* [*The Garden of Forking Paths*] (1941) and *Ficciones* (1944). This leading position was not, therefore, a matter of chronological but rather of theoretical priority, for perhaps more fully than

---

From *The Cardinal Points of Borges.* © 1971 by the University of Oklahoma Press.

any other of his fictions, it declares their basic principles, characteristically making of that declaration a fictionalized essay, a creation which studies itself. The subject, fittingly enough, is the enigmatic emergence of a new man-made universe, systematically designed and inserted into reality. For this reason, and for other reasons I will mention shortly, I would like to discuss this work in relation to the idea of utopia. My discussion will be divided into three parts: (1) some of the senses in which the world of Tlön is a utopia, (2) some anticipations of this idea in Borges' earlier writings, and (3) some of the ways in which the presentation of Tlön is dramatized. But first, a reminder of the tale's plot.

I

In a kind of memoir mingling essayistic discourse with anecdote, real names with inventions, Borges tells how his friend Bioy Casares discovers in an anomalous copy of a pirated edition of the *Encyclopaedia Britannica* an interpolated entry on a supposed country in Asia Minor called Uqbar, which diligent consultations elsewhere fail to verify. The entry mentions that the epics and legends of Uqbar never refer to reality but to the imaginary regions of Mlejnas and Tlön. Later Borges himself comes upon the eleventh volume of a so-called *First Encyclopaedia of Tlön*, which bears the unexplained inscription "Orbis Tertius" and contains fragmentary though methodical information on what is now said to be an entire planet. Astonished and delighted like a true bibliophile, after referring to various friends' polemics over the dubious existence of the other volumes and to vulgar distortions by the popular press, all of which the reader is presumed to recall, Borges proceeds to outline the *Weltanschauung* of this "brave new world."

Whereas our common concept of reality is materialistic, i.e. presupposes the independent existence of material objects and beings that the mind registers like a camera, Tlön's universal philosophy is a kind of ultra-Berkeleyan idealism according to which the only realities are mental perceptions. Not even space exists, only a dimensionless continuum of thought. This is first exemplified in an account of the planet's languages, which determine the nature of all its disciplines. In Tlön there are no nouns, only adjectives (qualities) or verbs (acts or processes), variable aggregates of which may comprise the entities designated by our nouns, and countless other entities as well. Both these and other constructs ranging all the way from causal links to scientific or theological systems are completely metaphorical, are "poetic objects," since only instantaneous perceptions are real, not their subsequent connections in memory. Hence in Tlön philosophies proliferate and compete wildly like avant-garde poetic styles, although the hypothesis that the universe is one supreme mind, that all phenomena are the somehow-associated thoughts of that mind, seems to prevail. The most scandalous heresy in Tlön is, of course, materialism, which the languages of Tlön can scarcely even formulate as an *aporia*. Borges' summary of this world concludes with a dizzying account of how its "things" multiply by thought and, conversely, vanish when they are forgotten.

To the sections on Uqbar and Tlön, Borges adds a concluding postscript already dated "1947" in the original 1940. Here curious discovery and eager discussion give way to a somewhat troubled report that Tlön has begun to intrude into our own everyday world. A letter discovered by chance reveals the history of its laborious creation over a period of centuries by anonymous groups of scholars, first in Europe, later in the New World. Strange objects from Tlön are found, the entire *First Encyclopaedia* is unearthed and widely excerpted, and everywhere people yield to the enchantment of an orderly, man-made universe of the mind come to supplant the divinely incomprehensible reality we know. One by one our sciences are reformed, our very memories replaced by others. In a hundred years, a projected *Second Encyclopaedia* will appear, announcing the even more ample but as yet undefined realm of Orbis Tertius, by which time our world will already be Tlön. As these events unfold, Borges finally assumes a resigned indifference, idly correcting his never to be published translation of Sir Thomas Browne's *Urn Burial*, which the advent of Tlön and its marvellous tongues will surely obliterate.

All this, rich with enticing allusion and ellipsis, is compressed into some twenty-odd pages. Even in rapid synopsis one can see that "Tlön, Uqbar, Orbis Tertius" comprises many interwoven levels of meaning whose relationships alone are exceedingly complex, not to speak of the levels themselves. Already a kind of palimpsest, a many-layered paraphrase of other paraphrases, the tale tends to make any critical résumé and commentary both desperately tautological and inaccurate, for at every turn one is also faced with sly reversals and subversions of the very schemes the work sets forth. For the moment, however, let us assume that, at least insofar as exposition is concerned, there are two main levels, one being that of the narrator's own progressive involvement with the events he relates, and the other (contained within the first) being that of the description and chronicle of Tlön itself.

The theoretical section of this second level (the summary of the Eleventh Volume) offers the outlines of a special kind of utopia, a most pure and extreme utopia, so to speak. Here is no new social order, but rather a new natural order, a whole new epistemology, a new relationship between mind and phenomena, worked out in myriad consequences of detail. Furthermore, this is done not in some single futuristic *roman de moeurs*, but in a vast, many-volumed compendium which registers not only the science and mathematics, the languages and literary theory, of an idealist cosmos, but also (according to certain oblique references by the narrator) its no doubt singular flora and fauna, topography and architecture. Literally, Tlön is an *ideal* world (a world of ideas) and a *utopia* (a no place, a world outside spatial coordinates). In its denial of matter, it constitutes a drastic case of what all utopias imply: the world upside down, a mirror image of habitual reality. (Remember the tale's first sentence: "I owe the discovery of Uqbar to the conjunction of a mirror and an encyclopedia.") This paradox (etymologically the word "paradox" means "contrary to opinion," that is, to ordinary opinion) is paralleled by another which also relates to an essential aspect of utopia. Utopias represent a convergence of reason and reality and are presumably objects of desire. In Tlön thought and reality are *one*, but desire or hope or even distraction may engender more or less faithful *duplicates* of anything (or duplicates of duplicates, and so on). These are known as *brönir*, which, among other properties, have a profound temporal effect. In the narrator's incomparable words:

> The methodical fabrication of *brönir* . . . has performed prodigious services for archaeologists. It has made possible the interrogation and even the modication of the past, which is now no less plastic and docile than the future.

He then points out the delicate differences between *brönir* of various degrees: "those of fifth degree are almost uniform; those of ninth degree become confused with those of the second; in those of the eleventh there is a purity of line not found in the original."

At this point, as it draws to a close, the whole scholarly review of the Eleventh Volume works up to a wild crisis beneath its calm, detached language. The idea of proliferation, of the endless rivalry and replacement of unverifiable mental constructs, was earlier introduced by referring to theories; now it operates with pencils, rusty wheels, gold masks, buildings. The gradual shift in vocabulary to familiar terms we construe as "concrete" forces us with growing perplexity to realize what is happening, to read these passages over and over, i.e. to produce our own succession of textual *brönir*. Furthermore, it would seem that in a world where supposedly "a later state of the subject . . . cannot affect or illuminate the previous state," forms and moments nevertheless minutely substitute for one another in a headlong rush toward indistinguishability, toward chaos. And yet, we are told, this world has been codified in an encyclopedia, this spaceless world divided into northern and southern hemispheres.

The narrator caps his summary of the Eleventh Volume with a very brief description of how objects fade and disappear *from view* when forgotten. The idea of proliferation is thus abruptly juxtaposed with that of loss, and, retroactively, the idea of forgetting suggests that the preceding discussion of *brönir* was, at least in part, an extended metaphor of the processes of memory, as well as of historiography. In his recent conversations with Richard Burgin, Borges recalls how, when a child, he heard his father speak of his own childhood memories as only memories of other memories, like a pile of coins each of whose effigies imperceptibly distorts the one before, moving further and further away from the now-unknown original. This "saddening thought," already a contradictory union of proliferation and loss like the idea of the *brönir*, is also found on a magnified scale at the end of "Tlön, Uqbar, Orbis Tertius."

Borges' utopia is an idealistic one because that philosophy represents, for him, a victory of mind over matter, over the "hard and fast," over all inert resistance and unreason. But his uncanny pursuit of its ultimate consequences, logically discarding Berkeley's coherence-lending God, swirls toward a total atomization where reason finds no foothold. Already in its discursive middle section we begin to experience the story's essential drama and can glimpse at least three implications: (1) intensifying the paradox of Tlön enlarges its scope to parallel or include our perception of the story itself, (2) Tlön is also a nightmare, an "anti-utopia," and (3) its states are not so fantastic or other-worldly after all. Perhaps I can make this more clear by showing how the main levels of the story interact, particularly in the very moving (and ambiguous) final pages. But first, I would like to trace some of the intimations of utopia in previous works by Borges.

II

Borges began his literary career around 1920 as an affiliate, first in Spain, later in Buenos Aires, of the so-called *ultraísta* movement, an enthusiastic but rather incoherent version of futurism which exalted the juxtaposition of violent metaphors as the sole poetic device. Borges, however, far from incoherent, tried to establish in his own manifestos and essays of the period a theory of metaphor based on clear philosophical principles. These writings repeatedly display three themes: (1) the use of Berkeleyan idealism to break down substantive reality—and even the continuities of space and personal identity—into a flux of immediate perceptions, (2) the combinational rearrangement of these perceptions by means of metaphor to form new poetic realities, and (3) the fervent hope that the future would bring a collective realization of his theories.

Argentine *ultraísmo* quickly evolved into another more nationalistically inspired movement now usually termed *martinfierrismo* (after its principal review, *Martín Fierro*), in which Borges also figured prominently. Now his futuristic vision ("futuristic" in the literal sense) also embraced a desire for a more lucid and authentic national literature, centered (for him) on images of the old quarters of his beloved Buenos Aires. The title essay of his book *El tamaño de mi esperanza* [*The Measure of My Hope*] (1926) exhorts his companions to join him in that task:

> Now Buenos Aires, more than a city, is a country, and we must find the poetry and the music and the painting and the religion and the metaphysics that correspond to its greatness. That is the magnitude of my hope, which invites us all to be gods and work toward its incarnation.

Here we can already glimpse something of the demiurgical, collective, and encyclopedic enterprise that engenders Tlön.

Another essay in the same volume, "Palabrería para versos" [Verbiage for Verses] outlines his concurrent and admittedly utopian aspiration toward a language of new and more comprehensive signs:

> The world of appearances is a rush of jumbled perceptions. . . . Language is an effective arrangement of the world's enigmatic abundance. In other words, with our nouns we invent realities. We touch a round form, we see a glob of dawn-colored light, a tickle delights our mouth, and we falsely say these three hetero- geneous things are one, known as an orange. The moon itself is a fiction. . . . All nouns are abbreviations. . . . The world of appear- ances is most complex and our language has realized only a very small number of the combinations which it allows. Why not create a word, one single word, for our simultaneous perception of cattle bells ringing in the afternoon and the sunset in the distance? . . . I know how utopian my ideas are and how far it is from an intellec- tual possibility to a real one, but I trust in the magnitude of the future and that it will be no less ample than my hope.

This, of course, reads like a preliminary draft for the section on language and "poetic objects" in "Tlön, Uqbar, Orbis Tertius," and is, in turn, a revision of passages from earlier *ultraísta* writings. All of these texts, placed side by side, suggest an essential oneness, a Janus-faced sense of time which in fact Borges often invoked in the 1920s by defining hope as "memory of the future" or "recollection coming to us from the future."

By 1930 the boom period of avant-garde solidarity and national optimism was over. The tone and concerns of Borges' work shifted, though not its underlying premises and implications. In a little-known address given in 1936 on the occasion of the four hundredth anniversary of Buenos Aires, he now spoke with uncertain pathos of his native city's mushrooming growth as a sacrifice of past and present in the name of an unknown future which hope must nevertheless somehow welcome:

> No one feels time and the past like a native of Buenos Aires. . . .
> He knows he lives in a city which grows like a tree, like a familiar face in a nightmare. . . . In this corner of America. . . men from all nations have made a pact to disappear for the sake of a new man which is none of us yet. . . . A most singular pact, an extravagant adventure of races, not to survive but to be in the end forgotten: lineages seeking darkness. [. . .] Buenos Aires imposes upon us the terrible obligation of hope. Upon all of us it imposes a strange love—a love of the secret future and its unknown face.

In those years Borges had abandoned poetry and ceased to theorize about metaphor, turning instead to the problem of fiction, whose aims and devices he first examined in the volume of essays called *Discusión* (1932), one of his most fascinating and unjustly neglected works. His earlier essays had brightly proposed a salutary reduction of common realities to an immediate swarm of perceptions. In *Discusión*, however, such a state lurks as a perplexing disorder to be resolved not by metaphors or a new poetic vocabulary but by a linear discourse of oblique allusions and internal correspondences which "postulate" a coherent reality existing only by virtue of the text itself. In a key essay entitled precisely "La postulación de la realidad" [The Postulation of Reality] Borges argues this in a most devious fashion, mingling as specimens both historical and literary texts, leaving his reader to deduce for himself that *all* discourse is "fictional." Another key essay, "El arte narrativo y la magia" [Narrative Art and Magic], concludes that imaginative or fantastic fiction is superior to other kinds because of its broader, "magical" notion of causality, linking elements by similarity and contiguity as well as by logical cause and effect.

Discusión is also the first of Borges' works to include essays of a type quite frequent in his later writings: examinations of fantastic cosmologies—the cabbala, gnosticism and (ironically, critically juxtaposed with these) the Christian conception of Hell—which, of course, are also "fictions." His interest in such theories suggests one of the reasons why Borges turned from poetry to narrative in those years: a need to treat in more dramatic form questions of human destiny, of time, illusion, and finality, and to do so within some closely reasoned world picture radically opposed to unthinking mental habit.

Another model or symbol of this enterprise was the concept of utopia, scarcely mentioned in *Discusión*, but emphatically used a few years later to invoke an ideal of pure, thorough inventiveness which most fantastic literature neglected. In March 1936 he opened his review of an early volume of stories by Bioy Casares with words which anticipate the subject of "Tlön, Uqbar, Orbis Tertius" and one of the story's passages:

> I suspect that a general scrutiny of fantastic literature would reveal that it is not very fantastic. I have visited many Utopias—from the eponymous one of More to *Brave New World*—and I have not yet found a single one that exceeds the cozy limits of satire or sermon and describes in detail an imaginary country, with its geography, its history, its religion, its language, its literature, its music, its government, its metaphysical and theological controversy...its encyclopedia, in short; all of it organically coherent, of course, and (I know I'm very demanding) with no reference whatsoever to the horrible injustices suffered by captain Alfred Dreyfus.

There is one more direct anticipation of "Tlön, Uqbar, Orbis Tertius" worthy of note, this time in the nature of a formal prototype which not only parodied both Borges' avant-garde theories and (before the fact) his ideas on fiction, but also showed how intimately a mad drive toward total disruption could coexist with his dreams of order. This prototype was revealed a few years ago in his remarkable preface to an anthology of writings by his late friend and mentor Macedonio Fernández (1874–1952). Onetime anarchist, genial eccentric, a kind of Charles Ives of Argentine metaphysics who improvised vast idealist negations of time and self, Macedonio became for the young *martinfierristas* a guiding spirit in disinterested speculation and absurd humor and was, in Borges' words, "the most extraordinary man I've ever known."

One of Macedonio's most curious fantasies was that of becoming president of Argentina, a goal toward which he felt he should first move by very subtly insinuating his name to the populace. Presumably sometime in the 1920s, Borges and a number of friends undertook collectively to write and place themselves as characters in a novel enlarging upon these imaginary machinations, a work to be entitled "El hombre que será presidente" ["The Man Who Would Be President"] of which only the two opening chapters were composed. The obvious plot, relating Macedonio's efforts, all but concealed another, concerning the conspiracy of a group of "neurotic and perhaps insane millionaires" to further the same campaign by undermining people's resistance through the gradual dissemination of "disturbing inventions." These were usually contradictory artefacts whose effect ran counter to their apparent form or function, including certain very small and disconcertingly heavy objects (like the cone found by Borges and Amorim toward the end of "Tlön, Uqbar, Orbis Tertius"), scrambled passages in detective novels (somewhat like the interpolated entry on Uqbar), and dadaist creations (perhaps like the "transparent tigers" and "towers of blood" in Tlön). The novel's technique and language were meant to enact as well as relate this whole process by introducing more and more such objects in a less and less casual way and by slowly gravitating toward a baroque style of utter delirium. In the end, Macedonio was in fact to reach the Casa Rosada, but, as Borges adds, "by then nothing means anything in that anarchical world." From this project for an idealist's devastating rise to power, let us return to the story of Tlön.

III

Borges' outline of "El hombre que será presidente" points up what is also one of the most striking formal aspects of "Tlön, Uqbar, Orbis Tertius": the mirroring of plot elements in the verbal texture of the tale. Consider, for example, Tlön's emergence. Within the story this comes about through a growing series of textual substitutions, ambiguities, revisions, and cross references which engender a whole new state of affairs and even seem to elicit rather palpable objects (more about these later). Borges' own text comprises an intricate network of word choices and juxtapositions that almost imperceptibly operate in a similar fashion. There is, of course, the mingling of real and invented names, and the narrator's self-revision in the postscript even as the *First Encyclopaedia* is revised in its second appearance. There are the word shifts I mentioned earlier, and others as well: at times a few adjectives seem to generate new degrees of "reality," one at the expense of the other. When Borges discovers the Eleventh Volume, the hitherto merely dubious Uqbar becomes "a nonexistent country" alongside the designation of Tlön as "an unknown planet"; later, however, Tlön is called "an illusory world" to make way for the "still nebulous Orbis Tertius." Very tenuous or even omitted indications can be curiously evocative. The name "Orbis Tertius" first appears in the Eleventh Volume stamped on "a leaf of silk paper that covered one of the color plates"; this subordinate allusion to a veiled image makes the volume and the name more vivid; later one may well wonder what manner of "thing" could be pictured there. In the postscript, we learn of the slave-owning, freethinking American millionaire Ezra Buckley and his role in enlarging the secret society's project to the creation of an entire planet, for all must be on a grand scale in America. This episode culminates with an abrupt syntactical leap: "Buckley was poisoned in Baton Rouge in 1828; in 1914 the society delivered to its collaborators, some three hundred in number, the last volume of the First Encyclopedia of Tlön." Filling in the dark gap between these two statements, following up other hints, parallels Alfonso Reyes' alleged proposal that Borges and his friends reconstruct the Eleventh Volume's missing companions *ex ungue leonem*, a proposal which, in turn, adumbrates a basic principle of Tlön: mental projection. The very first elements in the story—the mirror, the duplicated yet "false" encyclopedia, the debated narrative whose omissions or inconsistencies (not its direct statements) allow one to *guess* its "atrocious or banal" subject—set this process in motion by reflecting one another in widening patterns of self-reference. Indeed they signal that this is a text about its own principles, about the principles of all texts. Tlön is also the world of writing, of *escritura*, which consists in the meaningful permutation and alignment of signs according to inherent laws and not in the mere transcription of some prior, nonverbal reality.

The chronicle of Tlön can also be seen as a partial allegory of the emergence of Borges' own fiction over the years. The narrator's involvement with the events indicates, first of all, that Borges views his work as something revealed to him, as the heritage of many other writings over the centuries, the interplay of many more or less related texts animated by a suprapersonal spirit, with himself, Borges, serving only as their momentary reader. This conception that the literary work is really generated by the interaction of other works "dans l'espace sans frontières de la lecture"—a conception reflected in the critical theories of Tlön, in the creative method of Pierre Menard, in the essays of *Otras inquisiciones* [*Other Inquisitions*]—constitutes what Gérard Genette has called Borges' "literary utopia." But why do the last two pages of the tale so strangely combine notes of triumph and doubt, why does the narrator turn away at the end?

In his radio interviews with Georges Charbonnier in 1965, Borges said that all his stories are in the manner of games with two aspects, two sides of the same coin, one comprising the intellectual possibilities of a cosmic idea, the other the emotions of anguish and perplexity in the face of the endless universe. He added that any work, in order to last, must allow variable readings. In a conversation with me two years later, referring specifically to "Tlön, Uqbar, Orbis Tertius," Borges stressed this story's emotional side, which he defined as "the dismay of the teller, who feels that his everyday world. . ., his past. . . [and] the past of his forefathers. . . [are] slipping away from him." Hence, he claimed, "the subject is not Uqbar or Orbis Tertius but rather a man who is being drowned in a new and overwhelming world that he can hardly make out."

As the story concludes, Tlön does far more than win great droves of converts: it assumes all the obliterating scope and impetus of historical change itself, virtually annihilating the narrator, who in a hundred years, when the full transformation of our world occurs, will long be dead. Here again is the effect of simultaneous proliferation and loss. Hence the pathos of "I pay no attention to all this," the irony of translating *Urn Burial*, that magnificent set of baroque paradoxes on immortality. "Tlön, Uqbar, Orbis Tertius" is the first of a number of Borges' fictions which place an image of himself (to use Kierkegaard's phrase) "as a vanishing peculiarity in connection with the absolute requirement": Borges and the Aleph, Borges and the Zahir, Borges and the fate of Pedro Damián. This "sacrifice" lends poignant urgency to the new order enveloping him, or rather it visibly culminates an insinuation that has grown throughout the work: the mental powers, vicissitudes and vertigos of Tlön are *our own world*, our world of reality as shifting symbol, of relentless time and unknown ultimate pattern, here paradoxically turned about and fabled to help us perceive it more acutely as such. (This, by the way, would explain the words "atrocious or banal" at the beginning.) Northrop Frye has observed that all utopias present "unconscious mental habits transposed into their conscious equivalents." Borges concludes one list of Tlön's inroads with the words "already a fictitious past occupies in our memories the place of another, a past of which we know nothing with certainty—not even that it is false," a peril of all recollection, as the *brönir* implied, as well as an ironic reference to the feigned memoir we are being offered.

Tlön grows by revisions toward a "third orb" (which in turn implies a fourth and a fifth and so on), sprawling like some horrible map aspiring to coincide totally with the incalculable terrain it set out to represent within manageable coordinates on another plane. But this same self-revision can also be seen as the difficult virtue of a world of lucid thought, of multiple views. Gérard Genot, in his little book on Borges, believes that the narrator's lack of attention at the end signifies a loss of interest, because Tlön, now "real," has fallen from its former wealth of fictive potentialities. To this I would reply that the narrator may be rejecting what he has repeatedly noted to be a vulgarization of Tlön by the general public, who confuse its games with some kind of sacred order (a clear warning to readers and critics), and that Tlön clearly continues to evolve (in our minds). Genot goes on to observe, however, that the narrator's refuge in translation only confirms the extent of Tlön's influence, for the union of such disparate figures as Quevedo and Sir Thomas Browne into one text is but another version of its critical practices. Frances Weber, in her article on fiction and philosophy in Borges, claims that Tlön negates itself by replacing its variable theories and countertheories with an inflexible totalitarian order to enter our world. Again I would point to the popular misconceptions and continuing change, but I fully agree with the conclusions she draws from this and other stories: they are all "self-reversing tales" in which initially opposing factors coalesce and dissolve by a process of "negative thinking" that keeps us "aware of the conjectural character of all knowledge and all representation." The central focus we sense but cannot grasp in the midst of all these painful and playful contrapositions might be the true utopia, the true "no place," the supreme fiction.

CARTER WHEELOCK

Borges' New Prose

In 1966, some ten years after "God's magnificent irony" had given him "books and the night," apparently ending his career as a writer of prose fiction, Jorge Luis Borges published a short story, "The Intruder." His devotees sat up with interest, but many leaned back again because the new story – devoid of brain-rattling sophistry and erudite allusions – was not like the old Borges, whose three dozen gripping "fictions" published up to 1953 had made him the most important living writer in the Spanish language. Since "The Intruder," Borges has written more than a dozen new narratives, most of them collected under the title of one in the series, *Doctor Brodie's Report*. Two of them, along with several other short prose pieces, are interspersed with the poetry of *Elogio de la sombra* [*In Praise of Darkness*] (1969). A long story, "The Congress," was published separately in 1971.

This new prose has yet to be fully appraised. My effort here can be only a superficial beginning, and we must start by remembering the old Borges.

THE FORMER BORGES

Toward the end of the 1930's Borges turned from poetizing Buenos Aires and fictionalizing the hoodlums of the city's outlying slums (as in "Streetcorner Man," 1933) and took to playing literary games with time, infinity, destiny, and the nature of reality. He was well equipped for it, being multilingual and having spent most of his forty years as an eclectic reader, absorbing everything from Burns's *The Saga of Billy the Kid* to Berkeley and the Panchatantra. His

From *Prose for Borges*. © 1972 by Northwestern University. Northwestern University Press, 1972.

life, he has said, has been devoted less to living than to reading. In the following ten or so years he produced three small collections of compact fiction (the first two are now combined as *Ficciones* [1944; enlarged 1956]; the third is *The Aleph* [1949; enlarged 1952]). These stories, suggestive of highbrow detective fiction and of Symbolist poetic theory applied to prose, are utterly lacking in social consciousness or moral implication; unemotional, sexless, and uncontemporary, they wave no banners and press no points. They allude to everything and recommend nothing.

For the most part, these highly intellectual creations of the 1940's are clinical, cosmic tales peopled with almost faceless characters who are not really people but archetypal miniatures that move about in a purely cerebral universe. They often act like mythical beings in primitive cosmologies, or like dream figures: two men can be one, they can be dead but alive, and they can be only half real; they can pass in and out of mortal life ("The Immortal"), stare at magic coins until they go mad ("The Zahir"), behold the universe under the cellar stairs ("The Aleph"), live a year in a moment ("The Secret Miracle"), or dream other people into being ("The Circular Ruins"). Borges' people live in ignorance of the secret laws, or the secret will, which guide their destinies, and their actions are not finally their own. Borges surrounds them with the dicta of metaphysical philosophers who make all things logical, and their behavior is told in deftly ambiguous language. The reader finds himself acclaiming with emotion what he doesn't quite grasp and perhaps doesn't believe. He is floated into a kind of esthetic hysteria, feeling spoofed but also sublimated. Although Borges insists that he does not push a philosophical viewpoint (or any other), his underlying skepticism, or idealism, comes through.

Far from being verbose in proportion to their intricacy, these earlier stories are written in a wondrously frugal and exact style—richly suggestive, poetic, and full of ironic humor, baroque artifice, and rhetorical sleight of hand. Prominent symbols—mirrors, labyrinths, tigers, towers, knives—are repeated with unabashed regularity (Borges calls himself monotonous), and the repetition of other images or secondary symbols suggests an esoteric pattern with a meaning: circles, coins, pyramids, horses, swamps, cards.

But again, no messianism intrudes into Borges' work. The ideas of men are arbitrary formulations with infinite alternatives. Certitude is intellectual death; therefore, for Borges, even his basic philosophy is a conjecture. Speculation is the law of intellectual life. Out of this view come the irony and humor of Borges' prose. He mocks knowledge by displaying it lavishly, finally turning it against itself. But his jibes are gentle, because he relishes all ideas for their esthetic value.

Every strange figment of thought implies a whole new structure of reality, a realm in which the errant idea would not be strange at all. By piling up these pieces of heretical "fact," Borges overpowers us with the illusion that we almost understand that realm and that if we did we would know everything. The creation of this illusion of near-understanding seems, on the surface, to be the whole esthetic motive of Borges' older fiction. By attacking our conception of reality and implying another—a secret order in our chaos—he stalks the "esthetic occurrence" in an Olympian arena. In a short essay, "The Wall and the Books" (*Other Inquisitions*, [1952]), he tentatively defined the esthetic event or fact (*el hecho estético*) as "the imminence of a revelation, which never comes." But to say that Borges fabricates esthetic situations is a fundamental error; for he has not believed, apparently since the early 1920's when he split with Ultraism, that the esthetic is man-made.

Much light is thrown on Borges' fiction by his essays, his short prose thoughts, and his poems, where he often centers his attention on literature and philosophy, but where he just as often focuses upon a natural, historical, or literary event that strikes the sensitive intellect as marvelous because of what it implies (that is, what it does not reveal) of time, destiny, or reality. For example, a gaucho murdered by his son does not know that perhaps he died only to repeat Caesar's death along with the words "And thou, my son"; or when a man dies, an infinite number of things in his memory die with him and leave the world poorer, as when the last man died who had seen Woden's rites or the living Christ. These are not intellectual fabrications of an esthetic illusion but simple wonder at the mystery and suggestiveness of real facts. When Borges adds metaphysical half-explanations, the little miracle he is pointing to is only heightened. When he marvels at the strange spiritual likeness between Omar and FitzGerald, there are inevitable overtones of circular time, reincarnation, and Platonic form or of the primordial metonymy that makes two men one if they share merely a characteristic. When Borges writes that Shakespeare is nobody because he so long pretended on the stage to be other men, he conjures the old theological platitude that God, being everything, is not any one thing, therefore is no thing—nothing. Such logic is a trick of language—both intellectually palliative and spiritually cathartic. Such deliberate speciousness is rare in fiction, and its proliferation in Borges' prose has moved critics to treat it as an esthetic principle. Most readers of the old Borges, if pressed for a quick characterization of his typical stories, would call them dramatizations of intellectual propositions. This makes Borges a coiner of abstruse parables or fables, an allegorist; he is frequently defined as a writer who allegorizes heretical ideas, and more often than not there is the implication that he is some kind of truthseeker who uses literature as a megaphone for his anxieties or his agnostic faith. Borges knows this. In his new fiction he seems to be telling us that his strange literature of the past is not an intellectual destruction of reality but an esthetic affirmation of it.

THE NEW BORGES

The excellence of "The Intruder" appears to have been somewhat overlooked because many were disappointed that Borges' first story in many years was not of the old vintage. Borges punctured any hope that he would return to the "type" by telling an interviewer in 1967 that he was fed up with "labyrinths and mirrors and tigers and all that." In the future he would write "straight-forward" stories, somewhat after the manner of Kipling's early tales, with "little vocabulary" and "without tricks." What caused this change? Anyone who reads such recent stories as "Doctor Brodie's Report," "Guayaquil," or "The Gospel According to Mark" soon realizes that near-blindness has hardly impaired Borges' ability to produce organized intricacy in precise and frugal language. No, the real cause was visible as early as 1962, when James Irby noted that Borges regarded his older fictions as baroque and vain. Even before taking up fiction, Borges had abandoned (with Ultraism) the idea that literature can show us the essences of things or that art is any kind of key to metaphysical knowledge. He had abandoned faith in the reality of the "revelations" that can come out of new metaphors, contrived paradoxes, or juxtaposed antinomies. Now he has abandoned Ultraism's essentially baroque style; but he continues to espouse the idea that literature should "show us our own face," by which he means that it should show us *its* face, for to him the world and literature are the same thing: "If art is perfect, the world is superfluous." The "imminence of a revelation" is perhaps the ultimate knowable reality, and men do not create it. They comprise it, behold it, and try to transmute it into language. This idea precludes any esthetic theory—that is, any rule or formula for producing an imminent revelation.

Borges writes in the preface to *In Praise of Darkness* that he is not the possessor of an esthetic; and in the preface to *Doctor Brodie's Report* he seems to disclaim the attribution to him, by others, of an "esthetic of the intelligence":

> The art of writing is mysterious; the opinions we hold are ephemeral, and I prefer the Platonic idea of the Muse to that of Poe, who reasoned, or feigned to reason, that the writing of a poem is an act of the intelligence.

In the same preface, in answer to those critics who have deplored his lack of artistic concern for national and social issues, he says:

I want to make it quite clear that I am not, nor have I ever been, what used to be called a preacher of parables or a fabulist and is now known as a committed writer. I do not aspire to be Aesop. My stories, like those of the Thousand and One Nights, try to be entertaining or moving but not persuasive.

This may also be understood as Borges' justification for deserting those metaphysical fictions which have been taken as essentially allegorical, for Borges is well aware of the bad connotations of "allegory." He has called allegory "an error," although he admits to allegorizing. (In the foreword to the second part of *Ficciones* he calls "The Sect of the Phoenix" an allegory.) Apparently he does not mind being called an allegorist if only the implication of didacticism is removed. Stripped of its moralism, allegory becomes a valid and powerful esthetic device, a long metaphor rich in suggestion. In a recent interview Borges characterized himself as a former parabolist turned storyteller; speaking of the new stories he would write (those of *Doctor Brodie's Report*), he said: "They will not be like my former work, parables or pretexts for writing essays. I want to be a storyteller, a narrator of real stories, without tricks."

In "The Approach to al-Mu'tasim" (*Ficciones*), Borges says of the fictitious novel he is "reviewing" that the version of 1932 was somewhat symbolic, but that the 1934 version "declines into allegory." In the foreword to Robert Lima's translation of Ana María Barrenechea's work on Borges (*Borges the Labyrinth Maker*), Borges acknowledges his occasional recourse to allegory: "My best writings are of things that were striving to come to life through me, and not simply allegories where the thought comes before the sign." In other words, Borges strives for a true symbolism but thinks that he, too, may occasionally "decline into allegory."

NEW NARRATIVES

Borges' new manner is indeed more straightforward. Much of the stylistic complexity has disappeared, leaving his themes and plots more conspicuous. In these narratives the plots—the *fabulae*, tales as tales—are in my opinion superior to those of *Ficciones* and *El Aleph*, not because they are less fantastic but because truth itself is fantastic and these new tales, for the most part, are closer to it than are the stories about the equivocal verities of our mental life. In the eleven stories of *Doctor Brodie's Report* we do not get lost in limitless libraries or go wandering around inside the mind of the Minotaur. We go back, mainly, to the straggling outskirts, or *arrabales*, of Buenos Aires and to the pampa. These are the suburbs and plains as they were, or could have been, at the close of the nineteenth century or the early years of the twentieth, when *compadritos* (Argentine hoodlums, or gang toughs, with a lot of the classical gaucho in them) would hang around the saloons deciding who was the toughest, often by fighting with knives. Thus Borges continues to show his lifelong fascination with the cult of physical courage, which is present in "The Intruder" and commands at least five other *Brodie* stories.

These narratives about blustering *compadres* are among the eight in *Brodie* that are based on some type of interpersonal rivalry. Of the ruffians of the *arrabal* the most conspicuous is Rosendo Juárez ("Rosendo's Tale")—not because he is the toughest but because he is the same Rosendo Juárez who turned coward (apparently) in "Streetcorner Man," a story Borges wrote as far back as 1933. In the new story, Rosendo explains to Borges that his refusal to fight when challenged was due to disillusionment and disgust with his style of life. The most pathetic of the duelers are the gauchos Manuel Cardoso and Carmen Silveira of "The End of the Duel." These are two longtime rivals who have often faced each other knife in hand but have avoided killing each other because their rivalry gives meaning to their "poor and monotonous lives." Drafted into the army, they fight side by side, without speaking, until they are finally captured by the enemy. A sadistic captain, knowing their rivalry, orders that they die in competition. Their throats cut, they run a race to see who can go farthest before collapsing.

Borges plays many variations on the rivalry theme. "The Intruder" gives us a rivalry caused by a woman and transcended by a murderous brotherly love. The Nilsen brothers, a pair of illiterate Saturday-night brawlers, pick up and share a country wench, sell her to a brothel to quiet their growing jealousy, and later retrieve her when each of them begins going to the brothel on the sly. Unable to save their comradeship and affection with the girl between them, the older brother kills her. When the younger is told, the two embrace, almost in tears.

In "Juan Muraña" the personal conflict is more fanciful; it is hardly a rivalry, but it involves a tough whose knife was feared. Muraña, long dead, is a bloody legend, and his widow, sister, and nephew are about to be dispossessed by their landlord Luchessi. Muraña's widow, Aunt Florentina, is a bit daft; she keeps assuring the others that her beloved husband will not let the gringo throw them out. Luchessi is butchered one night in his doorway by an unknown knifer. Later, Aunt Florentina shows her nephew her beloved husband—the notorious knife of Juan Muraña.

In "Juan Muraña" the fanciful equation of a man with his knife is explicable as Florentina's mental aberration or as a symbol of Muraña's continuing influence. But in "The Meeting," Borges goes straight to the fantastic—to a mystical, metonymical equation of men with their instruments. Two men—not *compadres* but civilized upper-class Argentines—get tipsy at a stag party and quarrel over a card game. As if driven by something beyond themselves, they do the unthinkable. They go to a display cabinet, take out two knives made famous by a pair of rivals long dead, and fight. Neither knows anything about knife fighting, but they fight like experts. One is killed; the other is incredulous and ashamed. In a kind of postscript, Borges suggests that it was not the men who fought, but the knives; the men were instruments of an ancient enmity inherent in the weapons.

But of all these tales of the mythic outskirts of the city, "The Unworthy Friend" is perhaps the most ambiguous and intriguing. Don Santiago Fischbein (whose real name is Jacobo) tells his story to Borges. He was a Jewish boy and a confessed coward in a neighborhood where the physical courage of the *compadre* was admired. He was terribly eager to be accepted thereabouts, but also to be accepted as an Argentine and a good citizen. He fell in with a gang of hooligans headed by one Francisco Ferrari, not because he had what it took to run with that crowd but because he adulated the leader, who lured him in. Ferrari planned to break into a textile factory one night and assigned Fischbein to keep watch outside. But before the time came, Fischbein went to the police and told all, causing Ferrari's death.

After reading "The Unworthy Friend," one does not know who betrayed whom, who is really judged unworthy, and unworthy of what. In one way this story reverses the plot of "The South" (*Ficciones*), whose nameless old gaucho appears to correspond to the old man of "The Unworthy Friend," Eliseo Amaro, the only gang member who is named. Fischbein's betrayal of Ferrari is prefigured in his verbal denial, at one point, that he knows Ferrari (he feels unworthy of knowing him); this vaguely suggests Peter's denial of Jesus. (Borges' interest in Christ's betrayal is shown in "Three Versions of Judas" [*Ficciones*] and other places, and in his new fiction it is most prominent in "The Gospel According to Mark.")

The possible reasons why Fischbein betrayed Ferrari are numerous. He wanted to prove himself a good Argentine; his hero had tried to corrupt and use him; he lost respect for his idol when he saw him pushed around by the police; he saw him as a punk, the way Rosendo Juárez saw himself; he had to justify his own cowardice by causing his hero's courage to destroy him. The ostensible reason is psychological; men often betray those of whom they feel unworthy. The most probable explanation of the treachery is purely Borgesian: the inscrutable cosmos somehow required it; it repeated the Great Betrayal. Ferrari is a subverted Christ figure. Adored by his followers and persecuted by the authorities, he is first denied, then sold out, then killed.

Why is Peter suggested, however remotely, along with Christ's real betrayer, Judas? I think it is because the betrayal has somehow saved the traitor. The key to this lies in the reasoning of the strange Gutre, or Guthrie, family of "The Gospel According to Mark." Father, son, and daughter, all illiterate, work on a ranch being visited by the protagonist, a medical student named Baltasar Espinosa. Isolated with this rather stupid trio when the ranch is surrounded by floodwaters, Espinosa passes the time in the evenings by reading them the Gospel of St. Mark. Ordinarily unresponsive to the student, they listen with deep interest; when he treats their pet lamb for an injury, he wins their devotion. The rains destroy part of the roof of the tool shed attached to the house, and, according to the Gutres, this accounts for the hammering that goes on while Espinosa sleeps and dreams of the building of the Ark. One night the girl, a virgin, comes to his room naked and has intercourse with him without embracing or kissing him. The next day the father asks him whether even those who crucified Jesus were saved from hell, and Espinosa, whose theology is vague, says yes. After lunch Espinosa leaves his room to find the Gutres kneeling and asking his blessing; then they curse him and spit on him and push him to the door of the wrecked tool shed, from the timbers of which they have built a cross.

The transference of identity from Christ to Espinosa (whose name suggests Baruch Spinoza and also the word "thorny," like a crown of thorns) is plausible, given the superstitious mentalities of the Gutres. But the matter lies deeper. The idea of being saved by killing one's redeemer is a reversal of the idea of being killed *by* him, Job-like, as in "The House of Asterion" (*El Aleph*), where the Minotaur is "redeemed" by Theseus. While Borges equates salvation with death in that case, he makes it equivalent to life in this one, where the Gutres appropriate the virtues of their sacrificial victim through the symbolic ritual of cannibalism. Fischbein's cowardice, likewise, is somehow mitigated by the death of his superior, his "redeemer." In the story of the Gutres there are suggestions of correspondences between the death of Christ and the human sacrifices of primitive peoples. Just as the Gutre girl gave herself to Espinosa without the enthusiasm of love, as if in obeisance, the Aztecs (for example) chose sacrificial victims whom they coddled for a time, giving them luxury and women, before killing them. In a higher sense of the word, Jesus was "coddled" for a while, as during the triumphal entry into Jerusalem. The Gutres petted Espinosa, who, like Jesus, was thirty-three years old, a healer, bearded, and noted for oratory and goodness.

The cannibalism in these two stories is finally of an abstruse and philosophical kind, echoing the interplay of order and chaos that characterizes much of Borges' older work. Let me illustrate. The Gutres, who remind me of the oxlike Troglodytes of "The Immortal" (*El Aleph*), are of part-Scotch ancestry and are a mixture, Borges tells us, of Calvinist fanaticism and the superstition of the pampa Indian. Let us say they have a fixed and limited world-view. In words that paraphrase a reference in his confessional essay "The Maker" (*Dreamtigers*) and that allude to the Odyssey of Homer, Borges compares the Gutres to a lost ship searching the seas for a beloved island. The Odyssey and the Crucifixion are called the two histories which men, down through the ages, have repeated. On the symbolic level they are contrasted: the voyage of men lost in chaos, seeking a center, versus the exaltation through death (dissolution) of a supreme centrality on Golgotha. The medical student's mentality is contrasted with that of the Gutres; he is a freethinker who has no overriding or centered viewpoint, and no need for one. He likes to gamble, but not to win or to argue; he has "an open intelligence" and an "almost unlimited goodness." Unlike the world-view of the Gutres, then, his fluid and easy outlook seems magnanimous and noble. The Gutres, the lost ship, are searching for a secure idea, but Espinosa is not looking for anything. The Gutres see the Gospel as a conveyor of terribly important truth, but Espinosa reads it for its esthetic value. The Gutres seek order and meaning, but Espinosa is happy with a kind of agnostic equivocality, and, paradoxically, he is more ordered, more saved, than they. The narrow and fanatical Gutres believe that the sacrifice of their new pet, this other lamb, will redeem them.

How will it redeem them? We have to look back at Borges' older "system." Borges has made both salvation and hell equivalent to intellectual obsession (the inability to forget), as in "The Zahir" (*El Aleph*) where the narrator cannot forget a coin and goes happily, painlessly mad; or as in "Deutsches Requiem" (*El Aleph*) where the poet David Jerusalem is driven insane by an unnamed obsession inculcated by his tormentor, Otto zur Linde, who observes that any common thing, if not forgettable, is the germ of a possible hell; or as in "The House of Asterion" (*El Aleph*), where the Minotaur, bewildered by a house-universe that has too many galleries and doors, is "saved" by the world-simplifying sword that takes his life. In the story of the Gutres, as in Christian dogma, the death of the "Christ" is the vicarious death (redemption) of lost men; "Christ" becomes for the Gutres the holy obsession, the beloved island. Paradoxically, he represents not a limited, obsessive world-view, but its erasure.

"The Gospel According to Mark" is not one of the stories of rivalry. I want to go back to that type in order to mention "The Duel" and "Guayaquil." The first is a kind of parallel story to "The End of the Duel," mentioned earlier; the rivalry depicted is one that enriches the lives of the competitors. Two society women, Clara Glencairn and Marta Pizarro, compete in a friendly way in the field of painting. Painting is here analogous to literature, and I think we can infer that Borges is contrasting his own work—imaginative, ambiguous—both with the almost unintelligible literature of the vanguardist and with the clear-cut, rational literature of the *engagé* writer who tries to mirror the world and push a message. The story is humorous and satirical; in the artist Clara Glencairn we can perhaps see a caricature of Borges himself as he is seen, or thinks he is seen, by some Argentine men of letters who, on the one hand, have criticized his work for its universalism and aloof unconcern with national issues and, on the other hand, do not include him among the really "far out." Clara tried to be an abstract artist—a vanguardist—but that school rejected her work. She smiled and went on. Eventually she won a prize because some judges could not decide between two other artists, one of them too conventional and the other too "modern." Her friend and rival was the "straight" artist Marta Pizarro, a painter of portraits and patios with a nineteenth-century look. The two women painted against and for each other, and when Clara died, Marta's life lost its meaning. She painted Clara's portrait and laid her brushes aside for good. In that delicate duel, says Borges, there were neither defeats nor victories.

"Guayaquil" consists largely in the dialogue of two historians who are thrust into momentary rivalry. The narrator is a scholar whose specialty is the Independence movement and the life of the Argentine hero General San Martín. His adversary is a German Jew from Prague who has fled Hitler's tyranny, one Eduardo Zimmerman. Zimmerman is not a specialist in South American history but has proven himself adept at cleansing the biased histories of others (he has written on the Carthaginian Jews, who formerly were known only through the accounts of their enemies, the Romans). The two men are contending for the privilege of being officially chosen to go to another country to copy, appraise, and publish a newly discovered letter presumably written by Bolívar, which could clear up a famous historical mystery: what was said between San Martín and Bolívar, when they met in Guayaquil, which caused the former to retire from revolutionary activity and leave the destiny of the continent in Bolívar's hands. By conventional standards the narrator is better qualified to appraise the letter (a specialist, he is also the proud scion of revolutionary heroes), but he surrenders the privilege to Zimmerman after the two scholars converse. On leaving, Zimmerman divines that the narrator has conceded the honor because he intimately willed to do so. Still showing his penchant for alluding to philosophers, Borges weaves into the story a mention of Schopenhauer's "law" that no human action is involuntary; this serves a central purpose in the structure of the tale, which is about will and implies that volition—commitment—causes bad literature. I will comment on this story later in connection with Borges' esthetic ideas.

"The Elder Lady" shows Borges' ability to write in a charming and delicate way, with nostalgia for the glories of Argentine history and with both sympathy and satire of the *criollo* sensibility. The story is about the hundredth birthday of the last person who can claim to be the daughter of a revolutionary hero. The bustle and excitement of her anniversary celebration, which her countrymen turn into a celebration of national history and which she probably does not comprehend because she lives in the distracted world of the senile, hastens her end. She has long partaken of the glory of her famous father, hero of the battle of Cerro Alto; now she is somehow the last victim of that battle, for its celebration brings on her death.

Among the more ingenious of Borges' earlier stories are those in which he enumerates the irrational characteristics of some fantastic thing, apparently allegorizing an unnamed common reality. In "The Lottery in Babylon" (*Ficciones*), for example, he describes a "vertiginous country" where citizens are governed by pure chance, taking part in a lottery that awards them fame or ignominy, riches or poverty, life or death, on a day-to-day basis. Interpretation is up to the reader, and in this case the story seems to suggest the fortuitous and unstable nature of what men call reality. In "The Sect of the Phoenix" (*Ficciones*) Borges rounds up the random characteristics of a secret rite which is never identified but could be any number of things. In the new fiction, the title story of *Doctor Brodie's Report* is of this enigmatic type. It is an outrageous description of an incredible tribe called the Mlch, or Yahoos (the latter is the name of the degenerate humans in *Gulliver's Travels*). As a narrative device, Borges lays before us the incomplete manuscript of a Scottish Protestant missionary, David Brodie, who lived among the Yahoos. It reminds us of many things: Gulliver, a story by H. G. Wells, Pío Baroja's *Paradox Rey*, and other accounts of bizarre peoples. But mostly it reminds us of the old Borges, particularly of his description of the mind of Ireneo Funes ("Funes the Memorious," *Ficciones*), who could not forget details and was unable to form abstractions, "to think Platonically"; or it suggests the imaginary planet Tlön ("Tlön, Uqbar, Orbis Tertius," *Ficciones*), which is made of purely ideal—i.e., mental—elements. The Yahoos suffer the opposite of Funes' affliction; they have a language of pure abstractions and cannot remember details. They cannot combine phenomena except of a homogeneous, Platonic type. Unlike the people of Tlön, who can concoct anything at will, the Yahoos cannot fabricate at all. In the story of Tlön, the imaginary planet begins to concretize—to impose itself materially on the planet Earth; in the Yahoos of "Doctor Brodie's Report" we may see the grotesque end-result of that imposition. The Yahoos cannot count above four, can hardly speak, and appear to have no discrimination of time. In a limited way, they can predict the events of the immediate future (these appear to be only extrapolations). They remember almost nothing, and if they do remember an event they cannot say whether it happened to them or their fathers, or whether they dreamed it. They live in the present, they eat in secret or close their eyes while eating, they execute their fellows for fun, and if one of them is a poet (if he puts a few words together unintelligibly, but with moving effect) he is considered a god and anyone may kill him. Their king is blinded, mutilated, gelded, and kept in a cavern, except in war, when he is taken to the battle front and waved like a banner. Instead of declining into allegory, Borges' prose now tends to sharpen into satire, or even to move toward the intensive case of the modern novel, where the parable intersects with cultural anthropology, and whose characters obscure and overwhelm the symbols they encounter.

THE UNCHANGING BORGES

Borges' characters are still chessmen, however, and both character and action are subservient to situations of a chessboard kind. His settings are still indifferent; the *compadritos* could almost as easily be Chicago gangsters or western gunmen. Despite his return to the *arrabales*, Borges is not a portrayer of local color and customs; as somebody must have said before, his Buenos Aires is a situation, not a city. Many of his themes are still highbrow, esthetic, "irrelevant." References to systems of ideas, famous and arcane, are no longer profuse, but they have not vanished; we still find Spinoza, Euclid, Schopenhauer, the Kabbalah, Carlyle, Lugones, Carriego, Henry James, Hudson, and others. Still, these allusions seem to serve less purpose than formerly and to be more often literary than philosophical. Familiar Borgesian language crops up only here and there; in "The Intruder" we find "contentious alcohol" (*alcohol pendenciero*), a phrase he has used since the 1930's. Missing now are those very frequent words with which Borges used to point to the vast or infinite, such as "dizzying" (*vertiginoso*; this word used to do double duty, suggesting also the rise to an esthetic moment). Borges seldom plays with time and infinity, and instead turns to destiny, cosmic irony, and chance. Regrettably, we find no rich poetic images that suggest impossible intuitions like the plight of man before the chaotic universe: veiled men uttering blasphemous conjectures in the twilight ("The Lottery in Babylon") or old men hiding themselves in the latrines, with some metal disks in a prohibited dicebox, weakly imitating the divine disorder ("The Library of Babel," *Ficciones*).

Borges' language is still superbly laconic. It is less connotative, and conceits and etymological uses of words are no longer plentiful. Fantastic ideas still appeal to him, as we see in "The Meeting" and in "Juan Muraña," but they are no longer intended to rattle or astonish us; instead, they appeal to our esthetic sensibilities. There appears to be no significance, beyond Borges' personal whim, to the fact that the new stories are laden with Scotsmen (Brodie, Clara Glencairn, Glencoe, the Gutres), Germans (Zimmerman), and other North Europeans (the Nelsons or Nilsens of "The Intruder"). The prominence of red hair is consistent with all of these nationalities; all red things have symbolic meaning, I think, in Borges' work, and there may be a hidden significance here.

As before, Borges continues to throw in generalizations that are external to the narrative: "Carlyle says that men need heroes to worship" ("The Unworthy Friend"). Their effect is to give intellectual justification to a character's action, obviating a realistic or contextual explanation. This economy is fundamental to Borges' narration. He often inserts his own opinions; he tells us that the aged protagonist of "The Elder Lady" was gradually "growing dimmer and dimmer," and he justifies the metaphor by adding, "Common metaphors are the best because they are the only true ones"; and to explain Clara Glencairn's reason for taking up abstract instead of traditional art, he generalizes that "all esthetic revolutions put forth a temptation toward the irresponsible and the far too easy". These asides almost always have the value of esthetic commentary. In "Guayaquil," for example, Borges remarks: "The successiveness of language . . . tends to exaggerate what we are saying." This is given as a warning to the reader the Zimmerman's enumerated traits are "visual trivia," apparently not as important as the conclusion that he had lived an arduous life.

Borges has tallied, in the preface to *In Praise of Darkness*, a handful of his *"astucias"* — his stylistic and structural devices. The tabulation omits the majority of the subtleties that scholars have abstracted from his older works, and is obviously a declaration of present, not necessarily former, practice. Time, he says, has taught him to avoid synonyms, Hispanisms, Argentinisms, archaisms, and neologisms; to prefer habitual to astonishing words; to insert circumstantial details, "which the reader now demands"; to feign small uncertainties; to tell things as if he did not fully understand them; and to remember that former norms are not obligations. In the preface to *Doctor Brodie's Report* he says he has renounced "the surprises inherent in a baroque style." He does not call his new, "straightforward" stories simple: "I do not dare state that they are simple; there isn't anywhere on earth a single page or single word that is, since each thing implies the universe, whose most obvious trait is complexity."

Two of the devices he mentions are conspicuous because they preserve in Borges' new fiction an essential property of the old: namely, feigning small uncertainties and telling a story as if he did not fully understand it. Borges' chessmen — his people "seen through the wrong end of a telescope" (James Irby) — are not so much characters as props. Their faces are wiped off by Borges' aloof posture. He masks the activity of writing under the pretense of listening: "People

say (but this is unlikely) that the story was first told by Eduardo" ("The Intruder";
"Carlos Reyles . . . told me the story . . . out in Adrogué" ("The End of the Duel";
"here is the story, with all the inevitable variations brought about by time"
("The Meeting"). An occasional disclaimer, like "probably," keeps this objectivity
in front of the reader: "she was unable to keep hidden a certain preference,
probably for the younger man" ("The Intruder"). The only new story in which
he does not keep his distance is "Guayaquil," where he writes as the protagonist;
but it is also in this story that he speaks of the necessity of objectifying and
states the principle clearly: "I shall with all probity recount what happened,
and this may enable me to understand it. Furthermore, to confess to a thing
is to leave off being an actor in it and to become an onlooker—to become
somebody who has seen it and tells it and is no longer the doer." In contrast
to the narrator of "Guayaquil," who is so involved that he purports to understand only dimly what has happened, his rival historian, Zimmerman, is note-
worthy for his objective detachment from events and opinions; we feel that
Zimmerman understands everything—even the things he cannot express but
can only allude to.

THE ESTHETIC PHENOMENON

Borges' objectivity, his blurring of faces, is directly related to his esthetic.
I have suggested that in his older fiction Borges carries his reader to a mythic
awareness, an esthetic moment of near-revelation, and at the same time alludes
to that moment symbolically through images of dizziness: vertigo, fever, alcohol,
inebriation, exaltation, delirium. These images are part of a whole system of
secondary symbolism (i.e., below the level of such overt symbols as mirrors
and labyrinths) through which Borges used to create, in each narrative, a
background drama—a play of allusions in which the overt action of the story
is duplicated by symbolic forms as if these were the enlarged shadows of the
characters. In Borges' system there are symbols of order and being (blood, tower,
light, coin, tree, tiger, sword), symbols of chaos or nonbeing (circles, ashes,
mud, dust, swamps, plains, night, water, wall), and symbols of purely ideal
being and of world dissolution, made largely of combinations and interplays
of the images of order and chaos. They comprise an archetypal, almost Olympian
representation of the activity of the human consciousness as it creates, destroys,
and re-creates reality. In this shadowy undulation there is a moment between
the chaos of nonbeing (mere perception of meaningless things) and the lucidity
of full being (complete, meaningful abstraction) when the consciousness hovers
on the brink of a higher revelation. That revelation never comes; instead, what
occurs is a kind of short-circuit resulting in "language," the abstraction of a

bathetic reality small enough to be expressed. But that hovering instant when some kind of supernal truth seems imminent is the "vertiginous" moment to which Borges refers as the esthetic event.

We find far less evidence of this background drama of symbols in Borges' new fiction. Avowing his disbelief in esthetic *theories*, which he says are only occasional stimuli or instruments, Borges speaks continually of the esthetic *occurrence* or *fact*, "the imminence of a revelation." He built it allusively or allegorically into the fabric of such stories as "The End" (*Ficciones*); now it stares at us ingenuously from many of his new ones, and the forewords to the books he has published since 1960 are conspicuously concerned with the central point—the esthetic fact is not a collection of words on paper, but an experience: "A volume in itself is not an esthetic reality, but a physical object among others; the esthetic event can occur only when it is written or when it is read" (preface to *In Praise of Darkness*; translation mine).

Borges has shown that he is willing to judge literature good or bad using the *hecho estético* as a criterion. In the preface to his *Personal Anthology* (1961) he points to Croce's pronouncement that art is expression. To that idea, or to its deformation, he says, we owe some of the worst literature. He quotes verses from Valéry about a fruit whose form perishes in the mouth, giving delight by perishing, and other lines from Tennyson in which a boat fades into the distance and "vanishes into light." He doubts that anyone will finally include such verses among the best, saying that they represent a "mental process." We should infer that they carry an image or idea to its completion and that this is esthetically wrong. Borges adds: "At times, I too have sought expression; I know now that my gods grant me no more than allusion or mention" (translation mine). His comments do not finally cohere unless we understand that his "gods" are his ideas about how literature should be made. By opposing expression to suggestion he contrasts a finished mental process with one that is open-ended and indefinite, hovering over an unformulated idea. He seems to believe that allusion is not at all intellectual, hence the emphasis on event, on fact.

Borges likes the fruit image from Valéry. In another preface (to his *Obra poética* [*Poetic Works*; 1964]), he says he applies to poetry what Berkeley applied to reality: "The taste of the apple...lies in the contact of the fruit with the palate, not in the fruit itself.... What is essential is the esthetic act, the thrill, the almost physical emotion that comes with each reading." The bad writer, for Borges, is the one who *eats the fruit for us*, finishing the idea before we can savor its insinuations—or worse, letting his foregone conclusion shape the composition. Croce's "expression" is the complete verbal capture of a clear idea or feeling—the short-circuit that evaporates the pregnant myth. Borges points out in an essay on Nathaniel Hawthorne (*Other Inquisitions*) that Hawthorne's moralisms do not usually ruin his work, if only because they come in the last paragraph and because he did not fashion his characters to prove his conclusions. An "expressive" writer, an Aesop, builds a narrative that yields a simile between two realities (with the intention of giving one the color of the other), or between his fictitious events and the moral point or social theory he is trying to illustrate, while Borges himself wants only to distract his reader. Some quality held in common between two or more things links them secretly, and this is not something contrived by Borges but perceived by him. That perception, imparted to us, brings the momentary illusion that the chaotic world is somehow simplified or illuminated, and we are lifted toward a new insight or comprehension—which never solidifies.

Borges' esthetic idea is worked into his new fiction in at least two ways. In some stories he presents esthetically loaded situations, a "missing apex" type of suggestion which leaves the mystery incomplete. Usually this involves irony or paradox, and inevitably it raises the question of the character of God or of Destiny: an ironic competition between two dying rivals who had refused to kill each other in life; the redemptive crucifixion of an unbelieving, unsuspecting, unwilling "Christ"; a brother love that is no less admirable in itself (and perhaps is even more so) for having expressed itself in murder. The second way is that of the abstruse "allegory" (I now use the term inexactly, for lack of another) in which the esthetic event is pointed to by allusion as an objective idea. Only one of Borges' new stories is clearly of this kind, although others may be more subtly so; before turning to "Guayaquil," it will be helpful to look first at obvious allusions to the *hecho estético* in the short prose of *In Praise of Darkness*.

Borges uses, more often now, stories he has heard. Long ago he heard the one called "Pedro Salvadores," which is not really a story but a historical episode to which Borges adds his comments and shows his own esthetic reaction. Salvadores was an Argentine who, as an opponent of the dictator Juan Manuel de Rosas (deposed in 1852), was forced to hide in his cellar for nine years. This, plus the details, is his whole story. In the same way that Camus wondered, in *The Myth of Sisyphus*, what Sisyphus thought as he carried his eternal rock, Borges wonders at those nine years of dark isolation. (Internal elements lift the episode to a universal plane, and there is reason to suspect a parallel with Borges' blindness and his intellectual history). He conjectures about Salvadores' feelings, actions, thoughts, and very being—with no possibility of corroborating his intuitions. "As with so many things, the fate of Pedro Salvadores," he concludes, "strikes us as a symbol of something we are about to understand, but never quite do."

Very like that episode is the one called "The Anthropologist." Borges says he heard the story in Texas and he gives it to us without comment. Fred Murdock, a student of indigenous languages, goes into the desert to live with an Indian tribe and to discover the secrets behind its esoteric rites. After a long time he returns to the university and informs his disappointed professor that he has learned the secret but cannot tell it—not because of a vow or the deficiencies of language; in fact, he could enunciate it a hundred ways. But the secret is less valuable than the steps that lead to it, and "Those steps have to be taken, not told."

"The Anthropologist" is brief and deceptively simple; it is not a story about an anthropologist but about a young man in chaos, uncommitted, who tried to reduce the world to a facet of itself, hoping to find in it the centripetal vortex of vision that would explain or justify the whole. It is the same story as "The Library of Babel" (*Ficciones*) in which the inmates of the library go blind looking for the compendious book. It is the story of a frustration, like "Averroes' Search" (*El Aleph*), where Averroes is compared to the frustrated god "mentioned by Burton . . . [who] tried to create a bull and created a buffalo instead." It is the story told in Borges' poem "The Golem," where a rabbi tries to create a man and can only create a clumsy doll. Here we see vestiges of an allusive imagery that is much more evident in Borges' older work; it is not mere coincidence that the student dreamed of mustangs (in the Spanish, it is bison). He went into the desert to find a revelation and found only language. As he implies, the search was more valuable than the result, and the search has to be experienced, not told. The esthetic experience is in the contact of the fruit with the palate, not in the digestion of it.

Borges believes—I think it is clear—that the tales men tell and retell, the ones that comprise our myths, are all of the open kind. They respect and embody an esthetic of the unconsummated, rehearsing the cosmic mystery. All our science, philosophy, and explanations of the universe are buffaloes.

In a tiny poetic essay, "The Unending Gift," an artist promises Borges a painting but dies without sending it. If it had come, it would be a thing among things; but now it is limitless and unceasing, capable of any form or color. It somehow exists and will live and grow like music. "In a promise," Borges concludes, "there is something that does not die."

"GUAYAQUIL" AND *EL HECHO ESTÉTICO*

"Guayaquil," which I summarized earlier, is the story of a scholar who renounces intellectual fulfillment in order to preserve esthetic life. He sees more value in a myth than in an explanation, more virtue in an unformulated idea than in the language that purports to convey truth. The narrator of the story and his rival historian, Dr. Zimmerman, are contending for the privilege of appraising the newly found letter of Bolívar which will give Bolívar's answer to the renowned question of what happened in the interview with San Martín. We must remember that San Martín, after talking with Bolívar, withdrew from the revolutionary struggle; we might say that he, too, quit before his drama was done. Bolívar led his country's fortunes until his death, leaving his indelible stamp on the revolution and its aftermath. Transferred from the historical plane to the literary, San Martín's story is unconsummated and esthetic; but Bolívar's finished career (a completed "mental process") makes bad "literature." The conversation of the revolutionary heroes is somehow duplicated in that of the historians, who observe that it was no doubt Bolívar's will, not words, that determined the outcome at Guayaquil. The narrator finally concedes to Zimmerman the honor of publishing the letter in order not to repeat the action – the will – of Bolívar. To repeat Bolívar's error would be to turn an esthetically attractive historical event – a living myth – into mere short-circuiting language. The reason is this: there is mystery in the San Martín incident, and Zimmerman believes the letter cannot really clear it up because it gives only Bolívar's version, perhaps written in self-justification. If Zimmerman interprets the letter for the public, he will preserve the mythic ambiguity by weighing Bolívar's words in the proper perspective. But the biased narrator feels that if he publishes a commentary, the effect will be deadly; he is the descendant of revolutionists, very much involved in history and partial to San Martín, and his conjectural position on the matter is well known (although we are not told what it is). The public will link him with the letter, and the myth (the suggestive indeterminacy) will be destroyed by some miserable "explanation" which the public will suppose has been made by his conclusions on the subject. "The public at large," Zimmerman remarks, "will never bother to look into these subtleties." If the narrator imposes his will, he will act, as Borges expressed a similar urge in *Dreamtigers*, from "no other law than fulfillment," and the result will be "the immediate indifference that ensues" ("The Maker").

To show Zimmerman that he has understood, the narrator recites two parables in which we can see a tension between simple correspondence and the esthetic fact. In the first parable, two kings play chess on a hilltop while their armies clash. One loses the game and his army loses the battle; the chess game was a mere duplication of the larger reality. In the second, two famous bards have a contest of song. The first sings from dawn until dusk and hands the harp to the other. The latter merely lays it aside and stands up, and the first confesses his defeat. We can take the second parable to mean that the best song remains unsung – limitless, unending, like a promise. The narrator makes statements at the beginning and end of "Guayaquil" which can be understood to mean that he will not destroy the esthetic indefiniteness surrounding San Martín's talk with the Liberator. At the beginning: "Now I shall not journey to the Estado Occidental [Western State]; now I shall not set eyes on snow-capped Higuerota mirrored in the water of the Golfo Plácido; now I shall not decipher Bolívar's manuscripts." At the end the narrator, a man whose life has been dedicated to nailing down the definitive truths that explain history, seems to confess his conversion to an esthetic of the indefinite: "I have the feeling that I shall give up any future writing." Borges fashioned the opening lines of this story from Conrad's *Nostromo*.

In the original Spanish, "manuscripts" is *letra*, which means handwriting or letter. *Letra* is one of Borges' old symbols for clear conception, visible reality, or abstraction, as in "The Secret Miracle" (*Ficciones*), where God is a tiny letter on a map. Among other symbols of ordered or abstract reality in Borges' older stories are mountains and other kinds of upward projections. The things the narrator of "Guayaquil" says he will not do are all symbolic, it seems, of the production of intelligible reality through expressive language; he will not see a mountain duplicated, behold a "letter," or write his definitive conclusions. As for the "western country," it seems enough to say that "western" is the opposite of "eastern" with its implication of mystery. This, too, is consistent with Borges' old symbolism, in which all things eastern and yellow suggest the chaotic, mythic, and esthetic.

Borges is still building into his fiction the occasional guide-images or omens that facilitate interpretations but certainly do not corroborate them. For example, when Zimmerman enters the narrator's house, he pauses to look at a patio tiled in black and white (an old image in Borges' work), prefiguring the parable of the chess game and perhaps suggesting that the events to follow will be a kind of duplication. Indeed, during the conversation it seemed to the two scholars "that we were already two other people"; their encounter occurs at twilight, which in Borges' familiar work is a frequent symbol of change or suspension of reality. When the first bard sings, he sings from morning twilight to evening; his song is a daylight song, a finished and patent thing, superseded by the unsung music that belongs to the dreaming hours as day recedes. And at one point Zimmerman remarks: " 'Everything is strange in Prague, or, if you prefer, nothing is strange. Anything may happen there. In London, on certain evenings, I have had the same feeling.' " Zimmerman is from Prague, the native city of Kafka, and of the ambitious rabbi of "The Golem," who tried to create a man but produced only a monster. Also in "Guayaquil" is a reference to *Der Golem*, a novel by Gustav Meyrink of Prague. In converation Borges has said that the creation of the golem is "a parable of the nature of art."

One other important symbol deserves mention: blood. In Borges' older work, it is associated with fullness of being—with completeness, domination, victory, or will. The will in question in "Guayaquil" is not Zimmerman's, imposed upon the narrator; it is, rather, the narrator's, suppressed for a cause. Zimmerman observes that the narrator carries Argentine history in his blood, implying that he would treat Bolívar's letter with willful prejudgment. The narrator tells us that Zimmerman's words were "the expression of a will that made of the future something as irrevocable as the past," but we must understand that Zimmerman's "expression" delineated the undesirable willfulness of the narrator, which the latter willfully subdued.

This interpretation of "Guayaquil" suggests taking another look at such stories as "The Gospel According to Mark"; instead of comparing the mentalities of Espinosa and the Gutres in terms of order and chaos—or, to use a term from Borges, order and *adventure* ("The Duel")—we might infer a contrast between the open, uncommitted, mythic-minded writer (Espinosa) and the closed-minded, compromised, or committed writers (the Gutres) who are guided by their determination (their "Calvinist fanaticism") to get a point across, to find their "beloved island." The work of such writers is predetermined; its meaning is as irrevocable as the preconceptions of the authors.

If we can judge by "The Maker," even his blindness is to Borges analogous to the abandonment of Aesopism, somewhere in his past, and to his espousal of the idea that literature should be written "blind"—for its own sake, not for an intellectual or practical purpose. Most of his stories are punctiliously contrived allusions to the idea of art for art's sake; in that sense they comprise art about art.

ETHICS

With the appearance of *In Praise of Darkness* (as Borges notes in the preface) two new themes are added to his work: old age and ethics. What he calls ethics goes beyond and embraces much of his philosophy and its esthetic foundations.

"Fragments of an Apocryphal Gospel" could be called poetry or prose; it is a collection of numbered apothegms and injunctions modeled in part on the Beatitudes. They alter many of the sayings of Jesus and other moral or theological axioms, often contradicting them or seeming to. They reflect a point of view which denies heaven and hell, reduces men to predestined beings who are ignorant of their destiny, rejects the idea of morality for the sake of reward, believes in pursuing justice for its own sake, and looks with kindly, humanistic eyes at the human species. These dicta strongly imply a pessimism overcome by courage—not stoicism, which suggests a dogged refusal to be affected, but blind, Tillichian faith, which has only rigor to justify it. Borges' ethic, as he seems to declare in "A Prayer" (discussed below), consists in a devotion to lucid reason and just action.

In his "Fragments" Borges is satirical, warm, wise, heretical, moralistic, sly, and often majestic. "Blessed are they who know," he says, "that suffering is not a crown of glory," and "Wretched are they that mourn, for they have fallen into the craven habit of tears." He has no use for the poor in spirit, who expect heaven to be better than earth, nor for those who comfort themselves with feelings of guilt; and the actions of men, he says, deserve neither heaven nor hell. You can't judge a tree by its fruit nor a man by his works; they can both be better or worse than they look. "Give that which is holy unto the dogs, cast your pearls before swine: for what matters is giving." To one who strikes you on the cheek you may turn the other, provided you are not moved by fear. To do good for your enemy is to give him justice; but to love him is a task for angels, not men. Happy are the lovers and the loved, and those who can do without love, and those who forgive others and themselves, and "Happy are the happy."

The latter pronouncement has an esthetic motive, expressed in "The Unworthy Friend": "The only thing without mystery is happiness, because happiness is an end in itself." And there are other esthetic admonitions: "Swear not, for an oath may be only an emphasis." The moral and the esthetic are combined in: "Forgetting is the only vengeance and the only forgiveness." This idea is the theme of another new prose piece, "Legend," in which Cain asks Abel to forgive him. But Abel has forgotten who killed whom. Cain sees that Abel has truly forgiven, and says he will try to forget too. "Yes," Abel agrees, "as long as there's remorse, there's guilt." This idea is expressed also in "The Unworthy Friend."

"A Prayer" is perhaps the frankest and most intimate thing Borges has ever written and in my opinion the most magnificent. He begins by acknowledging that a personal prayer demands an almost superhuman sincerity. It is obvious, he says, that he cannot ask for anything. To ask that he not go blind (he is not entirely sightless) would be to ask for the suspension of cause and effect, and "Nobody is worthy of such a miracle." Neither can he ask pardon for his errors; forgiveness is an act of others, which purifies the offended, not the offender, and only Borges can save Borges. He can only give what he himself does not have: courage, hope, the urge to learn. He wants to be remembered less as a poet than as a friend; let someone recite a line from Dunbar or Frost and remember that he first heard it from Borges' lips. Faithful to his "gods" to the end, he combines the esthetic and the moral in a final observation: "The laws of the universe are unknown to us, but we are somehow sure that to reason clearly and to act righteously is to help those laws, which will never be revealed to us." When he dies, he wants to die wholly, "with this companion, my body."

The uncertain darkness of death and of blindness is the theme of *In Praise of Darkness*. In a piece called "His End and His Beginning," the two are united in superb metaphorical prose that subsumes all forms of transition into the unknown. Having died, and suffering the agony of being dead, Borges accepts death and it becomes heaven; blind, he accepts blindness and it becomes the beginning of an adventurous life in a new world. He praises his darkness, and in that praise there is a victory, as limitless as a promise, over all men's darkness. And somehow Borges extols the darkness of his own skepticism, his agnostic unknowingness, which is his philosophy; he translates it positively into an esthetic of conjectural expectancy. Borges' mind ranges over reality as the Vikings ranged over the world, plundering not for plunder but for adventure.

Reading this book, we are convinced of the sincerity of his apocryphal fragments, one of which says: "Let a candle be lighted though no man see it; God will see it."

"THE CONGRESS"

Not every story written by Borges in his heyday was a good one; "The Shape of the Sword" (*Ficciones*) has something fake about it. His story "The Congress," finished late in 1970 and published in 1971, does not "come off" on the first reading. Borges has said that he toyed with the plot for twenty years. Because of its long gestation alone, it is extremely important to the study of Borges' work. One gets the feeling that if it could be caught from the right angle and given a good shake, it would fall into the right pattern, shedding light on all Borges' major fiction. To be appreciated, I think, this long story has to be accepted as allegory and as exemplary technique, and even as Borges' deliberate circumvention of his own esthetic. In this story, the esthetic event, the sacred *hecho estético* which Borges upholds as the superior alternative to intellectual effort and "expressive" language, is itself, by implication, as meaningless as those other fruitless approaches to reality: philosophy and history.

The name of the story derives from the effort of one Alejandro Glencoe, a rich Uruguayan rancher living in Buenos Aires, to call together a "Congress of the World which would represent all men of all nations." This body would convene four years after the start of preparations. "Planning an assembly to represent all men was like fixing the exact number of Platonic types—a puzzle which had taxed the imagination of thinkers for centuries." One of the fifteen or twenty planners suggests that "don Alejandro Glencoe might represent not only cattlemen but also Uruguayans, and also humanity's great forerunners, and also men with red beards, and also those who are seated in armchairs." Glencoe finances the project, which consists largely in collecting books—at first encyclopedias, then the great books of the centuries, then random account books and Ph.D. theses. The narrator, Alejandro Ferri, visits Glencoe's ranch and sees him transformed into "the stern chief of a clan" of gauchos; later, Ferri is sent to London to find a suitable language for the Congress to use, and in that city he has a love affair with a girl named Beatrice, while Glencoe's nephew, Fermín Eguren, on the same mission in Paris, plays with prostitutes. Ferri goes back to Buenos Aires, where Glencoe, precisely at the end of the four-year period of preparation, has concluded that the Congress is impossible, for it embraces an irreducible world: "The Congress of the World began with the first moment of the world and it will go on when we are dust. . . . The Congress is Job on the ash heap and Christ on the Cross. The Congress is that worthless boy who squanders my substance on whores." At his order the group burns the collected books, and one member remarks: "Every few centuries, the Library of Alexandria must be burned down." Then, acting as if they had been cleansed of an evil and were on a somewhat languid holiday, the members of the Congress anticlimactically tour the city to "see the Congress."

The effort to classify all the world's men under a few abstract headings suggests the search for a syncretic philosophy, or for a literature that reduces chaotic reality to a recurring set of relations. One feels that if the Congress convened someplace, the world would be vacated. The members are relieved to discover that their efforts are futile, and as the books burn one remarks, "I wanted to do evil and I have done good." The story implies the spiritual or esthetic benefit of liberating men periodically from their structured certitude and restoring to them a perception of reality as an anarchy of things-in-themselves. Philosophically, this is a return to myth, to rebirth, to orgy; literarily, it suggests a return to uncontrived, straightforward storytelling about things as they are, unstructured and unmoralized. The book burning is reminiscent of the fire that swept the circular ruins in the story of that name (*Ficciones*) and the one that destroyed the dogmatists of "The Theologians" (*El Aleph*).

"The Congress" is complex, laden with familiar Borgesian images, symbolic names, and suggestions of identities: two Alejandros and an Alexandrian library. Again there is an allusion to the esthetic event: Ferri's amorous sojourn in London (like Prague, a dizzying sort of place, here called a red labyrinth) with a girl named Beatrice, like Dante's esthetic ideal finally unattainable (she refuses to marry Ferri). This episode comes just before what we may call the esthetic frustration or the loss of the impending revelation—in this case the end of hope for the fulfillment of the Congressional dream.

In all the episodes of "The Congress" the nearness of revelation, intellectual, linguistic, and esthetic, always leads to the same disillusion—a final return to reality as a mythic disorder incapable of being organized or interpreted with finality. The intellectual attempt to order the universe is the Congress itself; truth-in-art, by analogy, is not found in the classicist's attempt to reduce the world to abstract forms. The engaged writer's pursuit of art through direct, expressive language, used for a mission and therefore subordinate in its own right, is satirized in Eguren's visits to prostitutes; he "enjoys and forgets" like the protagonist of "The Maker," who acts from "no other law than fulfillment," with "the immediate indifference that ensues." Borges treats Fermín Eguren, whose first name suggests vermin and who has a very low forehead, with humorous disdain. (He is also of Basque ancestry, which Borges derides. A low forehead and Basque origin are qualities also assigned to Benjamín Otálora of "The Dead Man.") Ferri shows his superiority over Eguren in one episode; confronted by a ruffian with a knife, Eguren quails, but Ferri reaches inside his coat, as if to draw a knife, and faces the hoodlum down. Ferri and Eguren are in the company of a writer much admired by Ferri; he is the author of a fine work whose title, *The Marble Pillars*, strongly suggests the classical. The author, Fernández Irala, also symbolizes the Congress; he is perhaps its staunchest member. Considering the satirical nature of the whole story, there is possibly an intentional correspondence between Borges' literature of suggestion (his unproduced revelation) and Ferri's bluster with a hidden knife that is not really there.

Why does "The Congress" give the impression that it is not one of Borges' better stories? Its failure, if I can call it that, may be owing precisely to its accomplishment. It seem deliberately, successfully compendious, reflecting all the facets of a background idea which, I believe, has inspired the major part of Borges' fictional literature about literature. It closes the book. Though it is not a plain-language story with a clear meaning, it represents what Borges despises: a completed "mental process." Instead of symbolic allusion, it constitutes symbolic expression. There is a finished progression, by three implied routes, from chaos to near-order and back to chaos. Although this progression is depicted incidentally in some of his other stories, in "The Congress" it seems to be the whole purpose. The satirical denial of the esthetic event prevents the sacred event from seeming to be diffused into the structure of the story, embodied as a reality behind the symbols. For this reason I suggest that Borges is aware of the story's "failure."

It is hard to believe, moreover, that Borges, the supreme literary technician, could be ignorant of having violated his own techniques by overdoing them. In the episodes at the ranch, in London, and on the street where the hoodlum appears, as well as in the description of the Congress members, there is too much realistic detail to be consistent with an essentially fantastic plot. There is too much half-esoteric commentary of an autobiographical type, which yields clues to Borges' literary theories only after study and speculation. I venture to say that the story is not intended to be read but to be studied. Not only is "The Congress" heavy with hints and allusions and loaded with symbolic attributes (names, red beards, places), but it is slowed by superfluous actions (two knife episodes, the overlong love affair), and weighted with seemingly irrelevant descriptions (of the gauchos at the ranch, for example), so that it becomes ponderous. I said earlier that Borges' stories are floating tales; this one is too dense to float. I also suspect that "The Congress," being satirical, is full of intended humor that is too private, at least for an English-speaking reader.

This story is an overexpression which, purposely or not, stultifies its own inner insinuation that the esthetic phenomenon is a meaningless illusion. Borges' satire of himself and his esthetic is not convincing because it begs to be refuted. At the end, the Congressmen are not really joyful, as they appear; they are only disillusioned and released from struggle. The story seems to deny the value of that struggle—man's pursuit of the impossible. It denies the positive element in Borges' skepticism. The members of the disbanded Congress, who do not want to speak to each other again, cannot help reminding us of the disillusioned, bored and speechless Troglodytes of "The Immortal" (*El Aleph*).

The former Borges would have ended the story with an insinuation of positive conviction that the book burning was inevitable and right; but here he leaves us with the feeling that it is inescapably wrong. In "The House of Asterion" (*El Aleph*), where the miserable Minotaur is happy when Theseus comes to kill him, we are somehow happy for him because his bewilderment is dissolved in fatal meaning. But with the destruction of the books and the end of the Congress, Theseus has in some way faltered, and the Minotaur goes wandering on toward a meaningless end somewhere in his confusing labyrinth—a labyrinth whose anarchical variability no longer offers possibility and adventure. Again, this may be exactly what Borges has intended; at the beginning of the story Ferri explains that he is going on seventy-one (Borges' age); he came to Buenos Aires in 1899 (Borges' birth year), and a symptom of his age is that adventure no longer appeals to him: "novelties—maybe because I feel they hold nothing essentially new, and are really no more than timid variations—neither interest nor distract me." None of the infinite attributes of the universe, therefore, is a possible essence; no fortuitous position of the kaleidoscope can reveal anything; in the vast Library of Clementinum there is no tiny letter that is God, and we must not seek it in art, or philosophy, or language.

Perhaps the return to the nominalistic heterogeneity of things-in-themselves is only the symbol for Borges' decision to tell simple stories for their own sake. There is reason to wonder if he can do it consistently.

Borges' new inclination toward the simple and straightforward has been carried into English, not only in the translations of his new fiction but also in the recasting of stories written years ago. This is undoubtedly better than trying to produce in English the complicated linguistic effects of the Spanish originals. For example, as Norman Thomas di Giovanni, Borges' collaborator in translation, has noted, the special effect produced by writing Spanish while thinking in English, using English word order, cannot be duplicated in English even by reversing the process. But it would be absurd not to admit that something is lost, as it always is in translation. Judging from what I have seen (which does not include translations of some of the most cryptic and ambiguous of the old stories), I would say that di Giovanni's and Borges' translations are by far the best yet, particularly from the standpoint of their enjoyability to the average reader. Scholars will find them in some respects problematical.

By undertaking to translate Borges' works, Borges and di Giovanni have created a situation as ambiguous and subtle as one of Borges' tales. The case is reminiscent of "Pierre Menard, Author of the *Quixote*" (*Ficciones*), where Menard sets out to write *Don Quixote* in the exact language of Cervantes' original, by being the kind of man who would write, in the present century, what another man wrote centuries ago under different circumstances. With regard at least to Borges' older work, we cannot escape the fact that the translations are being made twenty years or more after the stories were composed, with all that this implies: slips of memory, changes in theory, the urge to improve the story, the influence of intervening criticism and the public's reactions, and the hand of a recent co-translator. Critics who are given to integrating an author's life and opinions with his work will lean heavily on the belief that Borges remains Borges across the years, and on his and di Giovanni's insistence upon being faithful to what Borges intended when he wrote. Others, who consider that a work is a work, to be isolated and beheld in itself—*res ipsa loquitur*—are likely to see the English versions as a body of fresh literature which neither affects nor depends upon the Spanish originals.

The independence of the English versions (I am still speaking of the old stories) will be strengthened to the degree with which critics judge them to be unfaithful to the originals, or even discrepant with more literal translations. The old fiction is full of involutions and nuances heavily dependent on a particular vocabulary, often shockingly ill-fitting, ambiguous, or otherwise strange. This puzzling prose has been in the public's hands for many years; Borges' fame is largely built on it, and much criticism has been based on its implications. According to Borges' own theory (very like Valéry's), he is now only one of his readers, and any clarification of strange language that he and di Giovanni might make must constitute in some degree a re-creation or an interpretation. In numerous interviews Borges has said—despite his incredible memory—that he has forgotten why he included an incident in a story, used a color, or wrote a certain word, and some of these forgotten things are of critical importance. Di Giovanni has been diligent in ferreting out the original reasons for the use of unusual language and equally diligent in making it rational. Borges wrote his early stories for a limited, somewhat erudite, and very Argentine readership, at a time when he was little known or appreciated; he and di Giovanni translate under the spur of fame and for a much larger and less intellectual readership that is largely ignorant of the context and tradition of Argentine literature.

In view of these special factors, I am not disturbed over the loss of such celebrated phrases as "unanimous night" (*unánime noche*), which has been rationalized into "encompassing night" in "The Circular Ruins." The change smacks of decoding poetry, and there is a loss of flavor; but it also points, without doubt, to what Borges now calls baroque trickery and indicates what in his opinion is not essential in his earlier work. A more radical deviation occurs when "enormous hallucination" (*enorme alucinación*) is changed to "populous vision." This phrase, also from "The Circular Ruins," refers to the college of imaginary students from which the magician tried to abstract one in order to insert him into reality. The antecedent of "enormous hallucination" is unclear in the original but can be inferred; the epithet suggests not that the students were numerous and imaginary (we already know that) but that the magician's very method was wrong. "Populous vision" makes the antecedent clear but loses all other implications, along with the insinuation of a second level of meaning.

Some of Borges' most conspicuous trademarks, such as his repetitious use of words like "notorious" and "attribute," seem to be suppressed in the translations. In the preface to *Doctor Brodie's Report* we find the words "most notorious attribute" (*más notorio atributo*) interpreted "most obvious trait." Given the frequent implication of evil that attaches to Borges' use of "*notorio*," particularly when it refers to the universe, "most obvious trait" loses or ignores the valuative tenor of the original phrase. Again, in "The Dead Man," the phrase which tells us that Bandeira's horse, saddle, and mistress are his "*atributos o adjetivos*" (a significant evocation of a substance-attribute or noun-adjective simile) is weakened to "attributes or trappings." The possibly metaphysical intention of the original is far less apparent in the English.

As another random example of the apparent decision of the translators not to carry certain insinuations into English, the name of the knife-wielding hoodlum of "The Congress" can be cited. This character's name is utterly unimportant to the story, but in his typical way Borges takes the trouble to give it: "Tapia or Paredes or something of the kind." The reader who does not know Spanish is unaware that both *tapia* and *pared* mean "wall," an image common enough in Borges' older fiction to raise an immediate question about its possible symbolism here.

One thing is obvious. The author-made translations now being published are most readable. They are smoother, in general, than the Spanish version; this diminishes the cerebral, deliberate quality conveyed by the more abrupt Spanish narrations, in which the uneven stops and starts give each word and phrase an intentionality and a singular authority. Conjunctions now smooth the path and relax the reader where semicolons used to jar him; transitions are made where there were only juxtaposed ideas. While such changes in the fluidity of language and idea can be attributed to di Giovanni's sense of clarity and polish, they also testify to Borges' abandonment of what he calls, in the preface to *Doctor Brodie's Report*, "the surprises inherent in a baroque style."

EMIR RODRÍGUEZ-MONEGAL

Symbols in Borges' Work

Borges' work is characterized, above all, by a plethora of symbols that is evident to even the most casual reader. Mirrors and labyrinths, rivers and tigers, swords and roses permeate Borges' fictions and essays, haunt some of his best poems. The permanence and reiteration of these symbols, the multiple and sometimes contradictory functions they perform, their omnipresence, makes them so notorious that, lately, even their maker feels uncomfortable about them. In an interview with César Fernández Moreno, published in 1967, Borges has stated:

> I am so fed up with labyrinths and mirrors and tigers and all that . . . .
> Above all when others use them . . . . That is the advantage of having
> imitators; they serve to cure one. Because one thinks: so many people
> are doing it. Let the others do it now, and get harmed.

Nevertheless, in his works these symbols do not have a purely ornamental function but constitute part of a code that allows a reading of the subtext, or intertext, of allusions hidden in the very fabric of his writing. One of his favorite authors, Thomas De Quincey, suggested once that "the whole world was a set of symbols or that everything meant something else," as Borges recalls in another interview. In the prologue to *El hacedor (Dreamtigers)*, Borges has referred to the hope that after death, time and chronology "will be lost in a sphere of symbols," and in his prologue to Ronald Christ's *The Narrow Act*, he has defined the writer as a "user of symbols."

From *Modern Fiction Studies* 19, no. 3 (Autumn 1973). © 1973 by Purdue Research Foundation, West Lafayette, IN.

Thus, I believe, it is in the examination of the symbols contained in Borges' work that the best key to the study of its ultimate significance can by found.

II

Like all writers, Borges uses symbols that come from the most distant traditions and that are often intimately incorporated into the common language. Those symbols serve to express eternal themes, and they are like metaphors created by that collective and ubiquitous author—"the spirit as producer or consumer of literature"—that Borges has evoked in one of his essays, with the help of a quotation from Paul Valéry. In Borges' texts, then, it is easy to recognize these traditional symbols, from the *rose*, which reveals at the same time the fragility of things and their perenniality, since each rose represents the immortal species, to the *sword*, which is generally presented as a favored emblem of his ancestors: heroes of the South American War of Independence or of the civil wars which brought about national unity. These same weapons also appear in his work in degraded forms, such as the *knife* or the *dagger*, to illustrate infamous aspects of courage: the murderous bravery of the thug, the gambler, the gangster.

Some of these traditional symbols—like that of the *river* which symbolizes at the same time Life, in its flow, and Time, in its irreversibility—appear so repeatedly in his texts that they become signs of personal obsessions and mark his imagery with an idiosyncratic seal. Even so, Borges uses them generally to underline their traditional significance. What gives them a Borgesian turn (what makes them Borges) is, always, the intensity of the reference. This also happens with the symbol of the *dream*.

When Borges uses the symbol of the river, or the symbol of the dream, he makes them function in a poetical and metaphysical context very much his own. By means of allusions, permutations, or even confrontations with other symbols, he ends by imposing his mark on these symbols worn out by tradition. One example: the well-known image of Heraclitus which illustrates that it is impossible to step twice into the same river, or as one of the versions says: "Upon those who step into the same rivers different and ever different waters flow down," is present in some lines of Borges' "Poema del cuarto elemento" ("Poem of the Fourth Element"). There Borges comments on the sacred character of the Ganges' waters; merging the formula of Heraclitus with the Hindu religious motif, he arrives at an original observation which transcends both traditional meanings: as seas communicate and are really one, so it is true to say that every man has bathed in the Ganges' waters.

By a subtle use of paradox, Borges inverts Heraclitus' image (with which he seemed to be in agreement) and contaminates it with an even more solipsist vision which suggests that as all water is one, all men are one. In the process, he makes a traditional image his, without ceasing to reflect (doubly, ambiguously) the image coined by Western philosophical tradition. In this way and by a technique that recalls the one used by the medieval copyists in creating a palimpsest, Borges suggests a second text hidden inside the space of the first, the visible one. The collision, the confrontation of images, the paradoxical inversion of meanings, allows him to take advantage of, and at the same time, to annihilate, the original content of the image. Both the metaphysical observation of Heraclitus and the Hindu religious beliefs emerge relativized and finally negated by the process of paradoxical contamination to which Borges submits them.

In another poem, ironically entitled "Arte poética" ("Ars Poetica"), the contradiction noted becomes more explicit and, thus, is more clearly accepted. Art is compared to a river

> That flows and remains and is the mirror of one same
> Inconstant Heraclitus, who is the same
> And is another, like the river with no end.

Heraclitus' image, Heraclitus himself as a metaphor for a certain vision of reality, is used in this poem for Borges' own ends: the traditional image has been charged with a personal, even private, meaning without losing any of its formal value. Like Mallarmé, Borges transforms the material belonging to all ("les mots de la tribu," as the French poet would say) into his own material and out of clarities produces a coded poetry.

III

The traditional metaphor of life as sleep or a dream (in Spanish, "sueño" means both), which generally serves to express the unreality of life and its illusory, almost fantastic character, allows Borges to illustrate a more personal and limited philosophical conception. On indicating, for example, the oneiric aspect that waking experience sometimes assumes, Borges says in the poem, "La noche cíclica" ("The Cyclical Night"):

> And the singleminded streets creating space
> Are corridors for sleep and nameless fear.

In another text, "Poema de los dones" ("Poem of the Gifts"), one of his most personal in that it refers explicitly to his near-blindness, the image of sleep allows him to represent his now impaired perception of reality:

> I watch the delectable
> World first disfigure then extinguish itself
> In a pallor of ashes, until all that is gone
> Seems at one with sleep and at one with oblivion.

This use of the image of sleep would seem to confirm the impression that Borges employs the image only for his allusions to a subjective experience: the excessive wakefulness is substituted gradually by a blindness that erases reality and converts it into sleep or a dream. But there is more to it than this traditional use of a common symbol. Even before he became blind, Borges was convinced that everyone's reality has a profound oneiric nature and that the distinction between waking and sleeping was finally illusory. All his metaphysical speculations, all the inquisitions of his best essays, are directed towards destroying the coherence of reality and superimposing on it a dream vision. Thus, the poem dedicated to Alfonso Reyes alludes to the vague chance or precise laws which rule "this dream, the universe." In another verse, also from "Arte poética," he will say more clearly:

> To be aware that waking dreams it is not asleep
> While it is another dream, and that the death
> That our flesh goes in fear of is that death
> Which comes every night and is called sleep.

The universe as dream dreamt by all (he calls it the "shared dream," in the poem, "El despertar," "Awakening"), death as another dream: little by little, Borges slips into the traditional symbol his own solipsist conception which denies external reality, denies time, denies the individual ego, going even further in all these denials than his acknowledged models: Berkeley, Hume, Schopenhauer, Nietzsche. The traditional symbols, like the meditations of those philosophers, serve Borges as stimuli, a starting point, means by which he always reaches his own private vision.

IV

It is obvious that Borges discovered, after psychoanalysis, that poetry uses the same mechanisms as dreams and that its symbols can be deciphered in a similar way. But his relations with clinical psychoanalysis do not go much further. Already in his first critical texts, written around 1921 in Europe at the time of Freud's first impact on literary culture, Borges indicated serious reservations about its techniques and subject matter, pointing out that its theories seemed to him "provisional psychological hypotheses." More recently, in the prologue to his *Obra poética* ("Poetic Works"), he has shown his disagreement by means of an ironic allusion:

> The dreary mythology of our time speaks of the subconscious, of what is even less lovely, of subconsciousness. The Greeks invoked the Muse, the Hebrews the Holy Ghost; the meaning is the same.

In a recent interview, he speaks of Freud as "a man laboring over a sexual obsession." Without using Nabokov's short and blunt expression to designate Freud ("a crank"), Borges attempts in a more ironic mode to find some justification for a man whose theories seem to him to limit themselves to a few "rather unpleasant facts." I frankly do not think Borges succeeds in understanding Freud. He tells his interviewer that perhaps Freud did not take things very seriously: "Perhaps he was just doing it as a kind of game," and adds: "I have tried to read him, and I thought of him either as a charlatan or as a madman, in a sense."

These peculiar reactions do not prevent one from finding in his interpretation of symbols, or in his conception of the symbolic nature of reality, many points of contact with the theories of psychoanalysis, especially those of Carl Gustav Jung. Borges' attitude towards him is very different. Not only does he admit to having read his works but also adds that he has always been a "great reader" of his. In contrasting him with Freud, he observes that "in Jung you feel a wide and hospitable mind." His recognition is not without some ironic undertones: he admits he has read Jung "in the same way as, let's say, I might read Pliny or Frazer's *Golden Bough*, I read it as a kind of mythology, or as a kind of museum or encyclopedia of curious lores." Thus even when he seems to accept Jung's psychoanalytical approach, he does not accept it to the letter.

By accentuating the oneiric character of art, and of reality, Borges comes to the conclusion that dreams put in question not only the objective world, but also the personality of the dreamer. In this, he goes further than Freud or Jung and returns (by the route of depth psychology) to the solipsist idealism which he had reached by way of Berkeley and Schopenhauer.

V

By means of his own fiction or those of others, Borges has often sought to define that abysmal experience of feeling oneself unreal: the dream or creation of another, a mere image, a simulacrum. Perhaps "Las ruinas circulares" ("The Circular Ruins") is the most elaborate expression of that experience which was also to surface in his poems and essays expressed as a metaphysical hypothesis as well. In that story, a magician from India decides to dream a man in order to insert him into reality. On succeeding, he discovers that his creation, his son, is distinguished from other real beings by only one characteristic: immunity to fire, the god both father and son are devoted to. He prays his god to spare his son the humiliation of knowing himself to be a mere phantom and sends him (unaware of his origin) to continue his teachings in a distant land. At the end of the story, when fire breaks out near the circular ruins, the magician will discover, "with relief, with humiliation, with terror," that he too is immune to fire, that he is a mere image, dreamt by another.

In one of his recent poems, "El Golem" ("The Golem"), Borges has developed the same theme with even greater economy and irony. Borrowing from Gershom Scholem's *Major Trends in Jewish Mysticism* but above all from the impact that the reading of Gustav Meyrink's novel *Der Golem* had upon him when a young man living in Geneva, Borges now reproduces in his poem the experience of Judah, the Hohe Rabbi Löw of Prague, who created a dummy and tried to teach it the "secrets of Time, Space, Being and Extension." That simulacrum (as Borges calls it), after years of training, learned only to sweep the synagogue:

> The rabbi gazed on it with tender eyes
> And terror. *How* (he asked) *could it be done*
> *That I engender this distressing son?*
> *Inaction is wisdom. I left off being wise.*
>
> *To an infinite series why was it for me*
> *To add another integer? To the vain*
> *Hank that is spun out in Eternity*
> *Another cause or effect, another pain?*
>
> At the anguished hour when the light gets vague
> Upon his Golem his eyes would come to rest.
> Who can tell us the feeling in His breast
> As God gazed on His rabbi there in Prague?

This is not the last of his vertiginous exploration of the symbol of the dream. In another poem, entitled originally in English "Adam Cast Forth," Borges shows the first man, the universal father, meditating on his fate, after the expulsion from Paradise, and asking himself: "The Garden—was it real or was it dream?" Almost as an afterthought, Borges slips in the hypothesis that perhaps Adam has also dreamed his God; perhaps the Garden

> was nothing but a magic fantasy
> of the God I dreamed.

The circle has closed itself. Starting from the traditional image of life as a sleep or a dream, Borges has unfolded the possibilities of that symbol to the point of investing it with the very personal forms of his own metaphysical vision, or charging it with meanings which transcend the traditional ones and point daringly toward his private mythology. The magician who dreams a man in the midst of the circular ruins of an Indian temple; the rabbi who creates a Golem in the ghetto of Prague, under the ironic gaze of his God; the first man who meditates on his fate and asks himself whether the Garden existed, whether he himself is not the creator of his own miserable fate: each of these images is more than a variation on a traditional theme. They become ciphers that point to certain constant obsessions in Borges' works: the unreality of the external world confirms the unreality of the individual personality; the fantasmal character of human beings accentuates the anguished vision. In a certain way, all these simulacra, pitiful creatures engendered by other pitiful creatures, are all monsters. Soon we will see that, by another route, also starting from a traditional symbol, Borges will face the theme of the monster that is hidden inside every human being.

VI

There is another universal symbol which appears so frequently in Borges' work that it has been used by his translators to entitle collections of his stories and essays which, in Spanish, had other titles: it is the *labyrinth*. Traditionally one of the most fertile symbols of all time, the mythical labyrinth of Crete was a palace created by the architect Daedalus to enclose and protect a monster the Minotaur, the offspring of Queen Pasiphaë's intercourse with a snow-white bull. (Daedalus also invented a mechanical cow to facilitate the union.) The labyrinth is, in a manner at once contradictory and complementary, a fortress erected to preserve and defend the monster and a prison to prevent his flight. A place of paradox it fixes symbolically a movement from the exterior to the interior, from form to contemplation, from multiplicity to unity, from space to absence of space, from time to the absence of time. It also represents the opposite movement: from within to without, according to a symbolic progression. In the center of the labyrinth is the monster, or the god, since monstrosity is sometimes a divine attribute as shown by the metamorphoses in Greek mythology. There could be something else in the center of the labyrinth: a secret, a revelation, or an epiphany. The labyrinth becomes then, from the traditional point of view, the image of a chaos ordered by human intelligence, of an apparent and deliberate disorder which contains its own key. It also represents, by analogy, nature in its least human aspects: an endless river is a labyrinth of water; a forest is a labyrinth of vegetation. In a similar way, it serves also to represent certain human constructions: a library is a labyrinth of books; any large city is a labyrinth of streets and houses. The same symbol can be used to allude to invisible realities: human destiny or the inscrutable will of God, the mystery of creation, either natural or human, all can be called labyrinthine.

Many of these allusions are naturally present in Borges' work. Some of his favorite authors, like Joyce and Kafka, have given the theme of the labyrinth an important place in their respective work. Of the two, Joyce seems closer to Borges from the point of view of the use of this symbol. It is possible to find in the work of the Irish myth-maker the same image of the city as a labyrinth (*Ulysses*), of human destiny as a cycle that repeats itself inexorably (*Finnegans Wake*), and also the idea of writers as creators of labyrinths of words. (Daedalus is the name of the artist in two of Joyce's novels.) Other coincidences, such as the systematic use of myth and parody, the strange and rather showy erudition both favor, the constant awareness of words and ideas as a game, the conception of literature as a sort of palimpsest constantly written and rewritten by its anonymous authors: all these characteristics serve to link these two writers. But the size and scope of their respective works—to the encyclopedic proportions of Joyce's work, Borges opposes his fragmentary and minimal art—and their final visions are very different. In the Joycean conception of the labyrinth and of a search for a center, the idea of a final epiphany, of a transcendental revelation, is always concealed. In Borges, the labyrinth has a center, of course, but what is found there is something else: something in the nature of a secret.

The similarities with Kafka are more on the surface. Like Borges, the Czech writer generally favors short, fragmentary texts and avoids the trappings of verisimilitude. But these similarities help to emphasize the differences. Although it would be possible to find in Kafka the idea of human destiny as an anguished search for a center, a search perhaps destined to fail, in his work this center is always occupied by a merciless God. In Borges, there may be a center, but there is no God in it. Neither, in general, is there an explicit search for God. Although there are, it is true, "theologies" and mystical "experiences," he often builds them with the remnants of those presented in obscure, unreadable books; they serve him not to present his own belief but to destroy, through parody, all of them in an endless game of confrontations and negations.

VII

Contrary to what one might think, Borges started using the image of the labyrinth rather late. It began to appear frequently in the stories he started writing after the accident of Christmas 1938 which almost cost him his life. The accident, which he fictionalized in a later story, "El Sur" ("The South"), liberated in him some obscure forces. Soon after it he was writing a series of related stories—"Tlön, Uqbar, Orbis Tertius"; "La lotería en Babilonia" ("The Lottery in Babylon"); "La biblioteca de Babel" ("The Library of Babel")—which present seductive variations on the theme of the world seen as a labyrinth, of human destiny and external reality as the creation of subaltern gods, inferior artisans, or just plain monsters. But it was only some years later, in the long short story entitled "El inmortal" ("The Immortal"), that Borges really succeeded in giving the theme of the labyrinth as destiny a distinctive expression. In this, one of his most elaborate texts, the image of the labyrinth is used to describe the monstrous city of the troglodytes which serves as a focal point of the narrative. At the same time, the labyrinth represents the hero's destiny: chronologically and successively, he will be Homer; a troglodyte who barely remembers some of Homer's verses; a Roman tribune who accidentally discovers the labyrinthine city; Alexander Pope, who translated Homer into eighteenth-century English; a bibliophile of our time; and (on a purely symbolic plane) the Wandering Jew. That is: a man who is everyone and no one as Borges later defined Shakespeare. In the texture of this and the other stories can be found the idea that human individuality is a delusion, that any reader of Homer is Homer (or: any reader of Shakespeare is Shakespeare, as Schopenhauer once said and Borges is always quoting); and also, that human reality, what we call reality, with its ambivalent aspects of order and chaos, sense and nonsense, pleasure and pain, happiness and terror, is nothing but the quest for identity, a search for the hidden center: of the world and of oneself. A search for a constantly receding faith, an epiphany, a meaning.

In Borges' poetry, the symbol of the labyrinth appears in an even later period. The first poem in which it is used, "Del infierno y del cielo" ("Of Hell and Heaven"), dates from 1942. Later, the image is repeated incessantly. Destiny as a labyrinth appears in one of his best texts, "Poema conjetural" ("Conjectural Poem"), which reconstructs the imaginary thoughts of one of his ancestors, Dr. Francisco Laprida, before being killed by gauchos in one of Argentina's civil wars. Another poem, "Página para recordar al coronel Suárez, vencedor en Junín") ("A Page to Commemorate Colonel Suárez, Victor at Junín"), shows the protagonist, one of his ancestors, confronting "the seething labyrinth of calvaries," whereas Borges himself, in the poem, "Mateo, XXV, 30" ("Matthew, XXV, 30"), is presented as listening while "The shunting trains trace iron labyrinths." One could quote endlessly.

The insistence in the use of the symbol more than justifies the association of the labyrinth with Borges' entire work. Nevertheless and in spite of this association, acknowledged by the critics and even ironically tolerated by Borges, there has been very little examination of one of the stories in which Borges peers (obliquely it is true) into the secret of the labyrinth: "La casa de Asterión" ("The House of Asterion"). An epigraph attributed to Apollodorus indicates, with misleading precision at the very beginning of the story, that "the Queen gave birth to a child who was called Asterion." The first and longest part of the narrative consists of a monologue by the protagonist who inhabits, all alone, an empty palace whose configuration (as it is gradually revealed) is similar to that of the labyrinth. Some words in Asterion's monologue convey the impression that he is a very vain and ignorant young man and that he does not know anything about himself and his destiny. He mentions, for example, a ceremony or rite in which he kills nine men, but he seems unaware of the meaning of the rite. In the same oblique manner, he reveals (to the reader but not to himself) the meaning of a "redeemer" he is waiting for who will take him to a place "with fewer galleries and fewer doors."

As it happens in other stories by Borges—"Hombre de la esquina rosada" ("Streetcorner Man") or "La forma de la espada" ("The Shape of the Sword"), for example—this one also utilizes a well-known technique of detective stories: it presents the action from the point of view of the protagonist. This device allows the true narrator (Borges) to subjectivize and limit the reader's vision, and, consequently, it allows him to leave out a part of the story the protagonist does not wish to tell or the "author" wants to reveal only at the very end. In "La casa de Asterión," the identity of the protagonist and of its "redeemer" is told only in the second and shortest part of the story: a third person narrative which transcribes a dialogue between Theseus and Ariadne after the Minotaur has been killed.

But Borges is not only interested in hiding until the very end of the story the real identity of "Asterion" but especially his monstrous nature. Only through allusions is this monstrosity shown. For example, when Asterion claims that he is not a prisoner in the empty palace, he adds:

> One afternoon I did step into the street; if I returned before night,
> I did so because of the fear that the faces of the common people
> inspired me, faces as discolored and flat as the palm of one's hand.

Here it is implicitly indicated that his face does have some color, and it is not flat. Further on, he admits:

> I am not without distractions. Like the rams about to charge, I
> run through the stone galleries until I fall dizzy to the floor.

These and other allusions slowly build a system of signs whose purpose is to reveal the monstrous nature of the protagonist. Toward the end of his monologue, Asterion asks himself what will his redeemer be like:

> Will he be a bull or a man? Will he perhaps be a bull with the face of a man? Or will be he like me?

It is possible to read this story as if it were a mere literary exercise, like Julio Cortázar's *Los Reyes*, ("The Kings") which was published by Borges in the same magazine he was then editing, *Los Anales de Buenos Aires*, and in which he had published some months before "La casa de Asterión." While Cortázar's exercise in bland verse can be easily linked to Gide's and Giraudoux's re-elaboration of Greek myths, Borges uses parody to mask, and thus better reveal, the horror at the center of the labyrinth. Borges himself seems to encourage a superficial reading of his story when he indicates, in the epilogue to *El Aleph* *(The Aleph)*, one of his sources, without further commentary:

> To a painting by Watts, made in 1896, I owe "The House of Asterion" and the character of its poor protagonist.

The only word which provides some clue is the adjective "poor." Even so, as happens almost always when Borges speaks of his own work, the explicit reference to Watts is more deceptive than illuminating. The importance of the story is only revealed by a careful reading. Far from being a fantasy in the more or less Modernist manner suggested by the too precise quote from Apollodorus and the reference to Watts, the story reflects a very personal symbol. For the first time, Borges confronts there the dismal destiny of the inhabitant of the labyrinth.

VIII

The labyrinth as a symbol has other possibilities than those already indicated. Above all, it is important to recall (as Ronald Christ does in his book) that the labyrinth itself is a symbol of the passage of life through death. In Egyptian mythology, the labyrinth was a place where the dead were buried: the site, then, of unbirth, which is another sort of birth. Moreover, the labyrinth is also a circle, that is to say, a mystical space whose center symbolizes suspended duration, an immobile place in both time and space, and also the place of origin. Another form of the circle, the Omphalos, is the symbol of creation. Perhaps for its significance as a passage from life to death, or, inversely, from death to life, the labyrinth is both in the origin and in the end; it is at once the Alpha and the Omega.

Keeping all this in mind and also recalling that in Jung's thought the labyrinth is a *mandala* (that is: a Hindu symbol of the mystical circle), one can perceive the infinite possibilities of allusion that the labyrinth may have in Borges' work. Of these possibilities, I think he has consistently preferred those which allude to the labyrinth as a symbol of the prison (real or imaginary) which encloses the self; the place where death is equated with the final destruction of the self, or, perhaps, with the liberation into nothingness. The labyrinth symbolizes the quest for a road to the center of oneself, as Mirce Eliade has indicated. This quest is always doomed in Borges' stories and poems. What is found in the center is a secret which conceals the monstrous nature of the self. In "La casa de Asterión," Borges presents the secret by means of allusions. The pathos of the final revelation is disguised, at least up to the end, by the deceptively light tone in which the protagonist talks. But in the last few words of the story (when Theseus speaks) the innocence and monstrosity of the Minotaur is revealed.

Rather than an elaborate construction *à la Flaubert*, the underlying text of this story reflects the ambiguities one normally finds in Henry James' tales. Asterión is unaware that he is a monster not only because he is naïve or plainly stupid (like the animal whose head he has), but also for the simple reason that none of us knows really who he is. He is at the center of his labyrinth (the labyrinth of his own self); he is in possession of its secret, but he is unaware of it: he is himself (a monster) and nobody. Like the hero of James' "The Jolly Corner," who, on confronting the phantom of what he could have become if he had stayed in New York instead of going to live in Europe, failing to recognize his other self in that mutilated being, the Minotaur does not recognize his own monstrous nature because he does not recognize himself.

It is not by chance that in one of his poems Borges links the symbol of the labyrinth to another mythical figure who also did not know who he was, although, unlike the Minotaur, he always tried desperately to reach his own center. In a poem entitled "A un poeta del siglo XIII" ("A Poet of the Thirteenth Century"), Borges imagines that perhaps in inventing the sonnet Jacopo da Lentini felt

> That the Arcane, incredible Apollo
> Had revealed an archetypal thing,
>
> A whirlpool mirror that would draw and hold
> All that night could hide or day unfold:
> Daedalus, labyrinth, riddle, Oedipus King?

Although here the tone is deliberately conjectural and seems confined to illustrate a rhetorical point—the sonnet is a mirror of the universe: an archetype—it is obvious that the allusions contained in its text point to a different matter. I find that the link established in the last line of the poem between the two symbols which correspond to the myth of the Minotaur and the two which correspond to that of Oedipus is very significant. More explicit still is the reference to Oedipus in the sonnet which carries his name ("Oedipus and the Riddle") and which evokes the confrontation with the Sphinx. What interests Borges is not the riddle but Oedipus' reaction to the secret:

> there came a person
> Deciphering, appalled at the monstrous other
> Presence in the mirror, the reflection
> Of his decay and of his destiny.
> We are Oedipus; in some eternal way
> We are the long and threefold beast as well—
> All that we will be, all that we have been.
> It would annihilate us all to see
> The huge shape of our being; mercifully
> God offers us issue and oblivion.

Like the Minotaur, Oedipus is also destroyed in discovering who he is, and if his destiny comes to him by a different route, the mutilation inflicted by his own hand is no less drastic (he will cease to "see") than that which the Minotaur suffers at the hands of his "redeemer." In fact, from a certain point of view, it is more tragic because it is possible to believe that the Minotaur dies without learning who he is (always blind to his own monstrous nature), whereas Oedipus suffers to the utmost the consequences of his self-recognition. Anagnorisis destroys him. As can be seen by this summary, Borges by no means concerns himself in his poem with the sexual aspects of the myth. (There is only an allusion in the last line when he mentions among God's gifts: "issue," a very ironical gift if one remembers what happened to Oedipus' issue.) But if Borges explicitly discards this important side of the myth, the one that is popularly called "the Oedipus complex," he does not deny himself a reference to the theme which is central in his work and in his philosophical preoccupations: the ultimate meaning of our fate, the true form of our being.

IX

Space will not allow us to pursue this analysis, which seems to promise valuable discoveries. Nevertheless, I would not wish to end this presentation without referring, however briefly, to other symbols which cast a spell on Borges' work. They are the symbols of the mirror, the tiger, and the library. Let us begin with the *mirrors*. Traditionally they underline appearance since they show an image of what is not in them, but outside them; moreover, their reflection is inverted. But they are also well-known symbols of consciousness and self-contemplation. The same word, "reflection," alludes both to thought and the images of a mirror. Because of the same reflective quality, mirrors are associated with water (the myth of Narcissus), and they can also be considered doors to another dimension of reality, as Jean Cocteau discovered after Lewis Carroll.

The symbol of the mirror is one of the most frequent in Borges' work, and it is one of the oldest. It is deeply rooted in his personal experience. As a child (his biographies tell us) he had a terror of mirrors, and he refused to sleep in a room which contained one. In a recent poem, "Los espejos" ("Mirrors"), he has tried to rationalize his fears, and although now his near-blindness has obliterated all mirrors, his poetry cannot forget that mirrors haunt us, that one is never alone in a room if there is a mirror. There is somebody else, he says: "the reflection that builds in the dawn a silent theatre." In "Arte poética" is found a similar figure which seems to underline even more the character of a sinister *double* or *doppelgänger* (in the romantic sense of the term) which belongs to the reflection in the mirror:

> At times in the evenings a face
> Looks at us out the depths of a mirror;
> Art should be like that mirror
> Which reveals to us our own face.

Like the riddle of the Sphinx, like the secret of the inhabitant of the labyrinth, that which the riddle of the mirror hides is the revelation of one's own being. That the revelation is painful and can be tragic (as it was for Oedipus) or totally destructive (as it was for the Minotaur) is something which Borges' work, in spite of its apparent rationality and its parodic or ironic mode, does not hesitate to insinuate. By way of the mirror, of reflection or duplication, of the double and horror of engendering a murderous issue, one can arrive at an even more abysmal vision of the secret of the labyrinth. But we must stop here, at least for now.

The symbols of the *tiger* and the *library* remain. Without the space to develop them now, I will confine myself to point out that the tiger is (as in the poem of William Blake) a symbol of nature's savage life and also a symbol of pure Evil. Borges has an obsession with tigers similar to the one with mirrors. It also derives from his childhood and has found expression in such representative texts as a prose poem, originally entitled in English, "Dreamtigers," or in "El otro tigre" ("The Other Tiger"). I chose this last one because it will bring us back, unexpectedly, to the library:

> A tiger comes to mind. The twilight here
> Exalts the vast and busy Library
> And seems to set the bookshelves back in gloom;
> Innocent, ruthless, bloodstained, sleek,
> It wanders through its forest and its day
> Printing a track along the muddy banks
> Of sluggish streams whose names it does not know
> (In its world there are no names or past
> Or time to come, only the vivid now)

Although the superficial contrast between the forest and the library masks the obvious connection (a library is a forest of books and, like the other, is also made of wood), the real contrast the poem wants to underline is between the tiger, who does not know the name of the river and is immune to time, and the librarian (Borges) who knows both time and the river's name. But in turn, he does not participate in the innocence, energy, and violence of the tiger in his elemental life. Further on, the poet will admit

> That the tiger addressed in my poem
> Is a shadowy beast, a tiger of symbols
> And scraps picked up at random out of books,
> A string of labored tropes that have no life,
> And not the fated tiger, the deadly jewel
> That under sun or stars or changing moon
> Goes on in Bengal or Sumatra fulfilling
> Its rounds of love and indolence and death.

Even so, he persists in seeking "the" tiger, not the one in the real jungle nor the one in the poem but a third tiger: "the beast not found in verse," the purely imaginary tiger. The ironic discrepancy between the real tiger and the dreamed ones underlines the discrepancy between what is symbolized by the tiger and what is symbolized by the writer who tries vainly to exorcize it with words, tropes, symbols. It is the contrast between life in the real forest and life in the forest of books. Thus, it seems natural to link Borges' devotion to the tiger to his similar devotion for the brave ancestors who died on the savage battlefields of South America or returned from them covered with honorable wounds. It is the same devotion, and nostalgia, toward all the action, blood, and violence which have been lacking in his life, which makes him invoke (again and again) in stories, poems, and essays ancient Scandinavian warriors, long lost gauchos and pirates, already faded gangsters and murderers. The violence missing from his sheltered life as a librarian has not been lacking in his books.

In this way, the tiger joins in the final unity of Borges' work, with the other symbols which illustrate the terrible and sad reality of this world of appearances, of mirrors, and labyrinths. If the tiger is admired and even envied by the poet, it is because it represents life in the raw, destruction as another way of creation, death as a path to life, whereas the librarian represents only life frozen, life changed into signs, into symbols, into tropes, into mere words. Into writing, of course.

ALICIA BORINSKY

Repetition, Museums, Libraries

This animal, common in the north, is four or five inches long; its eyes are scarlet and its fur is jet black, silky and soft as a pillow. It is marked by a curious instinct, the taste for India ink. When a person sits down to write, the monkey squats cross-legged nearby with one forepaw folded over the other, waiting until the task is over. Then it drinks what is left of the ink, and afterward sits back on its haunches quiet and satisfied.

WANG THAI HAI (1791)
BORGES, *The Book of Imaginary Beings*

The monkey sits back quiet and satisfied after having drunk what is left of the ink, what has been left unwritten by the writer. The monkey drinks the residue of ink and its silence is made of that which has been left *outside* but which is, nevertheless, also *there* as an excess that can only be brought forth by de-monkeying the monkey. What would that de-monkeying consist of? What would be the twist of the relationship—mimicry—that could escape from the specularity entailed by that sitting back, by the monkey's sameness to the writer, by the dependence of the inkpot? But in posing this question we veil yet another: who or what is the monkey? Who performs the role of silent imitator? Who works with the excess, with the residue of ink?

The texts by Jorge Luis Borges weave in the image of the monkey of the inkpot as an image for the kind of "originality" attained by the work of art. Borges' well-known notion of writing as an exercise of repetition of certain key metaphors approved by time, eternal because they come back said in a simpler tone suggests that the basic scene of writing is precisely a double relationship, at least, between a hypothetical writer and something or somebody

From *Glyph* 2 (1977), edited by Samuel Weber and Henry Sussman. © 1977 by The Johns Hopkins University Press.

assimilating what has been left *unsaid*, a something that is both unnecessary and pertinent. It belongs to the *same* inkpot but it has been left out. Nevertheless, the monkey is silent. The very notion of a simpler tone, of a certain economy of speech, a bareness, acquires simultaneously the qualities of silence, reticence, and excess. Why repeat what has been said before, why work out of the same inkpot? The inkpot, that *same* inkpot, performs the role of the language of *truth*. It is not a truth to be found out *outside* writing. It is the production of writing as a rereading, an interplay between sameness and difference that produces its own effects of clarity, economy, and bareness in a differential system of readings. That particular truth which Borges is talking about seems to elude the naiveties of realism; there seems to be no pointing outside the text, no belief in extraliterary referentiality. It is the inkpot. The position of the monkey regarding the writer is the double nature of authorship; no text is ever complete and finished; the authors are always two, one who writes the text and another one — at least — who profits from its excess.

Borges also speaks about authority, difference between monkey and writer. But the fragment about the monkey of the inkpot appears *already* as the result of the monkey's work. It is part of an anthology prepared by Borges, the author of the text is someone else. The anthologist sits behind Wang Thai Hai (fictional or not, it does not matter), his silence consists in showing that signature; the excess is worked into the very notion of an anthology, it is that which makes the arrangement possible, that *other* arrangement that takes it away from its context and integrates it as part of a miscellany. The anonymity implied by an anthologist is illusory; the disorganization of an order and the organization of a disorder effected by the selection, position and choice of quotes is hidden behind it. The monkey *is* the writer if every writing is a rewriting as Borges would have us believe.

> The yellow carrousel of horse and lion
> Whirls in the hollow while I hear the echo
> Of those tangos of Arolas and Greco
> I watched danced on the pavement
>
> On an instant that today stands out alone,
> Without before or after, against oblivion,
> And has the taste of everything lost,
> Everything lost and recovered

The monkey is a recoverer; his passivity in drinking the ink left in the inkpot is a way of preserving the materiality of the text written by the writer. Borges' texts tend to weave this preservation in a way that is apparently antithetical because the terms that come to mind to explain the relationship of rewriting are parody, lie, hoax, the building of versions. But it is precisely at that point, when the texts are telling us that they are not original, that they have already been written somewhere else, by somebody else, seemingly putting forth the notion of derivation versus originality, of a collective writing versus the individual authorship, that we may start to wonder about how collective this writing is, how radical the displacement is, what kind of substitution has taken place. This bracketing of the notions about writing to be "found" in Borges' texts takes, in the first movement of our reading, the form of posing the terms in which the monkey works as a witness of the others' writing. Our position entails a certain kind of specular exercise. For we—as many of Borges' narrators—are going to look for the Aleph, for that minimum that functions as a reduced model for the Universe, understanding by Universe, language.

It is not by chance that the image of the monkey of the inkpot does not tell us anything about what the writer is writing. The only things we know concern the economy of the ink. And that is precisely what Borges' texts will tend to effect: an effacement of that which is said by displacing any fixed information for the movement of informing itself. The proliferation of "witnesses" of all sorts (readers, reviewers, participants in events, friends, and family figures) helps to produce the illusion of secondariness and derivation at the same time that it is faithful to the kind of exchange between subject and object ridiculed in "Tlön, Uqbar, Orbis Tertius," according to which once you stop perceiving something, it disappears. But if this last development of the idealistic psychology of Tlön is devalued in the form of the example of the horse that faded after a man stopped looking at him, it is also strongly repeated in a displaced way in the very movement of the text that makes of the question of translation and reconstruction of Uqbar a task that can only be carried out by a group that is constantly defining its own "presence" by taking part in the kind of investigation that assures a bond between the belief in the "existence" of the subject matter and the researcher. The *emergence* of Uqbar is the result of the *convergence* of a mirror and a library. Whatever *outside* referent is attempted for the discourse appears already intertwined in a certain machinery of production, so that the task of naming it becomes a description of the obstacles that exist for pushing it back to a non-problematical identity to itself. That possibility of "going back to" functions as a certain otherness implied in the text, as the kind of opposition that would put into play what is involved in this fragment from Chesterton's *The Scandal of Father Brown*,

> From the very first minute I entered that big empty bar or saloon,
> I knew that what was the matter with all this business was emptiness;

solitude; too many chances for anybody to be alone. In a word,
the absence of witnesses,

with this fragment from Lactantius quoted by De Quincey in *Murder as One
of the Fine Arts*,

> Now if merely to be present at a murder fastens on to a man the
> character of an accomplice; if barely to be a spectator involves us
> in one common guilt with the perpetrator, it follows, of necessity,
> that, in these murders of the amphitheatre, the hand which inflicts
> the fatal blow is not more deeply imbrued in blood than his who
> passively looks on; neither can *he* be clear of blood who has coun-
> tenanced its shedding; nor that man seem other than a participator
> in murder, who gives his applause to the murderer, and calls for
> prizes on his behalf.

In Chesterton's fragment there are no witnesses; the "event" acquires the bareness
of the lack of any versions about it. The orator's speech in de Quincey's text
makes of the question of murder essentially a matter of complicity. Participation
in a murder is rendered possible by being a witness, someone who can build
versions about the "event." In very much the same way, Borges' texts show the
departure from a nonproblematic original language, intensifying that departure
through the narrator's participation in what makes the displacement more acute:
the construction of further versions of an *event* torn from its source.

LAUGHING IN THE LIBRARY

The most obvious embodiment of the monkey's work is probably "Pierre
Menard, Author of the *Quixote*." For Menard's attempt is to produce *Don
Quixote* while preserving, at the same time, the difference between himself and
Cervantes. At first, Menard thinks of the possibility of becoming Cervantes
but he soon abandons his attempt because he finds it too easy, "To be, in some
way, Cervantes and to arrive at *Don Quixote* seemed to him less arduous—and
consequently less interesting—than to continue being Pierre Menard and to
arrive at *Don Quixote* through the experiences of Pierre Menard. (This conviction,
let it be said in passing, forced him to exclude the autobiographical prologue
of the second part of *Don Quixote*. . . .")

Whatever verisimilitude we find as the final effect of a reading comes from
the strength with which a narrative builds for itself the fictionality of a voice
organizing it from "behind." A persuasive machinery of effects creates the illusion
of the existence of something or somebody at the very origin of its production
who is the giver of the information that we receive from the reading. But that

persuasiveness, the kind of hallucination — to use Macedonio Fernández' term — that makes us believe in a source of truth is there only because of a certain arrangement, a certain web by which the texts point outside themselves to create an authority that will give them a status different from fiction. When Pierre Menard decides to say the monkey's truth — since that is what is involved in his wish to be himself and Cervantes simultaneously — he puts into play the question of authorship as the production of voice and, in doing so, he questions the kind of continuity that exists between that hypothetical voice and its discourse. Menard learns the Spanish of Cervantes as a doubly foreign tongue (another language and another time), sets himself at the *other* end of the process and tries to posit his own voice as responsible for the text. Understanding the text becomes an understanding of the one who produced it because the only difference in the sense of the fragment reproduced lies in the separation between Menard and Cervantes. That is why we are asked to read the fragment twice. The interpretation provided by the reviewer constantly points to the question of authorship, "Equally vivid is the contrast in styles. The archaic style of Menard — in the last analysis of a foreigner — suffers from a certain affectation. Not so that of his precursor, who handles easily the ordinary Spanish of his time." The difference between Menard and Cervantes is pointed out in terms of style, tone, ideology, mastery of the language. Menard's work turns out to be superior because it is a higher level of artifice; he is a master of displacement and anachronism. A symbolist from Nîmes, Menard has been able to produce his own voice by rewriting with the exact words several fragments from Cervantes. It is through the reading of the text as voice that the reviewer is able to stress the artistry of Menard; the reviewer believes in the existence of such an entity behind the fragments and is, thus, able to exercise admiration for the producer. Menard has *re-enacted Don Quixote*.

But let us read closely the fragment that serves to build the difference between two producers and stress, at the same time, their existence as the voices responsible for what is said. It is precisely that part in *Don Quixote* where one is told that the novel may be a translation of a work by a Moor — all liars in the coded literary morality of the time — Cid Hamete Benengeli. Cervantes would have been a Menard already; his relationship to that text is no different from Menard's. Cervantes had a monkey relationship to his own text; the question of original authorship is pushed back to an undecidable "before."

> He remembered that the dreams of men belong to God, and that
> Maimonides wrote that the words of a dream are divine, when
> they are all separate and clear and are spoken by someone invisible.

The reviewer warns us from the beginning that there are two main divisions

in the works of Menard, his *visible* works and his invisible ones. The fact that
he first discusses the visible ones in order to have material for the invisible
is important. Menard's visible work is mostly some kind of displacement of
other writings. He plays with irony, translation, attributions. What we read,
therefore, is the intellectual biography of a symbolist whose task consists in
creating illusions of duplication or a critique of univocal meanings. The invisible
work is nothing but the culmination of the same nihilistic esthetic; in the last
analysis an esthetic that is supported by a notion of derivation. Rewriting *Don
Quixote* is part of the same attempt; it is the production of a double of the
novel through the preservation of the words and a redefinition of meaning
by the voice that produces it. The particular situation of the fragment in the
original work functions as a bracketing of the very notion that the rewriting
wants to convey. For if Cervantes was not himself the author of *Don Quixote*,
what sense is there in his having become split, in being at the same time
Cervantes and Menard? Menard does not understand the status of the piece
he has written. He believes that the "original" has been the result of Cervantes'
spontaneous work. In a letter quoted in the review he says "My affable precursor
did not refuse the collaboration of fate; he went along composing a little à
la diable, swept along by inertias of language and invention. I have contracted
the mysterious duty of reconstructing literally his spontaneous work." What
Menard believes to be a new task is already inscribed in *Don Quixote* so that
his rewriting is, in fact, a misreading. But the form of his error is such that
it turns out to be the most faithful kind of reconstruction; it is a simulacrum
of the "original" situation which is, already, devoid of the kind of anteriority
conveyed by a fixed producer.

What is the status of the reviewer? To what extent is his own account
outside of Menard's system of false derivations? The reviewer signs his text
in Nîmes, 1939. In doing so he repeats De Quincey's speech about murder;
his exercise will take him back to Pierre Menard and his followers. His snobbish
discourse, the way in which he quotes the supporters and friends of Menard,
the enemies he builds in order to sort out arguments for his credibility are
there in order to introduce him as a character and bracket his objectivity. What
does this bracketing involve? How important is it for the understanding of
the Menard enterprise? The reviewer himself has participated in the Nîmes
cenacle; the many digressions in his text suggest a complex network of personal
intrigues that link him to Menard's friends and enemies. His review is but one
of the elements through which he attempts to make an intervention in the
same literary circle. In this way, the reviewer emerges from the "beginning"
as *the character* hidden in the surface of his own discourse. In talking about
Menard, he talks about himself, he gains a literary voice which coincides with

Menard's; his text is one of the figurations (*figuraciones*) of a conspiracy for granting sense to the Nîmes project; his specular relationship with Menard is revealed by the complicity involved in the belief in his invisible works. As soon as we pose the way in which the reviewer becomes a displaced version of Menard who is a displacement of Cervantes who, in turn, is a displacement of an undecidable Cid Hamete Benengeli, we realize that this kind of interplay effects a figure (*figura*) for another exchange, which is the virtual exchange that makes humour possible. It is now time to work our way out from the specular movement of our reading, to abandon the monkey's position and to pose the question that will help us come to terms with the interplay that overdetermines our laughter in reading this text. What is it in the rewriting of this project of rewriting that builds the possibility for the detached laughter?

> In the last analysis, says Lane, it's always best to stand in front of
> a mirror with the pipe in your mouth and study the effect. Some
> pipe smokers consider it vanity to scrutinize themselves in the mirror.
> But it is well worth their while. After all, a pipe is an investment
> in a man's future.

Menard and the reviewer have chosen for themselves a pipe that does not belong to them. The reviewer and Menard are each other's mirror; they are trying to smoke – to use up – Cervantes who, in turn was using up Cid Hamete. But if Cervantes was able to write a masterpiece, Menard can only come up with a faulty artifact praised by a reviewer who shares his *bad* taste for useless intellectual games.

The reason why the pipe smoker has to study the effect of the pipe in the mirror is *class*; he has to discover which one really corresponds to him. It is hopeless to get a pipe that will not fit you because your looks and your manners will clearly indicate to *us* that in spite of your being able to get through all the motions of smoking, there exists a basic discontinuity between you and the pipe. Some characteristics of that discontinuity – according to Schnitzer – are lack of elegance, subtlety, etc. In short, a certain "I don't know what" that indicates very precisely, nevertheless, good and bad in the world of taste. Who are *we*, the ones who know about the pipe? Who are we, readers, laughing against Menard and the reviewer and why is that inevitable? The answer lies in the kind of interplay liberated by the signature of the article in Nîmes. That signature – a reduced model for the games showing the pettiness and ignorance of the reviewer, his bad Spanish, the admiration for Menard's most useless enterprises, his friendship with lady readers, the general participation in a shallow cultural circle – serves the purpose of producing the space of separation that will be taken over by another complicity; the one between a narrator writing the text behind the reviewer and a reader who shares his grammar, his library, his sense of good Spanish; a complicity between good pipe smokers, owners of the strict set of rules of that "I don't know what" which is the same "I don't know what" that separates good repetition from pointless rewriting. The monkey of the inkpot is the qualification of the distance that separates it from the writer; it works out of the *same* inkpot but it still remains a monkey; it has not been able to produce an inkpot that would be a repetition in difference of the "author's" work; it has a derivative relationship to the text it wants to rewrite; in very naive terms: there is a good and a bad repetition. Menard is the bad difference. He has read the question of repetition literally. Although he has been able to produce a simulacrum of *Don Quixote* by reproducing the movement already present in Cervantes, what he does puts him in the position of the silly monkey. The reader and the narrator behind those explicitly at play in the text conspire to reveal that the Nîmes enterprise is to be scorned because it involves a basic misunderstanding of what good literature is all about.

Our laughter is the effect of that conspiracy overdetermining the reading. It is a laughter *with* the owners of the library of good literature and correct language; it pushes aside certain literary movements seen as the result of ignorance. (At this point let us remember that we find in Borges numerous texts of this nature. *El Libro de arena* [*The Book of Sand*] is perhaps one of the clearest examples. The loss of the infinite book in the story that gives a title to the collection is a substitute for the destruction of that book and, perhaps, the volume in which the reader finds the story. The intricate network leading to this "end" alludes to the dialogue between an implied reader and a narrator who conspire to deny credibility to the one explicitly in charge of telling the story.) In laughing at Menard, then, we participate as accomplices in the enterprise of building the figure of the able practitioner of repetition.

We know that the pipe is not being well smoked; Menard and the Nîmes cenacle are not the ones to master the art of literature because they have a naive, literal understanding of repetition. The literal understanding of repetition *is* Menard and, to a certain extent, the monkey. It involves preserving the earliest appearance of the thing and taking it up as the source for further work – a map of natural size, as we read in *Las Crónicas de Bustos Domecq* [*The Chronicles of Bustos Domecq*] – or the loss of voice by preserving the ownership of the inkpot as we learn from the fact that there is an inescapable difference between author and monkey.

What is involved in the scorn for Menard is not a simple opposition between originality and rewriting; it is rather a complication of the notion of *going back to*. Due to our mistrust we have gone back to *Don Quixote* and found out that the passage is not *even* the earliest appearance of the thing. The method is suspect from the very start; going back in search for a univocal source is hopeless because the "event" is torn from the beginning. Rewriting is, nevertheless, what Borges attempts to do in his literature. His works suggesting the constant recurrence of the same metaphors with the effect of producing one single anonymous text, the enlargement of the notion of text by posing, as in "The Garden of Forking Paths," a system of exchanges where a detective plot that leads to a real crime may be better inscribed in a newspaper or in marble or, perhaps, in an in-between that is neither one nor the other; the games with false attributions where the Aleph and the Zahir may operate as reduced models for a simultaneity that includes succession. These are but ways in which he takes part in attempts not altogether different from Menard's.

But Borges' repetition has little to do with a historical anteriority. It is the building of a system of translations and reinscriptions where the original source is blurred to effect a neutral space for what is "said," a radical anonymity that makes Menard's reviewer a fool because he believes in the importance of voice and individual producers. In posing the ways in which Menard and the reviewers become characters punished by laughter, we have started to doubt the anonymity, we have discovered that it hides an exchange between good readers. It is now time for thinking about the library of these good readers, their authority, the ways in which they earn their right to laugh, their card catalogue.

TOWARDS A MUSEUM

> but it wasn't a voice it was voicing
> JOHN BRICUTH, *The Heisenberg*
> *Variations*

The explicit project in Borges is the substitution of the notion of *voice* by *voicing*; there is no locus for the one's overdetermining the texts. Their neutrality is their truth, the truth of undecidability. But the undecidability that wants to dissolve itself as having any single effect attempts, nevertheless, to teach us how to read well. It wants to remain hidden not as voice, but as the eternal recurrence of a neutral *voicing*. Our bracketing of laughter returns it, nevertheless, to a locus where neutrality becomes impossible. In searching for clues against neutrality a rather brutal move is required, the dating of the aristocracy of intelligence in Argentine political history.

After the wars of Independence a conflict between Buenos Aires, the port city, and the rest of the country developed. The economic problems involved in these struggles are obscured in the years that follow the Independence by the cultural dichotomy posed by Sarmiento in terms of "Civilización y Barbarie ["Civilization and Barbarism"]." By a twist not altogether foreign to the rest of the Romantic movement in Latin America, the native groups of the country are seen as the evil forces of Barbarism and ignorance. The project of gaining the hegemony of Buenos Aires over the rest of the land is closely linked to an educational campaign where European culture is equated with the only possible literacy; the fight for democracy becomes, in Argentina, an effort of importing the model of the American Constitution and the ideas of French Liberalism. Sarmiento, praised as the great pedagogue, founder of the first schools, becomes simultaneously one of the most influential ideologues against the local provincial caudillos and their task force, the Montoneros. Bartolomé Mitre founds the most important organ of opinion for the epigones of the port city, the newspaper *La Nación* and becomes the translator of Dante. Literacy is seen as a violent battle for Europe; whatever exists already in the country is perceived as an obstacle, to the extent that the campaign to eradicate the Indians from the South is called euphemistically "Campaign of the Desert" thereby presenting itself as a populating effort. The killing necessary to turn the region into a real desert is hidden by the name of the campaign.

This group does not see itself as particularly violent; on the contrary, it fights against violence and irrationalism. Its project is to speak the language of a neutral truth, to integrate Argentina in the world scene as a European country, the only kind of country to be considered educated; the model of progress in America being the United States. Two distinct lines are formed in the country, one that poses the continuity of the anti-liberal forces in the triad San Martin-Rosas-Perón and another one that takes up the Mitre tradition. It is still puzzling to see the recurrence of the terms of the old struggle in contemporary Argentine politics. The left wing of Peronism takes up the name of Montoneros in direct reference to the provincial soldiers; the anti-Peronists speak against the barbarism of Perón in very much the same terms they spoke against Rosas. The cultural battle is re-enacted time and again, both sides claiming to represent one of the old lines.

Borges' notion of an aristocracy of intelligence, which emerges from the kind of complicity between good readers that we have discovered in the reading of Pierre Menard, is one of the figurations of this old struggle. The infinitude of the Library of Babel hides in its surface the refusal of another card catalogue (the one we discover as being punished by humour); the neutrality of its truth is the one of the good pipe smokers. He is teaching us how to read well by exercising the right of laughter against ignorance. It is already a commonplace to say that Borges' literature blurs all distinctions between dreaming and reality, sanity and madness. But this undecidability only gives way to another opposition, intelligence versus ignorance. A pair of opposites putting into play the great fight for literacy that currently assumes the form of a sense of "good" Spanish fighting against any attempts at destroying syntactic laws.

In one of the many fictional genealogies that Borges attributes to himself he posits his own name as the result of the recurrence of certain political figures in his own blood:

> This, here, is Buenos Aires. Time which brings
> to men either love or money, now leaves to me
> no more than this withered rose, this empty tracery
> of names from the past recurring
>
> out of my blood: Laprida, Cabrera, Soler, Suárez . . .
> names in which secret bugle calls are sounding,
> the republics, the horses and the mornings,
> glorious victories and dead soldiers.

The names that recur are the ones of distinguished soldiers of the educational effort; the cycle will be constantly repeated—differently—as for Perón. Perón heard the names of Rosas and the Montoneros. He saw himself as nothing but one instance of their repetition. The duel between those two recurrent forces does not take place any longer in a space where their efforts are contradictory. They come to be united—as in "La Milonga de los dos hermanos" ["The Milonga of the Two Brothers"]—under a common flag by dint of a third term in the political struggle, that new class that has redefined the fighters and displaced the neutrality of their libraries to an ideological museum.

ON CURATORS

> *Not that I believe that people raised this statue to me,*
> *I know as well as you that I commissioned it.*
> *Nor that I thereby hope for inmortality:*
> *I know the people will one day destroy it.*
> *Nor that I wished to give myself in life*
> *the monument you will not raise when I am dead:*
> *but that I had it raised knowing you hate it.*
>> ERNESTO CARDENAL, "Somoza unveils the statue
>> of Somoza in Somoza Stadium," *Marilyn*
>> *Monroe and Other Poems*

Who would be the curators of such a museum? Who the cataloguers, the ones to tell us what is what? How would that present tense able to build a history for the fighters be elaborated?

The narrative that has presented two opposing traditions—the *sarmientista* founding of the schools vs. the *montoneros's* barbarism—as forces that jointly disregard their previous disagreements to fulfill the task of oppressing a new class implies the existence of a third term delineating a new battlefield. The anecdotal history of this phenomenon would present us a Borges that celebrates the military dictatorship in Argentina, one who is decorated in the Chile of Pinochet. The Perón that emerges in this context is the theoretician of what he called "El Pacto Social [The Social Pact]," an attempt to efface the nature of the class struggle in Argentina by posing the problems of the country in terms of a fight between the *pueblo* [people] and the *antipueblo* [those who are against the people] while forcing the left wing of his own Peronist movement into the underground. The fight against the left initiated by Perón's last government is being continued by those who were seemingly his adversaries, the Army praised by Borges. At this level, the story has the devastating clarity of a news item in the daily paper. The Montoneros praised by Perón in their common opposition to *Sarmientismo* become enemies of the people in much the same way as for Borges. The tradition of intelligence-and-truth-versus-the-ignorance-of-*barbarie* makes it possible for Borges to praise the barbaric practices of a fascist military elite that continues the task started by Perón.

But our reading has attempted to produce something that is located in a different node of the same network; it has tried to show how the neutrality of Borges' discourse may be re-inscribed as the interested discourse of an ideological elite. By thinking of some of the humorous effects of his texts as the result of a complicity among good readers we have found a *place* for an exchange that would otherwise remain unmarked, neutral, universal. Our reading opens up puzzling analogies between the Borges we encountered and a Perón eager to dilute any direct reference to class antagonism through his Social Pact.

An ideological museum. Freezing some effects of texts in a way that would seem to be faithful to their most intense reading. All of this cataloguing and exhibiting is rendered possible not by a romantic belief in any wisdom of a militant working class but by the suspicion that "neutral" discourses work against themselves.

JOHN STURROCK

Odium Theologicum

Not least among the admirable tortuosities of "Pierre Menard, autor del Quijote" ["Pierre Menard, author of the Quixote"] is that it culminates in the one truly abortive conclusion open to the maker of fictions: a coincidence between his own invention and the invention of someone else. Menard's ambition, like that of any true author, is antithetical, but it is also so perverted that the synthesis he eventually produces is identical with the thesis from which he first began. The dialectical process seems to be short-circuited. The identity, however, is purely textual; as soon as a reader is introduced into the scheme, that textual identity lapses. From the reader's point of view there can be no ideal coincidence between Menard's chapters of *Don Quijote* and the original. Indeed, from the reader's point of view there have never been two identical texts of any book because no book has ever been read with identical responses by two people, nor by the same person twice.

Before the great day comes when he accomplishes the coincidence he is seeking, Menard experiences a great many failures. He has to go through a lot of rewriting before he rewrites Cervantes. These failures are fictions—faulty translations of *Don Quijote*, it could be said—which we are not invited to read; in fact we have the story's word for it that Menard has destroyed them, that it was his custom to walk at dusk through the outskirts of Nîmes and "to make a merry bonfire." These evanescent works of literature have perished, like those tossed into the flames by the Hunnish cavalry. They are condemned by their author in conformity with his "polar rules," whereby all unjustified innovations— and that, in this case, means *all* innovations—must be annihilated. By first

From *Paper Tigers: The Ideal Fictions of Jorge Luis Borges.* © 1977 by Oxford University Press.

inventing fictions and then abolishing them again. Menard is playing a double game; in the very appropriate jargon of espionage services, he is a double agent. He is, as I have said, engaged on a game of chess against himself. The *Quijote*, as it happens, is not the first Spanish book he has "translated," he has also published a French version of Ruy Lopez's *Book of Liberal Invention and Art of the Game of Chess*. The "liberality" of that title prefigures the spontaneity which Menard is anxious to correct in the work of Cervantes. There is nothing at all "liberal" about the inventions he approves of.

Unlike other of Borges' inventors, unlike Dandy Red Scharlach, say, Menard requires no adversary but himself. But in order to be an inventor he has got to find, within himself, a principle of division, a germ, as it were, of schizophrenia, since until a man be divided internally he is not able to launch himself on the creation of a fiction. That fiction is dialectical through and through: dialectical in respect of the fictions which already exist at the moment of its creation, dialectical in respect of its narrative form, which is a whole series of potential contradictions, dialectical in its "characterization." That word, in Borges' case, must go into quotation marks because it is used in an etiolated, formal sense. The characters in his stories are not psychological entities, merely proper names. They are, as all fictional characters are to a greater or lesser extent, functions of the plot, and Borges gives them names as a concession to the protocol of fiction; they could as well have been identified more symbolically, perhaps by an algebraic notation.

Characters, like any other element in a literary structure, derive their meaning in the first instance differentially: it is by comparing one character with another, and seeing what the differences are, that we get our first understanding of their presence in the fiction. The differences between them matter, and so, equally, do the similarities, for if there are no similarities between two characters then there is no incentive to measure the differences between them. So the first step towards classifying the characters in a narrative is to observe what is common to any two of them and what is unique.

With most fiction we should normally set about doing this in psychological terms, distinguishing one character from another by the way they behave and deducing that these are alternative psychological "types"; in one situation we observe two different reactions. With Borges, however, that possibility is removed, since his characters have no psychology, no inner life worth speaking of. It is always *possible* to interpret any act psychologically and to take it as evidence of a distinctive personality, but it would be perfectly sterile to attempt that with the acts which Borges' characters perform. His characters are there to serve the plot, they are "mere subjects of the action" as the preface to the printed version of two of Borges' and Bioy Casares' film scenarios puts it.

There are characters in any narrative because there can be no narrative without them; they may not be human characters but animals or even inanimate objects, but they are characters none the less, and the actions of the narrative will be distributed purposefully amongst them.

If there are no psychological characteristics to distinguish one character from another in a story, then we are thrown back on their names to do the job. Proper names matter far more in fiction than is sometimes allowed, and far more than in real life. They matter because they are distinctive. When people are present to us we do not distinguish them by their names but by their looks; when they are absent it is quicker and more effective to distinguish them by name, rather than by some brief résumé of their appearance. In a fiction, where there are no physical presences, we depend greatly on having the characters identified for us by their names, even if, as the fiction develops, we come to "recognize" characters by their mannerisms and obsessions. (An extreme Formalist might argue, with reason, that those mannerisms and obsessions are themselves demanded by the conventions of narrative, that the content thus stems from the form.) There has been much resentment when novelists deliberately fail to name their characters, so that they become harder or impossible to keep apart. In some instances, as looks to be the case with Virginia Woolf, they may want us to identify them by their intimate foibles; in others, as is certainly the case with Nathalie Sarraute, they may not want us to identify them at all, when so much even of our secret, psychic life is quite lacking in "authenticity" and therefo.e undeserving of attribution to one person rather than another. In general, hough, characters *are* distinctive, and much more distinctive than real people. This extra distinctiveness we acknowledge almost every day when we encounter real people who, because of the extravagance of their behaviour, we call "characters."

It was the distinctiveness of "characters" as opposed to the homogeneity of real people which, we saw [elsewhere], alerted the shrewd Isidro Parodi to the plot against Montenegro in "Las noches de Goliadkin" ["Goliadkin's Nights"]. Alert spectators of *Murder on the Orient Express* might, though I doubt it, have likewise penetrated the plot on that train. But the diversity of Agatha Christie's characters on that occasion is rich and overwhelming, and reinforced by the need to give a variety of important film actors their chance in a "character" part. Borges could never be so florid in his exposure of convention.

It is a principle of linguistics that meaning may be instituted by very small differences between linguistic units, by the minor, acoustic variation, say, between the words *pull* and *bull*. The variations through which meaning may be instituted in a fiction will need to be more decisive than that, but not exaggeratedly so. In one of Borges' later stories, "El encuentro" ("The

Encounter"], there is an allusion to two old *cuchilleros* [knife-fighters] called Juan Almanza and Juan Almada. They bear each other a grudge for the apparently frivolous reason that "people mixed them up." The pair of them never in fact meet, even though both are recorded as having died, Almanza of a stray bullet, Almada of natural causes. They story into which this ill-differentiated pair is introduced is the story of two other men who *do* meet, in a knife-fight. Unlike Almanza and Almada these two, by name Uriate and Duncan, are not knife-fighters. When they fight, however, they show an unexpected expertise and one kills the other. Their expertise is an attribute not of the men themselves but of their weapons, which have been taken from a show-case full of famous knives dating back to the legendary past of Buenos Aires' *cuchilleros*. "El encuentro" is a story in which the encounter matters a great deal and the identity of the rivals little. They fight because an encounter, *any* encounter, requires two adversaries; they are functions of the plot, a necessary, formal duplication. The story is doubly archetypal: it is archetypal as an Argentinian story, approximating to the Platonic ideal of the story of a *duelo a cuchillo* (knife-fight); and archetypal for being founded on conflict, on the disjunction without which there could be no story.

It is this disjunction for which Almanza and Almada fail to qualify because their names are too alike and people confuse them. It is to them, however, that the weapons used in the fight by Duncan and Uriarte are eventually traced back: the encounter between the two bourgeois is the fulfillment of the rivalry between the two *cuchilleros*. The tone has been raised, and in the future it will be raised still further, because the witnesses to the duel agree amongst themselves that they will "lie as little as possible and raise the duel with knives into a duel with swords." This, it seems, will keep the authorities quiet; the encounter is now in circulation as a narrative and can progress towards the status of a myth. The names of the duellists, Uriarte and Duncan, are distinctive, as are their persons and the weapons they fight with, and the story, as Borges tells it, contains regular hints at the inevitability of its conclusion. The name of Duncan, who is eventually murdered by Uriarte's "dagger," is presumably an echo of *Macbeth*, planted, as by Nolan in "Tema del traidor y del heroe" ["Theme of the Traitor and the Hero"], so that we shall recognize the story's plot to be a conspiracy, part plagiarism and part improvisation.

I have said that the reason why Almanza and Almada hate one another is the "apparently frivolous" one that people get them muddled up. It is only "apparently frivolous" judged by the psychological criteria we normally bring to the discussion of motive in fiction. As a psychological explanation of a rivalry it looks most inadequate; but it is not a psychological explanation. It is a formal, literary explanation, in terms of narrative. Almanza and Almada have, in their names, everything it takes to be two characters in a fiction: they are similar but not identical. They invite comparison. The fact that they are, to judge by the story of "El encuentro," a little too similar to be made into fully blown characters does not disqualify them. They can be listed among the embryonic, apprentice characters in Borges, like others we have considered. Their deaths are random, they have failed to take the chance their names offered them of a significant conjunction.

But they embody the principle of bifurcation, or division, and that is the reason they hate one another. Hatred is the emotion which divides, the emotion most obviously appropriate if we want to establish a motive for the dialectic principle itself. Where love brings together, hatred drives apart, and the various pairs of rivals in Borges' stories hate one another because they are rivals, they are not rivals because they hate one another. It is hatred which is justified by the disjunctions of the story and, very strikingly, by the disjunction within a single character whereby the story originates.

In the course of the highly creative fever which follows his operation in the sanatorium, Juan Dahlmann, the protagonist of "El Sur" ["The South"], "hated himself meticulously (*minuciosamente*); he hated his identity, his bodily necessities, his humiliation, the beard that bristled on his face." This is his cue to divide himself, like protoplasm, into two, to inaugurate an alternative, fictive self which will suppress his identity, or oneness, set him temporarily free from biological constraints, and compensate him for the shortcomings of reality (a theme in Borges I shall return to [elsewhere]). I have no good explanation for Dahlmann's animus against his beard, unless it represents the facial contingencies he will rise above on his subsequent expedition in search of his definitive, "eternal" face. The important thing is that Dahlmann has now duplicated himself and will soon be on his way to his Romantic death in the South. This duplication, into a sedentary and a heroic self, is one conditioned, as so often in Borges, by his ancestry, in which there are German pastors—the Protestant or dialectical element again—and Argentinian military heroes. Dahlmann himself is the secretary of a public library and feels "deeply Argentinian." He will die what is, in literary terms, a "deeply Argentinian" death, in a knife-fight. Like Uriarte and Duncan in "El encuentro" he does not know how to wield a knife, for if he did his fate would be evitable.

Dahlmann's self-hatred turns him literally from a patient (in a sanatorium) into an agent, or into an agent who is both agent and patient in one, true to the assertion of Schopenhauer, that "I demonstrate the same being in the actor and the sufferer." But patients may well not enjoy their transformation into agents, since the process of bifurcation does not end there; indeed, it only *begins* there. The alternative self stands at the head of a sequence of narrative choices, the labyrinth through which he has to pick his way to his inevitable fate. He may feel, like another of Borges' fever patients, Dandy Red Scharlach, that all this duplication is too arduous. The presence which dominates Scharlach's inventive sickness is that of the "hateful" two-headed Janus. His feelings towards his suffering body are like Dahlmann's but more negative: "I came to abominate my body, I came to feel that two eyes, two hands, two lungs, are as monstrous as two faces." For Scharlach the human body itself has labyrinthine possibilities.

Hatred, whether of one person for himself or of one person for another person, results in fictions. Haters are no respecters of facts. In the story of "La busca de Averroes" ["Averroes' Search"] the philosopher dines in the house of Farach, the local theologian or "Koranist"; among the other guests is the traveller Abulcásim Al-Asharí, whose memory, like that of any potential Borges hero, is "a mirror of intimate cowardices":

> Abulcásim said he had reached the kingdoms of the empire of Sin (of China); his detractors, with that peculiar logic which comes from hatred, swore that he had never set foot in China and that in the temples of that country he had blasphemed against Allah.

The "peculiar logic" of hatred thus thrives on contradiction. The two charges made against the traveller—the teller of tales—by his adversaries are incompatible. Those adversaries want the best of both worlds, want Abulcásim both to have been in China and not to have been in China. They are dialecticians on principle, who disregard the incompatibility of the premises from which they are arguing. Their two fictions against Abulcásim can never be reconciled, so if they were ever to coexist in a narrative—apart from their coexistence in Borges' narrative, as a specimen paralogism—one must be annihilated. If hatred inspires disagreement with existing narratives, it has subsequently to be controlled by logic of an orthodox sort in order to ensure that such disagreements are not mutually exclusive. Logic works by excluding middles, or the coexistence of contradictories, and so, once it is finalized, does narrative, but, as Borges repeatedly demonstrates, a narrative still on its way to being finalized works by discarding alternatives which are incongruous.

Of the alternative charges laid against Abulcásim, that he was a liar or a blasphemer, there is more to be gained by studying the second. To blaspheme is a peculiarly literary act: it is to depart verbally, from the prescribed formulas of devotion. Blasphemy is a minor, less elaborate branch of heresy, and there is, very logically, nothing that Borges likes better than a systematic heresiarch. The heretic is someone who distinguishes himself by his departure from orthodoxy; his motive is *odium theologicum*, supposedly the most visceral of all hatreds. Heresy, with Borges, is identical with authorship in general, both in its motives and its products: it reorganizes the old fictions which it hates into new ones.

The most persistent and outrageous of Borges' heretics is Nils Runeberg of Lund, protagonist of the "Tres versiones de Judas" (Three Versions of Judas"). Runeberg, dissatisfied by the Gospel story as given, invents three theological fictions of his own, which we are bound to see, from the narrative point of view, as improvements on the original. He is interested not in the story as a whole, but in its conclusion, with the betrayal of Jesus. He is interested in fact in the relationship of Jesus with Judas. Now these two names, in view of what we have just been saying, are something of an *hasard objectif* for Runeberg (or Borges), a coincidence in "nature" which invites their incorporation into a story. The names are similar but not identical, like those of Almanza and Almada.

Runeberg's variations on the New Testament account of Jesus and Judas are exercises in what he calls "the economy of redemption," but he does not use the word "redemption" in quite its normal theological sense. He wants to redeem Judas Iscariot, and to do so by giving him a more and more decisive role in the narrative of Jesus' betrayal. The gravest sin which, as a maker of fictions, can beset him, is the sin of contingency, or the haphazard, and it is this sin he plans to redeem by integrating it within a story. Judas' betrayal of Jesus will be treated like the betrayal of Scharlach by his impulsive henchman, Azevedo, in "La muerte y la brújula" ["Death and the Compass"]: it will be ransomed by being turned into a different, more satisfactory, and more "interesting" narrative. As an act of redemption this is unorthodox but not wholly unorthodox, since the redemption of the human race through the sacrifice of Jesus also works by endowing our collective and individual histories with finality: it is a proof, if we accept it, that the world is not fact but fiction, a story willed by God.

Runeberg starts from what he sees as a crucial weakness in the Gospel account: the superfluity of Judas' treacherous kiss in the Garden of Gethsemane. This is superfluous, he argues, because everyone must have known what Jesus looked like already, so that there was no need for him to be identified in this way. Now a fiction, as we have several times remarked, has as one of its functions to establish the identity of its hero, to trace his essential features; if that identity is already established, further fictions are redundant. But such redundancy is a virtue, because it means that whatever further fictions are elaborated they cannot affect the "historical" record: the history of Jesus remains unscathed by Runeberg's speculations. A superfluous action in a narrative, however, is an offence for a mind as rigorous as his, and he will work to justify it: "To suppose an error in the Scriptures is intolerable; it is no less intolerable to admit a casual fact into the most precious occurrence in the history of the world. *Ergo*, Judas' betrayal was not casual; it was a predetermined fact which has its mysterious place in the economy of redemption."

Runeberg's successive reinterpretations of Judas' value in this economy promote him rapidly and scandalously from the most ignominious of roles to the most glorious. His first version has Judas being sacrificed in order to mirror, on the merely human level, the sacrifice of God himself on the divine level. In the second version Judas is seen as a supreme ascetic, mortifying not his body but his soul for the greater glory of God, and becoming the equivalent in Hell of Jesus in Paradise. In the third and final version Judas, having first reflected and then equalled Jesus, supplants him; it is now he, and not Jesus, who is seen as the Son of God, God having decided to espouse humanity in its lowest form. Runeberg's Redeemer is thus to be found in Hell, which must rank as something of a last word in Christian heresy. But the last word in heresy is also a triumph of narrative logic, and Runeberg ranks high on the list of Borges' methodical makers of fiction. The weakness of the Gospel has been repaired. Judas, a traitor not to Jesus but to the rigorousness of the story, is redeemed.

Borges comes back to the story of Jesus and Judas in a later story, "La secta de los treinta" ("The Sect of the Thirty"), in terms exactly similar to the story of Nolan's Festspiel in "Tema del traidor y del heroe":

> In the tragedy of the Cross . . . there were voluntary and involuntary actors, all of them indispensable, all of them inevitable . . . Only two were voluntary: the Redeemer and Judas. The latter threw away the thirty pieces of silver which were the price of the salvation of souls and immediately hanged himself. At that time he was 33 years old, like the Son of Man. The Sect venerates them as equals and absolves the others.

The Sect are advanced students of fiction. They know that, in structural terms, there is equality between all the elements of a narrative, and that they all contribute to the one end. Nothing could make the point more succinctly than the provocative reasoning whereby the money which Judas received for his treachery becomes "the price of the salvation of souls." This is teleology taken to its limits: the Sect, which has taken its name from these thirty ill-gotten shekels, argues that but for Judas' betrayal there could have been no Redemption, that whatever is part of the story leads to the culmination of the story. Jesus needs Judas just as much as Judas needs Jesus; but for the one's infamy the other could have not known glory.

Runeberg's three fictions have the effect, therefore, of transforming the lowest of the low into the highest of the high. Fiction, for Borges, glorifies. The protagonist of a story, after all, however villainous, is technically its hero. Many of Borges' protagonists are, by their own confession, cowards, or alternatively are shown to be cowardly and treacherous. In a fiction they can, like Judas Iscariot, change places with the loyal and brave. Like another of Borges' traitors, Zaid in the story of "Abenjacán el Bojarí, muerto en su laberinto" ("Abenjacán the Bojarí, Dead in his Labyrinth"), they can become king for a day. This is another of the A to Z stories. Zaid is the cousin of an African king, Abenjacán el Bojarí, who is himself the architect, in exile, of an imposing labyrinth in the wilds of Cornwall. Abenjacán lives in his labyrinth guarded by a lion and a Negro slave and tells his story to the local rector (Rector Allaby, a character borrowed by Borges from Samuel Butler's *Way of All Flesh*, where Rector Allaby is the father-in-law of Theodore Pontifex). In alliance with his cousin, Zaid, Abenjacán has despoiled his people and then, when they rebelled, fled his kingdom with his cousin and the loot. Subsequently he has murdered Zaid and built his labyrinth as a refuge. But this account proves false; Abenjacán calls on the Rector again and tells him that Zaid is alive and pursuing him, indeed that he is already inside the labyrinth. His own body, together with that of his lion and his slave, are later found in the labyrinth, their faces carefully expunged.

The "explanation" offered of these events is that the inhabitant of the Cornish labyrinth was not the brave Abenjacán at all but the treacherous Zaid, that the labyrinth has been built not as a refuge but as a lure, in the knowledge that when Abenjacán heard of it he would travel to Cornwall in pursuit of his cousin, who, in the flight together, has robbed him of his treasures. When Abenjacán finally arrives and penetrates into the labyrinth, Zaid murders him and flees back to Africa. This murder and ensuing flight are the realization of the fictive murder and ensuing flight in Zaid's story to the Rector. In that story he has impersonated his enemy and so turned himself into a hero. He has alienated his treachery from himself by projecting it on to the third-person Zaid of his narrative, and that Zaid is "dead." The story of "Abenjacán el Bojarí, muerto en su laberinto" is one of the replacement of the King by his cousin, of the letter A by the letter Z. Hero and villain are interchangeable because it is only their names, and above all the initial letters of their names, which separate them; the face of the dead man in the labyrinth has been destroyed, so that they can no longer be identified by their bodies. "He pretended to be Abenjacán, he killed Abenjacán and finally *he was Abenjacán*" (Borges' italics) is the story's dying verdict on Zaid. The traitor has been transformed into a hero, except, of course, for us, before whom the actual deceitfulness of that transformation has been exposed.

The glory Zaid achieves, like the glory Runeberg procures for Judas, is a reflected glory. Both are usurpers of a dignity which, "historically" speaking, belongs elsewhere; Zaid is not a "real" king, any more than Judas is a "real" redeemer. A reflected glory is one which comes from moving to the centre of a story. In Zaid's case it comes from telling one's own story as if one were its hero rather than its villain. As a story-teller Zaid subscribes to a fundamental principle of narration, which is that the stories we tell can make men of us; his story comes very much under the heading of what, in *Evaristo Carriego*, Borges calls "the narratives of iron which shed their valour on whoever is recounting them."

It is this acquisition of a reflected glory which seems to be supported in Borges, albeit rather obscurely, by certain astronomical (or should it be astrological?) arrangements in the stories. In several of the stories play is made of the relationship between sun and moon. We have come across the moon at least once already, reflected in the rectangular *fuentes* [fountains] of London when Ebenezer Bogle sets off through the streets in search of creative inspiration. Elsewhere, as in the story of "El inmortal" ("The Immortal"), it is associated with the onset of "fever," and we know by now what that means. The moon is the planet appropriate to Borges' fictions because, as "controlled dreams," they are pointedly nocturnal. But the moon is a source of illumination only by the grace of the sun; its glory is a reflected glory. It may replace the sun during the hours of darkness but it cannot shine without it. As a bringer of light, the moon is a fraud if not a fiction.

There is evidence of a sun/moon relationship in the relationship between Abenjacán and Zaid. When the presumed Abenjacán first lands in Cornwall with his lion and his Negro slave, the lion, the King of Beasts we may assume, is described as having "the colour of the sun," while the slave has "the colour of the night." Abenjacán himself, who is Zaid pretending to be Abenjacán, is, rather surprisingly for someone emerged from darkest Africa, "a man of lemony (*cetrina*) skin." He is, one might say, yellow: literally yellow in the colour of his skin and figuratively yellow, as it will turn out, in his cowardice. Thus in addition to the King of Beasts who is the colour of the sun, and the slave who is the colour of the night, we have an intermediate presence who is the colour of the moon. As the story develops, Zaid is a moon who substitutes himself for the sun, for the King, a substitution he achieves as both hero and narrator of a story, that is to say as the elucidator of a mystery.

This symbolism may seem alembicated and incredible. It is repeated, however, perhaps more clearly, in another story: "La forma de la espada" ("The Form of the Sword"). This is also a story of treachery told by the traitor himself, and it is set in that privileged location, Ireland, much of it indeed in the country-house of a certain General Berkeley, conveniently removed for the duration to another of Borges' occasional campaign-grounds, India. Ireland is in a state of civil war, which we can take to be that very state of internal dissension we have seen to be the nursery of fictions. The story is told *to* the narrator in Uruguay, by an Englishman "whose real name does not matter"; since his "real" name is Moon, we may dispute that casual aside. It concerns a young recruit to the cause of Irish independence against the English, a twentieth-century Fergus Kilpatrick. His name is John Vincent Moon. Moon propitiously for a Borges story, is a "dialectical materialist" and also strongly deterministic, being convinced that "the revolution was predestined to triumph." And triumph it does, as with Kilpatrick; only it is not the conspiracy against the English which comes to fruition, it is the conspiracy against reality.

Moon, alas, is a coward. He betrays the fellow-conspirator who has, being a true hero, risked his life to save Moon from capture. It is this hero who, so it appears, is now telling the story of the treachery. After hearing Moon arranging, on the telephone, like some more technological Judas, to have him arrested as he crosses the garden, he pursues the "informer" through the "black corridors of nightmare and deep staircases of vertigo" of General Berkeley's labyrinthine house. Eventually he takes down a sword and marks his adversary for life: "with that half-moon of steel I put my mark on his face, for ever, a half moon of blood." This tell-tale mark is one we have been introduced to already, as crossing the face of the nameless Englishman who is telling the story. John Vincent Moon, the Judas, has appropriated the glory of the nameless Irishman whom he has betrayed by the simple, grammatical expedient of turning himself into the third person "he" and his saviour into the first person "I." The "I," as the narrator of the story, is automatically its hero, the "he," or its narratee, is the infamous traitor in need of redemption.

Moon, the provisional source of light, is ultimately exposed as a sham. He is also a man in a state of civil war, a man divided. He is both agent and patient. As agent he inflicts on his patient half the mark—a half-moon—which symbolizes his divided state. But that division lasts only as long as his narration lasts, it is a division forced on him by the necessary disjunction of narrative itself. Once the "solitary game" is over, Moon can revert to being a full moon again, instead of two warring halves. The true hero of his story has been shot by the English, and it is, as ever, the death of that "reality" which has opened the way for Moon's own fiction of self-aggrandizement. There is a last irony, however: by telling his own story to a stranger Moon negates the redemption that story was invented in order to achieve. Should we admire him or despise him all the more for the expertise of his deception?

NANCY B. MANDLOVE

Chess and Mirrors:
Form as Metaphor in Three Sonnets

"To the Looking-glass world it was Alice that said,
I've a sceptre in hand, I've a crown on my head;
Let the Looking-glass creatures, whatever they be,
Come and dine with the Red Queen, the White
Queen and me!'"

—LEWIS CARROLL

The mirror appears frequently in Borges' work as a symbolic representation of the infinite multiplication and repetition of human experience. In his short stories, Borges often uses mirrors and mirror images to show that human nature endlessly repeats itself, that a single character exists in both the past and in the future, or that he exists simultaneously in places widely remote from each other. The mirror image in the short stories generally serves to reflect and support the theme of the work. A very different use of the mirror image appears in much of Borges' more recent poetry, where the form of the poem itself becomes a mirror which captures and reflects the infinite variety of human experience. Through the image of the mirror, form becomes metaphor; the structure of the poem points beyond itself to the structure of human existence.

Critics Guillermo Sucre and Zunilda Gertel have both emphasized the fact that Borges turns away from the visionary images and free verse of the early *ultraísta* period (1918–1929) in favor of traditional, timeless metaphors and conventional poetic forms in the later work (1958 to the present). According to Sucre: el poeta, para él [Borges], es aquél que busca secretamente los

From *Kentucky Romance Quarterly* 27, no. 3 (1980). © 1980 by The University Press of Kentucky.

arquetipos, las formas esenciales; aquél que busca un orden superior de la que
la obra sea un símbolo y donde el azar se vea cada vez más reducido [the poet
for him, is he who secretly looks for archetypes, the essential forms; he who
searches for a superior order where the work can be a symbol and where chance
can be reduced]." The more recent poetry of Borges is then, a search for forms,
for forms which reveal a superior order, the order of the universe itself. The
work becomes symbolic of a higher order because Borges uses archetypal images
and metaphors within conventional poetic forms in such a way that both the
formal structure and the content of the poems reflect the same basic structural
pattern of human existence. The archetypal content of the poems is a metaphorical representation of a higher order. The form of the poems, too, becomes
metaphorical through the image of the mirror. Ana María Barrenechea has
observed that the mirror image in Borges' work alludes to "the Gnostic idea
that the universe is an inverted copy of the celestial order." Functioning like
a mirror, the formal structure of the poem directly reflects a greater structure,
that of the universal order. Thus one finds in Borges' work not just a harmony
of form and content, but poems in which both form and content are parallel
vehicles of a metaphor in which the tenor is the greater, universal structure.
The poems produce an ever expanding pattern of reflections, mirror images
into which the reader too, is drawn, recognizing himself as part of the pattern,
as one of the multiple reflections in the mirror of the poem. As Borges notes
in "Arte poética" ["Ars Poetica"]: "A veces en las tardes una cara/Nos mira
desde el fondo de un espejo;/El arte debe ser como ese espejo/Que nos revela
nuestra propia cara [At times in the evenings a face/Looks at us out of the
depths of a mirror;/Art should be like that mirror/Which reveals to us our
own face]" (*Selected Poems*, tr. W. S. Merwin).

It is Borges' use of the sonnet which, as the most ordered and conventional
of poetic forms, best illustrates the way in which form becomes metaphor.
In a sonnet entitled "A un poeta del siglo XIII" ["A Poet of the Thirteenth
Century"], Borges suggests that the sonnet form—the structure of the sonnet—is
archetypal, that it is not the result of trial and error, of an arbitrary arrangement
of quatrains and tercets on the part of the great poet Petrarch, but rather the
reflection of a divinely revealed archetypal structure. The sonnet form itself
is a mirror, a metaphor reflecting another, greater structure.

> Vuelve a mirar los arduos borradores
> De aquel primer soneto innominado,
> La página arbitraria en que ha mezclado
> Tercetos y cuartetos pecadores.
> Lima con lenta pluma sus rigores

Y se detiene. Acaso le ha llegado
Del porvenir y de su horror sagrado
Un rumor de remotos ruiseñores.

¿Habrá sentido que no estaba solo
Y que el arcano, el increíble Apolo
Le había revelado un arquetipo,

Un ávido cristal que apresaría
Cuanto la noche cierra o abre el día:
Dédalo, laberinto, enigma, Edipo?

[Think of him laboring in the Tuscan halls
On the first sonnet (that word still unsaid),
The undistinguished pages, filled with sad
Triplets and quatrains, without heads or tails.

Slowly he shapes it; yet the impulse fails.
He stops, perhaps at a strange slight music shed
From time coming and its holy dread,
A murmuring of far-off nightingales.

Did he sense that others were to follow,
That the arcane, incredible Apollo
Had revealed an archetypal thing,

A whirlpool mirror that would draw and hold
All that night could hide or day unfold:
Daedalus, labyrinth, riddle, Oedipus King?
                    (*Poetic Works*, tr. W. Ferguson)]

In the first stanza, before the original sonneteer has finished his poem,
it appears that the composition of the sonnet is a matter to be determined
by the creative power of the poet as he labors meticulously over his work.
The random arrangement of tercets and quatrains indicated by the words
arbitraria and *mezclado* suggests that the poet is seeking the proper form for
his expression through an act of his own creative will. However, in the second
stanza, when he suddenly discovers the precise combination of stanzas for the
sonnet, what were once "tercetos y cuartetos pecadores" now seem to be distant
and timeless echoes of a dimly intuited sacred form.

In the first tercet Borges speculates on the possibility that the random pattern
selected by Petrarch for the sonnet is not a matter of chance or freely determined
creative activity, but the recognition of a greater, archetypal, pattern older than
poetry. He associates the revelation of the form with Apollo, god of beauty,

law, civilization and supreme authority in matters of ritual, suggesting that
the form itself is, in some way, a reflection of an Ideal structure, a structure
basic to human civilization which acquires ritualistic dimension through its
repetition in diverse areas of man's endeavor.

In the last stanza, Borges compares the form to a mirror which both contains
and reflects "cuanto la noche cierra o abre el día." The form captures and contains
all the possibilities of human existence, the dark, evil, malevolent as well as
the enlightened; at the same time, it serves as a direct formal reflection of those
polar opposites because it too is part of the same pattern. The last line of the
poem mirrors the four part structure of the sonnet and incorporates the opposites
introduced in the preceding line by "noche" and "día." It begins with Dedalus,
the archetypal representative of man's highest aspirations, and ends with Oedipus,
symbolic of man's deepest anguish. In the middle is the form—a labyrinth,
a mysterious mixture of chaos and order, a puzzle. The sonnet is a formal
structure which mirrors another, greater formal structure, whose pattern is
known, but whose meaning remains an enigma. The form is a mirror image
of its content and, as the content may comprise the full spectrum of human
existence, the structure of the sonnet, according to Borges, is a microcosmic
reflection of the structure of the macrocosm. The form becomes a metaphor
linking the lesser world with the greater world.

In two sonnets dedicated to the subject of chess, Borges expands and
elaborates the concept of the sonnet as an archetypal pattern which mirrors
the structure of man's existence. In these two sonnets, the mirror image is not
presented directly, but is created through formal patterns which are mirror
images of each other. The black and white pattern of the chessboard becomes
the background for a cosmic game in which man is both player and pawn.
In "Ajedrez I" ["Chess I"] the sonnet structure reflects the structure of the chess
game, creating a pattern within a pattern. Metaphorical structure mirrors
metaphorical content.

> En su grave rincón, los jugadores
> Rigen las lentas piezas. El tablero
> Los demora hasta el alba en su severo
> Ambito en que se odian dos colores.
>
> Adentro irradian mágicos rigores
> Las formas: torre homérica, ligero
> Caballo, armada reina, rey postrero,
> Oblicuo alfil y peones agresores.
>
> Cuando los jugadores se hayan ido,
> Cuando el tiempo los haya consumido,

Ciertamente no habrá cesado el rito.

En el oriente se encendió esta guerra
Cuyo anfiteatro es hoy toda la tierra.
Como el otro, este juego es infinito.

[Set in their studious corners, the players
Move the gradual pieces. Until dawn
The chessboard keeps them in its strict confinement
With its two colors set at daggers drawn.

Within the game itself the forms give off
Their magic rules: Homeric castle, knight
Swift to attack, queen warlike, king decisive,
Slanted bishop, and attacking pawns.

Eventually, when the players have withdrawn,
When time itself has finally consumed them,
The ritual certainly will not be done.

It was in the East this war took fire.
Today the whole earth is its theater.
Like the game of love, this game goes on forever.
                    (*Poetic Works*, tr. A. Reid)]

The first stanza of this sonnet sets the stage for the interplay of opposing
forces which gives form to both sonnets. The setting in which the chess game
takes place is stripped of all but the essential details. It is completely impersonal,
formal and almost abstract. The game takes place in a "grave rincón," a "severo
ámbito." The adjectives "grave" and "severo" lend formal dignity to the game,
while the noun "rincón," the place where the nameless players sit, reflects the
square shape of the chessboard. Neither the players nor the pieces are named
in this stanza. The game proceeds almost mechanically according to strict, logical
rules, without haste or emotion. When night falls and the game is suspended,
the pieces are frozen, motionless and trapped in their fixed pattern until the
game continues. The last line of the stanza ("ámbito en que se odian dos colores")
is both abstract and impersonal, yet charged with tension and emotion. The
two sides of the game are reduced to pure antithesis, black against white, which
implies the opposition of all opposing forces. At the same time, the verb "odiarse"
makes the antagonism between them something personal and emotional which
is then not confined to the two opposing factions, but spreads out to dominate
the entire atmosphere in which the struggle takes place.

While the first stanza presents the exterior, logical, rational nature of chess,
the second stanza elaborates the interior, irrational logic which operates within

the game. The chessmen on the board are subject to a rigorous set of rules which govern their moves and appear to be of a formal, logical nature and yet behind that logic there are irrational, mysterious forces at work. The figures on the board are not pieces now but forms, a change which raises them from mere markers in a game to the level of archetype. Each form is named and modified to correspond to its function in the game, according each one a character of its own.

In the tercets, Borges moves away from the temporal and specific into the realm of the eternal. The chess game is a ritual, a rite symbolizing the perpetual struggle between opposing forces. The last stanza links chess, a game of war to the greater game, the microcosm to the macrocosm, for "el oriente" refers both to the Eastern origins of chess and to the dawn of man and civilization. The world is now a chessboard and the game is infinite.

In "Ajedrez I" Borges presents the game of chess as an archetypal conflict between opposing forces by reducing the game to an essential pattern of forms in opposition, black versus white. He locates that pattern within another archetypal pattern, the sonnet, which is a direct reflection, a mirror image of the same archetypal structure. The sonnet, like the game of chess, is subject to a rigid and predetermined pattern. Both forms are based on the number four, a number symbolic of rational order, of human civilization and logic. The game of chess is played on a four-sided (square) board divided into eight rows, each one composed of alternating colors—four black and four white. The pieces, too, are based on the number four: bishop, knight, rook and pawn governed by the king and queen. The structure of the game reflects the structure of human society. The terminology used to designate the pieces changes according to the culture and period in which it is played, from terms implying strategic warfare to those reflecting the European court structure, but the game is universal and the patterned movement of the pieces never varies. Whether viewed as a game of war or of court intrigue, chess is an archetypal representation of man's attempt to reconcile chaos and order, to provide a rational, logical structure for the irrational conflict of opposing forces. The sonnet structure into which this game of chess is woven represents the same symbolic ordering of threatening, chaotic oppositions. It too is based on the number four: four stanzas, including two quatrains, symbolic of rational order. Just as the chessboard is composed of symbolic opposites, the sonnet structure also reflects a balance of oppositions. The two tercets complement the quatrains and represent (through the symbolic number three) the irrational dimension of existence, the world beyond man and his society. The tightly knit rhyme scheme of the sonnet further supports the integration of symbolic opposites and contributes to the tensive nature of oppositions held in perfect balance. In the quatrains, the ABBA rhyme scheme, dependent on two rhymes, reflects the tension found in the content between the pairs of opposites: black and white, the opposing players. The CCD/EED rhymes of the tercets also support the tension between opposing forces in the two rhyme sequence found in each tercet, but the pattern here goes beyond that of the quatrains to include a third rhyme when the tercets are considered together, thus contributing to the irrational dimension symbolically represented in the tercets by the number three.

In "Ajedrez I" Borges uses the pattern of the two quatrains to reflect the pattern of the chess game. The form of the game, like the quatrains, represents the external, rational, human ordering of forces in conflict. In the tercets, however, the game extends beyond the limits of the chessboard and encompasses the greater world. The three line stanzas reflect the internal, irrational dimension of the game which is now cosmic. While the order which governs the opposing sides in the game extends, in Borges' poem, to include the universal order, logic is lost when the game becomes infinite. Both the sonnet and the game of chess are man's civilized attempts to bring order out of chaos, to provide a logical structure for irrational forces, to encompass the infinite within the finite, to control the uncontrollable. In chess the moves of each piece are limited and well defined, while the possible variations within those limitations are infinite. In the sonnet, too, the form is limited and pre-determined, but the material contained is limitless. Thus, this sonnet is a mirror image of its content, an archetypal pattern reflecting an archetypal pattern. The form of the poem is a metaphorical vehicle of the same nature as the content and points beyond itself to a higher order.

In "Ajedrez II" ["Chess II"] the archetypal pattern is extended still further to add two more dimensions to the same structure. In "Ajedrez I" the symbolic chess game expanded in space, converting the world into a chessboard where man waged war against chaos. In "Ajedrez II" the pattern expands in time as well as space and incorporates the literary tradition into the archetypal pattern.

> Tenue rey, sesgo alfil, encarnizada
> Reina, torre directa y peón ladino
> Sobre lo negro y blanco del camino
> Buscan y libran su batalla armada.
>
> No saben que la mano señalada
> Del jugador gobierna su destino
> No saben que un rigor adamantino
> Sujeta su albredrío y su jornada.
>
> También el jugador es prisionero
> (La sentencia es de Omar) de otro tablero

De negras noches y de blancos días.

Dios mueve al jugador, y éste, la pieza,
¿Qué dios detrás de Dios la trama empieza
De polvo y tiempo y sueño y agonías?

[Faint-hearted king, sly bishop, ruthless queen,
Straightforward castle, and deceitful pawn —
Over the checkered black and white terrain
They seek out and begin their armed campaign.

They do not know it is the player's hand
That dominates and guides their destiny.
They do not know an adamantine fate
Controls their will and lays the battle plan.

The player too is captive of caprice
(The words are Omar's) on another ground
Where black nights alternate with whiter days.

God moves the player, he in turn the piece.
But what god beyond God begins the round
Of dust and time and sleep and agonies?
                    (*Poetic Works*, tr. A. Reid)]

In the first stanza Borges again names the chess pieces and modifies each with an adjective which both designates its function in the game and contributes to the personification of the individual forms. The black and white pieces, personified by such adjectives as "tenue," "sesgo" and "encarnizada" appear to function as free agents ("buscan y libran su batalla armada"). The pattern of the board, which was represented as a static, spatial pattern in "Ajedrez I," now becomes an active pattern extending into the dimension of time. The opposing pieces are no longer in fixed positions, but are actively pursuing their own destinies in time and space "sobre lo negro y blanco del camino." The quatrains present the relationship between player and pawn. In the first stanza the chessmen appear to forge their own destinies, while in the second the illusion is broken by the hand of man which controls their every move. But it is still the rational world of human civilization, in which man assumes control by methodically ordering his circumstances.

In the tercets of "Ajedrez II," Borges extends the game to include the universal order — the order beyond man and his world. The alternating black and white pattern of the static chessboard in sonnet I became, in the tercets, a spatial pattern encompassing the world. In sonnet II the alternating black and white path followed by the chessmen becomes the eternal cycle of day and night in which man is a prisoner. The pattern expands in time now, as well as in space. In the final stanza, the levels of the game extend to encompass the universal order where the relationship of player and pawn is an infinite series of master and subject. Once again the order is precise, logical and predetermined, but the rational gives way to the irrational when the game becomes infinite, for although the order is clear, the meaning is a mystery. The function of the three line stanzas again contrasts with that of the four line stanzas by providing the irrational dimension.

The form of sonnet II, like that of sonnet I, is a mirror image of its content, a pattern within a pattern. However, in the second sonnet Borges includes still another representation of the pattern which was only hinted at in the first sonnet. The image of the eternal cycle of day and night as a chessboard on which man works out his destiny is not only a continuation of the theme the poet presents in the first stanza, but is a direct reference to *The Rubaiyat* of Omar Khayyam ("la sentencia es de Omar"). "'Tis all a Chequer-board of Nights and Days/Where Destiny with Men for Pieces plays:/Hither and thither moves, and mates, and slays,/And one by one back in the Closet lays." Thus Borges incorporates within a twentieth century Argentine sonnet, an image taken from a twelfth century Persian poet based on the same archetypal pattern. The Persian poet weaves together the pattern of man's fate and the pattern of the chessboard. Borges fuses that pattern, now a part of the literary tradition, with his own re-creation of the same archetypal concept of order and uses the sonnet form, a literary convention to mirror that structure. Furthermore, the version of the original poem which Borges relies on for his poem, is that translated for the modern world in the nineteenth century by Edward Fitzgerald who has added his own stamp to the archetypal pattern. The result is a complex structure of interwoven patterns: the chess pattern within the sonnet pattern, two literary traditions within a literary convention.

While in "Ajedrez I" the incorporation of the literary tradition was not as central to the poem as it is in "Ajedrez II" it was, nevertheless present, and added resonance to the sonnet. In the second stanza of that poem where he named the chess pieces, Borges referred first of all to the rook calling it, "torre homérica," giving an epic quality to the struggle between opposing factions. The reference to Homer in this context also calls to mind the Trojan War and the strategic Trojan horse designed like a giant chess piece in which the real players are contained. That brief allusion to the literary tradition recalls a whole series of archetypal references which support the pattern of the poem: the parallel between war and chess, man as a pawn in a greater game, the infinite repetition and variation of the epic struggle between opposing forces.

The last line of "Ajedrez II," ("de polvo y tiempo y sueño y agonías") despite the fact that it is an ordered, parallel construction conforming to the symmetrical structure of the sonnet, reveals a certain sense of chaos and mystery. Even though man imposes order on his creations, God orders man's world and an infinite series of gods behind God impose the same order on their creations, the meaning is still an enigma. The sonnet form, like the game of chess, is an attempt to capture and reflect the universal order, but there is a point at which, when it becomes infinite, the order breaks down and reveals the chaos and disintegration which are the other side of order. The last line of Borges' "Ajedrez II" recalls that of Góngora's famous sonnet in which the perfectly ordered world of physical beauty disintegrates with the passing of time, "en tierra, en humo, en polvo, en sombra, en nada [into earth, smoke, dust, shadow, nothingness]." The world of order once again returns to chaos, to nothingness. Whether by design or by coincidence arising from the archetypal nature of both sonnets, Borges' sonnet is linked to Góngora's which expands the literary resonance of that last line to include another tradition.

Finally, returning full circle, the last line of "Ajedrez II" forms a direct parallel to the last line of Borges' own sonnet, "A un poeta del siglo XIII," in which he speculates on the archetypal nature of the sonnet. "Dédalo, laberinto, enigma, Edipo." "De polvo, y tiempo y sueño y agonías." The sonnet form captures and reflects the human experience. It gives order to experience but it does not explain it. The form reflects the full spectrum of existence, the chaos and mystery as well as the order. In "Ajedrez II" Borges moves from the specific archetypal content of "A un poeta" to a more general archetypal content when he questions the meaning of the whole pattern. The archetypes, whether embodied in a symbolic hero, form or concept—Dedalus and Oedipus, the sonnet and chess, the labyrinth—provide man with a symbolic framework in which to order his experience, but again, the order is lost when the concept becomes infinite. When these two last lines are contrasted, Dedalus (and by extension, all man's aspirations) returns to dust, the labyrinth is an eternal labyrinth of time, the enigma is the infinite world of dream and Oedipus is only one representation of man's eternal anguish in the face of the unknown.

The artistry of Borges' sonnets does not depend on the themes, which are common, on the form, which is conventional, nor on the uniqueness of the language, but on the skillful manipulation and inter-weaving of archetypal patterns. The sonnets work through the pattern itself which expands in ever widening circles and produces the effect of a mirror with infinite reflections. The theme of free will versus predetermination apparent in "A un poeta del siglo XIII" is reflected in the sonnet structure. The same theme predominates in the two sonnets on chess but it acquires greater dimension by becoming fused with the pattern of the game and with the parallel structure of the sonnet, creating a multiple fusion of the pattern. The chess pattern then expands in time and space through the literary tradition and through the extension of the game to universal proportions. Borges suggests that the pattern is universal but the variations are infinite. The reader identifies with the archetypal content of the sonnets, recognizes the same archetypes in the literary tradition incorporated within the poems and becomes a participant in the expanding pattern. Thus the world of Alice, the Red Queen and the White Queen with which this essay begins is, in a sense outside the sonnets, and yet a part of them, for it is another variation, another extension of the same pattern into which Borges has drawn the reader and the reader's own experience. The multiple pattern in the sonnets triggers a reaction in the reader which tempts him to continue expanding that pattern, to see Lewis Carroll's White Queen as part of Omar Khayyam's pattern of days and nights, to watch the chessmen work out their destiny against the background of Stendhal's *The Red and the Black*, to see himself on the chessboard through the looking-glass of the sonnet.

SHLOMITH RIMMON-KENAN

Doubles and Counterparts:
"The Garden of Forking Paths"

That the governing structural principle of Jorge Luis Borges' "The Garden of Forking Paths" is the analogy among fictional levels goes almost without saying. In the fashion of Chinese boxes, many parallels are established between the characters Yu Tsun, Stephen Albert, and Ts'ui Pên, forming a chain that modern psychoanalysis would call "intersubjective repetition."

Pên's novel is a labyrinth, a "garden of forking paths"; Albert's garden abounds in zigzagging footways and, like Borges' own story, is named "the garden of forking paths" after the title of Pên's novel (or is it only a metaphor for the novel?). On the way to Albert's house, Tsun must turn always to the left, following a road that "fork[s]," as one goes in order to discover the central point of certain labyrinths. Labyrinths are familiar to Tsun since he grew up in a symmetrical garden of Hai Feng, and like the garden, a certain Fang is mentioned in Albert's explanation to Tsun of Pên's mystery. War dictates Tsun's behavior, and war is described in the contradictory chapters of Pên's novel. To write that novel, Ts'ui Pên retired to "the Pavilion of the Limpid Solitude," and Albert, upon meeting the narrator, says, "I see that the pious Hsi P'êng persists in correcting my solitude." Similarly, Ts'ui Pên was murdered by "the hand of a stranger," and Albert, too, is killed by "a stranger, one Yu Tsun," who is himself about to be hanged for that crime. Yu Tsun is Chinese, a former professor of English at the service of a Western power, and Albert, an English professor of sinology, puts himself at the service of a Chinese labyrinth/book. In explaining Pên's concept of diverse futures to Yu Tsun, Albert gives the example of the different possible outcomes, all simultaneously maintained in

From *Critical Inquiry* 6, no. 4 (Summer 1980). © 1980 by The University of Chicago.

Pên's fiction, of an encounter between a certain Fang and a stranger who calls at his door and whom Fang resolves to kill. This is obviously analogous to the events of the diegesis, but it also reverses them; for in the example it is Fang who resolves to kill the stranger, whereas in the diegesis it is the stranger who intends to kill Albert. However, the result in the example, as Albert says, may be different from the intention and thus may parallel the events of the diegesis. And the pattern of analogy and reversal thus created is itself similar to the mutually contradictory chapters of Pên's novel which, in turn, resemble the opposed accounts of the First World War by Liddell Hart and the narrator in Borges' own story.

The above are the most conspicuous examples of a principle of analogy which, I believe, is almost self-evident. What is less self-evident is that the analogies between the diegetic and the metadiegetic levels of narration function to collapse classical oppositions either by identifying them with each other or by rendering them interchangeable. Thus a message addressed to the public becomes esoteric, whereas an esoteric transmission appears in a public medium; the best form of revelation is omission, while the most effective method of concealment is exposure; the same speech act is both a success and a failure; speech itself (or writing) is shown to be an action, and action, in turn, becomes a form of speech (or writing); time is characterized both by the uniqueness of transitory moments and by the (time-negating) eternity of repetition; and these repetitions simultaneously disintegrate and define the self.

Both Ts'ui Pên and Yu Tsun are faced with the task of transmitting a message, and both do so through indirection. Pên's message is a philosophy of time and is addressed to "the various futures (not to all)" in the form of a book, a public medium. Nevertheless, as Albert acutely perceives, it is Pên's belief that the most effective form of revelation is omission:

> "*The Garden of Forking Paths* is an enormous riddle, or parable, whose theme is time; this recondite cause prohibits its mention. To omit a word always, to resort to inept metaphors and obvious periphrases, is perhaps the most emphatic way of stressing it."

Such concealment for the sake of revelation turns a work written for the public into an esoteric message, deciphered only by one person: Stephen Albert. Is Pên's speech act then infelicitous through its failure to utter crucial words, meaningful to all appropriate participants? Yes and no. From a conventional point of view, Pên does not succeed in imparting his thought to the large, though selective, audience he had in mind. But because of Albert's discovery and the triple identification it effects between himself, Pên, and Tsun, the famous novelist succeeds not merely in discursively conveying his view of time but in dramatizing it through live repetition.

Unlike Pên's novel, intended for the many and decoded by one, Tsun's secret information is meant for one person only. But because of the absence of normal communication channels, it is addressed to the many. The spy-narrator pointedly formulates his predicament by the use of oxymoron:

> If only my mouth, before a bullet shattered it, could cry out that secret name so it could be heard in Germany . . . My human voice was very weak. How might I make it carry to the ear of the Chief?

Crying out a secret, and doing so without being heard; both tasks seem paradoxical and infeasible. And yet, the solution devised by Yu Tsun is no less paradoxical than the problem with which it is intended to deal. It resolves the oxymoron by reasserting it. Yu Tsun decides that the best way to transmit the secret is by crying it out, by making it appear in the newspapers. Whereas Ts'ui Pên believes that the most effective method of revelation is omission, Yu Tsun discovers, rather like the queen and the minister in Poe's "The Purloined Letter," that the best form of concealment is exposure, or rather pseudoexposure, since the newspaper item, formally available to everyone, is here used as a code whose real import can be deciphered only by the appropriate person. For the sake of his message's double status, Tsun devises a speech act of referring or naming from which the crucial "utterance of R" is missing and, in the fashion of Pên's novel, replaced by "inept metaphors." Nothing is said about the British artillery park, but the murder of the sinologist who carries the same name as that park is a metaphoric disclosure of the secret to the initiated. A city is named by killing a man—an indirect speech act, successful from the viewpoint of the Chief, guilt-provoking for its ingenious and insincere performer.

It is not only the indirectness of Pên's and Tsun's speech acts and the inverse relations they entertain between concealment and revelation that make the two episodes mirror images of each other. The constituent elements of speech acts, speech and action, are also interestingly juxtaposed and equated in these episodes. On both occasions—the one diegetic the other metadiegetic, the one concerned with a book the other with a crime—speech and action are first presented as separate activities and are then equated with each other. At the metadiegetic level, we are told by Stephen Albert that the famous Ts'ui Pên renounced worldly power "in order to compose a book and a maze." The "and" leads us, as it has led Pên's relatives and admirers, to believe that he had two projects in mind: the verbal act of writing and the physical act of constructing a labyrinth. This misleading impression is reinforced by memories of the spy-narrator, himself a descendant of Ts'ui Pên. His illustrious great-grandfather, he recalls, retired "to write a novel that might be even more populous than the *Hung Lu Meng* and to construct a labyrinth in which all men would become lost." The "and" again acts as a *leurre*, further developed by the narrator's explanation that Ts'ui Pên devoted thirteen years "to these heterogeneous tasks." No one discovered the labyrinth after Pên's death, and the book was found to be incomprehensible and self-contradictory. It fell to the British sinologist, Stephen Albert, to solve the mysteries of the loss of the maze and the incoherence of the novel by postulating an identity of the seemingly "heterogeneous tasks": "the book and the maze were one and the same thing." To write, for Pên, is to construct a labyrinth; speech is action.

At the diegetic level, an analogous situation occurs. Two newspaper items which initially seem disparate prove in fact to be intimately related: the Germans' bombing of the city of Albert and the murder of the British sinologist by a stranger. No one but the "stranger"—the narrator—and the Chief of Berlin knew that the murder of Albert was the only way of imparting to Germany "the secret name of the city they must attack." The bombing is a result of the killing, and the murder itself is an action which replaces impossible speech— impossible because of the war conditions and the imminent arrest of the spy-narrator. Thus whereas at the metadiegetic level speech is seen as action, here action is seen as speech; the two episodes reflect each other as if in inverted mirrors.

This interchangeability of speech and action can easily be juxtaposed with post-Borges attempts to subordinate one to the other. Both speech-act theory and semiotics make such attempts, though with mutually opposed intents: while the former sees speech as a kind of action, semiotics views action as a type of language. Nor is this merely a semantic difference or a shift in emphasis. The disagreement is in both world view—Do we inhabit a verbal world or a world governed by action?—and methodology—Should linguistics become the stock of models for translinguistic practices or should it derive its own models from some other sign system? These are stimulating questions in themselves, but for the purpose of my study it is more profitable to note that Borges, like Ts'ui Pên, refuses to choose between the two contrary positions. In his story both views are correct: speech is action and action is speech.

A correlation emerges between this equation and the paradoxical treatment of another classical opposition, one that is prominent in the whole of Borges' work as well as in that of his fictional labyrinth producer: time versus timelessness. At first sight it may seem that language parallels timelessness, whereas action is time-bound. By its very nature a sign is reproducible, capable of being repeated by different people in different circumstances at different periods, hence time transcending and in a sense "eternal." On the other hand, action, and in particular a radical action like murder, is irreversible, irreproducible, and hence bound to the flux of time. But the story shows that just as speech and action can be identified with each other so can each of them manifest both the transitory and the eternal, and time itself must paradoxically be both negated and affirmed. For, to start with the language end of the equation, although it is true that a sign transcends time through repetition, it is also true that no repeated occurrence is identical with another, since the context in which the sign appears automatically changes it. This double nature of the sign is utilized by the narrator: it is precisely because the word "Albert" can be repeated in different circumstances that the narrator can refer uniquely to the object he intends (the city) through the one quality this object shares with another, that is, its name. But it is only because the referent of this name changes with the context that Tsun can disguise his reference and make it indicate one thing to the Chief and an entirely different thing to the ordinary newspaper reader.

In principle, Tsun's reference could have been made verbally; but owing to the specific conditions in which Tsun finds himself, it must be replaced by action. And action, it would seem, is bound to the moment of its performance. Endorsing this view, the narrator emphatically declares:

> Then I reflected that everything happens to a man precisely, precisely *now*. Centuries of centuries and only in the present do things happen; countless men in the air, on the face of the earth and the sea, and all that really is happening is happening to me.

As if sharing the narrator's view, the diegesis (narrated, of course, by the same person) emphasizes the transitory, moment-bound nature of events by making Albert's death "instantaneous." And if action is instantaneous, occurring only in the present, it has no past and no future, no prospect of being changed or repeated—hence the emphasis on expressions of finality, such as "inexorable death," "irrevocable determination," and "irretrievable details."

Given such expressions, how do we explain the presence of expressions like "innumerable," "infinite," and "various futures"? If Albert's death is really bound to the moment of occurrence, how can we account for the narrator's "innumerable contrition and weariness"? If the details of Pên's book are indeed "irretrievable," how has Albert "re-established" their "primordial organization"? And if everything happens only in the present, how could Ts'ui Pên "create a labyrinth which would be strictly infinite," illustrating "an infinite series of times" and "innumerable futures"? Action, it seems, is paradoxically both bound to the moment of performance, hence transitory and irrevocable, and capable of "continuing indefinitely," being reestablished or repeated, and hence time transcending. On the one hand, "everything happens to a man precisely, precisely now," and on the other, "*the author of an atrocious undertaking ought to imagine that he has already accomplished it, ought to impose upon himself a future as irrevocable as the past.*" Not only can the future be imagined as a past, but both dimensions are grasped as a proliferation of several alternatives rather than as uniform, absolute times. "In one of the possible pasts," says Albert to Yu Tsun, "you are my enemy, in another, my friend," and "Time forks perpetually toward innumerable futures. In one of them I am your enemy." Pên's book dramatizes this divergence of times by its self-contradictory narrative technique: "in the third chapter the hero dies, in the fourth he is alive." And the narrator subtly does a similar thing when he describes Albert's face a short time before his death as having "something unalterable about it, even immortal." In one future he is going to die, but in another he is immortal; only the dead cannot die.

Perhaps the most striking way in which action can transcend time is by the coincidence or repetition of the same occurrence in different temporal dimensions and/or in the lives of different people. In an article which bears the appropriately paradoxical title "A New Refutation of Time," Borges describes such a duplication and comments: "Time, if we can intuitively grasp such an identity, is a delusion: the difference and inseparability of one moment belonging to its apparent past from another belonging to its apparent present is sufficient to disintegrate it." Thus the various analogies between Pên, Albert, and Tsun function to disintegrate time through mirroring and repetition.

These analogies also disintegrate the concept of self or identity. Consistent with the pattern which governs all opposites in the story, however, the self is both lost through an identification with the other and at the same time more authentically defined by it. The phenomenon of repetition described in "A New Refutation of Time" serves to deny not only temporal succession but also the autonomy of the self:

> We can postulate, in the mind of an individual (or of two individuals who do not know of each other but in whom the same process works), two identical moments. Once this identity is postulated, one may ask: Are not these identical moments the same? Is not one single repeated term sufficient to break down and confuse the series of time? Do not the fervent readers who surrender themselves to Shakespeare become, literally, Shakespeare?

Like the fervent readers of Shakespeare, Albert becomes Ts'ui Pên through his devoted discovery of Pên's labyrinth, so much so that like Pên he is murdered by a stranger. In being killed by Tsun, Albert is revealed as a victim of the same device he so ingeniously unearthed in Pên's work, and Tsun, in turn, duplicates Albert by using the same technique in an inverted form. Significantly, Tsun is also the great grandson of Ts'ui Pên, and his thoughts before reaching

Albert become, in retrospect, a divination of Pên's secret as formulated by the British sinologist: "I [Tsun] thought of a labyrinth of labyrinths, of one sinuous spreading labyrinth that would encompass the past and the future and in some way involve the stars." The identification thus becomes threefold, and the self is to some extent lost in the other.

Analogy among characters is not the only structural device which blurs the boundaries of the self. The very repetition of the act of narration, involving a chain of quotations, makes the story a perfect example of what Jakobson calls "speech within speech" and divorces the various characters from their own discourse. In addition to the real author's speech to the real reader, crystallized in that of the implied author to the implied reader, the whole story is the speech of an extradiegetic-heterodiegetic narrator who, in the footnote, calls himself "editor" and who sums up Liddell Hart's account and juxtaposes it with Yu Tsun's dictated statement. Just as the editor quotes Tsun, so Tsun, an extradiegetic-homodiegetic narrator, quotes Albert who in turn quotes Ts'ui Pên, sometimes verbatim, as in the case of the crucial letter, sometimes by conjecture, as in the instance of Pên's supposed declarations about the book and the maze. Quotation, then, is a dominant narrative mode in this story, and quotation is the appropriation by one person of the speech of another. Since a person is to a large extent constituted by his discourse, such an appropriation implies, at least partly, an interpenetration of personalities. Thus both repetition through analogy and repetition through quotation threaten the absolute autonomy of the self.

Or do they? Is not a sinologist most truly a sinologist when he identifies himself with the object of his research? And is not a spy most truly a spy when he obliterates his own personality in an identification with another? Tsun's colleague does this by changing his name: "The Prussian spy Hans Rabener, alias Viktor Runeberg." And Tsun himself acts in complete opposition to his real emotions. He endangers himself for the Chief in Berlin, "that sick and hateful man," he risks his life for Germany while "car[ing] nothing for a barbarous country which imposed upon [him] the abjection of being a spy," and he kills "a man from England—a modest man—who for [him] is no less great than Goethe," kills him and feels "innumerable contrition and weariness." He has indeed bidden farewell to himself in the mirror figuratively as well as literally, and in so doing he has become a successful spy. But the identification with Albert is not limited to a definition of the narrator's role as a spy. It also defines something essential to the real face in the mirror, something which is to a large extent responsible for his decision to associate himself with Berlin. "I didn't do it for Germany," he says, "I did it because I sensed that the Chief somehow feared people of my race—for the innumerable ancestors who merge within me. I wanted to prove to him that a yellow man could save his armies." And it is precisely the culture of his ancestors that is "being restored to [him] by a man of a remote empire, in the course of a desperate adventure, on a Western isle." The identification with Albert, it transpires, leads to an identification with Ts'ui Pên, and this return to his ancestors most intimately determines an essential aspect of Tsun's authentic personality.

Thus the same phenomenon of repetition which disintegrates the autonomy of the individual also defines it, and Borges is far from being unaware of this paradox. After a dazzling discussion of time and the self in "A New Refutation of Time" he concludes:

> *And yet, and yet* . . . Denying temporal succession, denying the self, denying the astronomical universe, are apparent desperations and secret consolations. Our destiny (as contrasted with the hell of Swedenborg and the hell of Tibetan mythology) is not frightful by being unreal; it is frightful because it is irreversible and iron-clad. Time is the substance I am made of. Time is a river which sweeps me along, but I am the river; it is a tiger which destroys me, but I am the tiger; it is a fire which consumes me, but I am the fire. The world, unfortunately, is real; I, unfortunately, am Borges.

The real "scandal" in this story, I suggest, is not merely the disintegration of classical notions but the simultaneous denial and affirmation of a given concept and the interchangeability of mutually opposed ones. The world thus created is one which constantly, vigorously, and ingeniously courts paradox. And what can one expect when an irresistible force flirts with an immovable object?

RICARDO GUTIÉRREZ-MOUAT

The Center of the Labyrinth

"writing is the destruction of every voice, of every point of origin . . ."
—BARTHES, "The Death of the Author"

"Tlön, Uqbar, Orbis tertius," perhaps Borges' most anthologized story, narrates the interjection of one world into another or, to be more precise, of a *fictitious* world into the order of reality. The fabulous planet of Tlön is a fiction contrived by an obscure collectivity of scriptors who record in a meticulous encyclopedia the planet's topography and metaphysics, its languages and literatures. The anonymity of the authors is in accord with the literary orthodoxy of Tlön, where

> The idea of a single subject is . . . all-powerful. It is uncommon for books to be signed. The concept of plagiarism does not exist: it has been established that all works are the creation of one author, who is atemporal and anonymous.

One of the more notorious wonders catalogued in the encyclopedia is the *hronir*, a category of objects which materialize out of the imagination and which exist in multiple versions of themselves, much like the encyclopedia that records them, itself a revised edition of a nebulous original. The typical self-referentiality of Borges' narrative is patent: the *hronir* and the encyclopedia are both avatars or transformations of the ultimate referent, that is, of the Borgesian text itself, also a product of the imagination inserted into reality and characteristically a labyrinth without a center, a writing without a signature (or with a false one).

The Borgesian text displays this *ex-centricity* in the same evident manner as it displays the artifice of fiction. In some of the stories the motif of the

From *Romance Notes* 21, no. 2 (Winter 1980). © 1980 by the University of North Carolina.

fallacious center operates at the level of *histoire*, a case in point being "The Library of Babel" in which a futile search is undertaken for the Book of Books. In others, such as "Pierre Menard, Author of the Quixote," the narrative voice shifts uneasily and gradually from a tone of parody to direct statement, thus questioning the possibility of a central, authoritative voice to articulate the text. Still in others, the labyrinth with its tantalizing center appears as a structural paradigm. In "The Approach to Al-Mu'tasim" a law student searches for the eponymous character by pursuing his radiant reflection in other people. When this oblique, indirect approach is about to culminate the "novel comes to its end." There is no revelation but only the *imminence* of one which, of course, is Borges' tentative definition of the aesthetic phenomenon. Neither is the perverse symmetry of labyrinths absent from this text: the law student's search is *doubled* by the reviewer's search for an analogous kind of center: Mir Bahadur Ali's novel, in itself a double of Borges' text since they both have the same title. The circumlocutory reviewer arrives at the novel in question indirectly, after a textual periple whose stages are the two published reviews quoted by him. The arrival at the center, however, is problematic: the novel exists in two versions and, furthermore, it is an "uneasy combination" of an Islamic allegory and a detective story.

This structure of displacements, curiously enough, is also apparent in some of Borges' essays, particularly in "A Note on (toward) Bernard Shaw," whose self-correcting title should alert the careful reader as to the shifting, unstable quality of the text. Borges opens the essay by enumerating diachronically the different formulations of an idea, that of "making metaphysics and the arts into a kind of play with combinations." This idea, which implies the exhaustion of literature, is then questioned by Borges: "Literature is not exhaustible, for the sufficient and simple reason that no single book is." After further elaboration of this position, the discredited idea is restated in order to submit it to another dialectical attack: "If literature were nothing more than verbal algebra, anyone could produce any book by essaying variations." But the new attack is mounted by way of a detour, since Borges does not choose a writer as his object-lesson but a philosopher:

> The lapidary formula "Everything flows" abbreviates in two words the philosophy of Heraclitus: Raymond Lully would say that, with the first word given, it would be sufficient to essay the intransitive verbs to discover the second and obtain, thanks to methodical chance, that philosophy and many others. Here it is fitting to reply that the formula obtained by this process of elimination would lack all value and even meaning; for it to have some virtue we must conceive it in terms of Heraclitus, in terms of an experience of

Heraclitus, even though "Heraclitus" is nothing more than the presumed subject of that experience.

It is clear that in order to dispute again the idea of literature as a combinatorial exercise Borges postulates the *existence* of the author and a genetic relationship between author and text, at which point the elusive Bernard Shaw is introduced:

> Can an author create characters superior to himself? I would say no and in that negation include both the intellectual and the moral. I believe that from us cannot emerge creatures more lucid or more noble than our best moments. It is on this opinion that I base my conviction of Shaw's pre-eminence.

This defense of the author's rights (of his copyright) seems blatantly to contradict Borges' literary theory and praxis. But the antithesis ceases to be so radical when one realizes that Borges' *apologia pro auctore* is itself contradicted a few lines below its postulation:

> The biography of Bernard Shaw by Frank Harris contains an admirable letter by the former, from which I copy the following words: "I understand everything and everyone." From this nothingness . . . Bernard Shaw educed almost innumerable persons or dramatis personae: the most ephemeral of these is, I suspect, that G.B.S. who represented him in public and who lavished in the newspaper columns so many facile witticisms.

The essayistic text, then, is structured as some of Borges' fictions: there is an indirect, circuitous approach to its central theme (Bernard Shaw) followed by a postulation of a center: Bernard Shaw as author or creator of characters, but this center is immediately subverted when Bernard Shaw appears as one of his own characters, dispossessed of authorial autonomy, of authority. His condition thus resembles that of Shakespeare and also of God, the ultimate Author:

> The voice of the Lord answered from a whirlwind: "Neither am I anyone; I have dreamt the world as you dreamt your work, my Shakespeare, and among the forms in my dream are you, who like myself are many and no one."

The disappearance of the author in Borges liberates the text to an infinite play of allusions in the "homogeneous and reversible space of literature," that is, it defers its meaning both intratextually (by means of displacements and self-corrections) and intertextually. Like the nebulous land of Uqbar, the Borgesian text cannot be bounded nor its origin determined. To read it induces a perplexity and an uneasiness similar to those experienced by the readers of volume XLVI of the *Anglo-American Cyclopedia*: "Reading over again, we discovered beneath its rigorous prose a fundamental vagueness." Borges' reader cannot situate himself at the center of the text. A classic mode of passage to that center afforded by the realist or psychological novel is the character, but the character in Borges is undermined by a series of techniques which disfigure, mask, or fragment him, precluding any identification with the reader: Pierre Menard is a character presented through a bibliography; Pedro Damian's identity in "The Other Death" is lost in the labyrinths of time and memory; the narrator in "Tlön, Uqbar, Orbis Tertius" admonishes that the story he is narrating is "not the story of my emotions but of Uqbar and Tlön and Orbis Tertius," and when he records his personal reaction to the *First Encyclopedia of Tlön* he does so indirectly, by means of a literary allusion. Along with the questioning of character one must consider the anxiety produced by the intimidating erudite apparatus which Borges typically sets in motion, for regardless of his cultural baggage no single reader will be able to reconstruct the heterogeneous body of citations which occupies the space of the text and blocks access to its center.

If the Borgesian text exists in that shifting space between an author and a reader who are both unable to claim it, it is because the experience Borges writes about is primarily the experience of reading. Since reading always involves a previous writing, writing can only be re-writing, a predicament which Borges readily acknowledges. When asked about *Ficciones* in a recent interview, for example, he replies: "Oh, I think it's made of half-forgotten memories. I wonder if there is a single original line in the book." In "Borges and I" he declares that the legitimate space of the text is that of language and tradition, both peculiarly mobile entities. One might recall that in the languages of Tlön nouns are unknown; they are either replaced by impersonal verbs or constructed by an arbitrary and theoretically infinite accumulation of adjectives. This conception of a language perennially in flux (doubled at the end of the story by a revision of an "uncertain" Quevedian translation of *Urn Burial*) has a counterpart in Borges' conception of tradition. Pierre Menard's re-writing of the *Quijote* results in a richer, more provocative text, not only because three centuries of history have elapsed, but also because Pierre Menard, a peripheral French symbolist, has arrived at the *Quijote* through Valéry, D'Annunzio, Leibniz, and other writers not available to the initial readers of Cervantes nor to Cervantes as reader. These successors of the Spanish novelist deflect the reading of his work just as Kafka modifies the reading of Browning and Lord Dunsany, his unsuspecting precursors.

Devoid of a center around which to assemble itself, the Borgesian text cannot but allude to its own absence. Like Pierre Menard's invisible masterpiece,

Ts'ui Pên's impossible novel, or Hladik's secret miracle, Borges' *écriture* would seem to claim a paradoxical poetics of silence for its realization. If every text is a tissue of anonymous, untraceable citations, of "quotations without inverted commas," the *visible* writing of Jorge Luis Borges, lucidly aware of its absent center, by naming the citations and restoring the commas, erects a frame of reference that is self-consciously literary and in which it is possible to show an absence, to articulate a silence.

Borges' Ultraist Poetry

Beginning in 1919 when he met some of the contributors to the first ultraist publication, *Grecia*, in Seville and continuing through the next two years in Madrid, Borges "collaborated" with the Ultra movement in Spain; and he did so at a high pitch of enthusiasm. As might be expected, this early eagerness to join the movement, and his important role there as theorizer and as translator of other European vanguardists, affected some of his own earliest poems, which do reflect the new avant-garde ideals. While in Spain Borges regularly published, in the avant-garde magazines *Grecia, Ultra* and *Tableros*, poems with either ultraist or expressionist traits.

Though clearly not a committed expressionist poet even at that time, Borges' interest in translating those German poets also led him to produce his own versions of that type of verse. He did not share their experiences of intergenerational and sociological upheaval, nor did he have any direct involvement with the first world war; but despite his own sheltered personal situation the expressionist poems that he wrote compare favorably with the Germans' efforts. If they must be considered as imitative works, they are excellent copies and are of better quality than the finger exercises one expects from a beginner.

"Rusia," ["Russia"], a poem which shows to what extent expressionism left its mark on Borges, was published in the magazine *Ultra* in 1921; it was probably intended to have a niche in the never-to-be-published collection from his years in Spain, *Salmos rojos* [*Red Psalms*] ("red" referring to the 1917 Soviet Revolution and "Psalms" to the Judaic inclinations of the "Master," Cansinos Asséns).

From *Borges' Ultraist Movement and its Poets.* © 1981 by International Book Publishing, Inc.

Russia

La trinchera avanzada es en la estepa un barco al
    abordaje con gallardetes de hurras
mediodías estallan en los ojos
Bajo estandartes de silencio pasan las muchedumbres
y el sol crucificado en los ponientes
se pluraliza en la vocinglería de las torres del Kremlin.
El mar vendrá nadando a esos ejércitos
que envolverán sus torsos
en todas las praderas del continente.
En el cuerpo salvaje de un arco iris clamemos su gesta
bayonetas
que portan en la punta las mañanas.

[Russia

The advance trench is in the steppe, a boat
    to be boarded with pennants of yells
middays explode in the eyes.
Multitudes pass under banners of silence
and the sun crucified on the western horizon
is pluralized in the shouting from the Kremlin towers.
The sea shall come swimming to those armies
that will wrap their bodies
over the prairies of the continent.
In the savage body of a rainbow let us cry out their geste
bayonets
which carry mornings on their points.]

War and its associated terminology fill the poem. From the metaphor of the first line, with its startling juxtapositions of distant realities (the trench is a boat to be boarded with pennants of yells), violence prevails. The expressionist use of nature to reflect and crystalize the poets' anguish provides the basis for many of these images of violence. Middays *explode*, the sun is *crucified* and "pluralized" in the *shouting* from Kremlin towers. The rainbow's *savage body* represents the cry for [bayonet-carried] mornings. The middle image (lines 6–8) stands out for its lack of overt violence. The personified sea swims to the troops who, though dead, so dominate the scene that they have the power to wrap themselves in all the meadows of the continent. The extreme understatement of these images (the swimming sea and the meadows suggest only peacefulness) belies the true violence that has been done to the dead soldiers. This reversal of expected descriptions presents, in violent terms, nature just going about its business; and a scene of mass death in a peaceful setting prefigures the irony that will become so prevalent in all of Borges' subsequent work. Here, however, the effect of irony is not humorous; the litote emphasizes the pathetic result of violence (a violence integral to the poem's theme, as opposed to the often gratuitous harshness used by the dadaists and futurists to underscore their artistic rebelliousness).

Borges has other early poems in this vein, such as "Trinchera" ["Trench"] and "Gesta Maximalista" ["Maximalist Geste"], and expressionist images are used in other, more cosmopolitan, poems: "with guns on their shoulders the streetcars/patrol the avenues," in "Tranvías" ["Streetcars"] for example. Far removed in his personal situation from the actual violence, Borges "as a foreigner, feels the pain of war less deeply and takes greater pleasure in an occasional metaphorical discovery." Experimentation with metaphors, integral to the expressionist poems, continues in his other early pieces such as "Aldea" ["Village"], a poem more in tune with those he will write in Buenos Aires a few years later. In fact, this and "Sala vacía" ["Empty Drawing Room"] (originally published in *Grecia* in 1920) represent the only items of poetry from the years in Spain that will be published in Borges' first collection of poems. A tinge of expressionism remains, but ultraist technique, combined with Borges' own sensitivity, give this poem the qualities that he will be developing in *Fervor de Buenos Aires* [*Buenos Aires' Fervor*].

Aldea

El poniente de pie como un Arcángel
tiranizó el sendero
La soledad repleta como un sueño
      se he remansado al derredor del pueblo
Las esquilas recogen la tristeza
dispersa de las tardes
        la luna nueva
es una vocecita bajo el cielo
      Según va anocheciendo
vuelve a ser campo el pueblo.

[Village

The west wind on foot like an Archangel
tyrannized the pathway
Solitude full as a dream
      has formed an eddy around the town

> The small bells gather in the afternoons
> scattered sadness
>   the new moon
> is a little voice under the sky
>   As it grows dark
> the town turns again into country.]

Expressionist influence is obvious at the beginning of the poem in the personified natural element (the west wind on foot), the religious reference ("Like an Archangel"), and the violence of the action described ("tyrannized"). But then a passiveness, which will predominate in most of Borges' poetry from this point on, sets in. Isolated human emotions—solitude and sadness—are made concrete. Solitude, "full as a dream," has formed an eddy; treated as if it were tangible, like water, the image almost forms a visible pool of solitude. In a similar manner, sadness (which here is a property of, and personifies, "afternoons") is "gathered in" by the little bells which in turn are governed by the moon personified into a "little voice." The emotions herded away under the tyranny of the wind, the town now ceases to affect its surroundings and blends once again into the countryside.

"Aldea" fits Borges' definition of correct ultraist poetry: metaphors reign supreme within the free verse setting. He manages to "synthesize two images into one," fulfilling another prime value of ultraism: solitude is like a dream and is also dammed up like water while sadness is both a property of afternoon (and of the people in the village) and something to be herded up. All of the images in the poem are made up of "distant realities" (there is no expected or logical connection between "moon" and "little voices," for example). The starkness of both the images and the poem's language contrasts completely with *modernista* verse, to which he is already showing a complete aversion. The overall serenity which the poem evokes fits into the ideal of dehumanized structural purity, although the emotional unity which that serenity gives the poem is an unexpected quality because of the usual avant-garde proscription of sentiment. The overriding sense of tranquility, however, gives "Aldea" a validity which an otherwise uncohesive string of metaphors would not necessarily have. Because it is so successful as a poem, Borges deigns to preserve this single sample from his Spanish experience of ultraism in his first collection published in Buenos Aires in 1923, although for some reason he changes its title to "Campos atardecidos"—from "Village" to "Fields in the Dusk."

Borges continues to spread the avant-garde message after his return to Argentina and successfully recruits a number of talented poets to the ultraist ranks. The "banner waver's" own first book of poetry, however, produced a shock wave among his old friends in Spain: they could not believe that he excluded all but one of the earlier poems, and they were surprised at the nature of the new ones. The title of the book itself, along with the themes of the poems it contains, provide sufficient grounds for those ultraists' puzzled reaction. Concern for thematic development does not fit into "pure" ultraism, and the personal and intellectual ambitiousness of Borges' poems do seem to place them at great divergence from the movement. As the title would suggest (it either indicates Borges' affection for Buenos Aires, or is a personification of the city's *élan*: Buenos Aires' fervor), Borges' home city is a central concern in many of the poems. Other themes in the collection are love (one poem is dedicated to his "novia [girfriend]," Concepción García), Berkeleyan idealism ("I am the only observer of this street,/if I stopped seeing it, it would die," from the poem "Caminata" ["Long Walk"]) and, pervading the majority of the poems, the topic of time.

As many of Borges' critics (Rodríguez-Monegal, Sucre, Gertel, Stabb, Videla) correctly point out, with this first book of poems he already senses what central ideas are going to preoccupy him in his next half-century of literary creation. Borges himself admits, in spite of his generally negative view of this period in his life, that regarding *Fervor de Buenos Aires*, "looking back on it now, I think I have never strayed beyond that book. I feel that all my subsequent writing has only developed themes first taken up there; I feel that all during my lifetime I have been rewriting that one book." By going against the grain of his own ultraist pronouncements condemning ideological subject matter, Borges both avoids and transcends one of the movement's self-imposed limitations and allows himself freedom to encompass a larger poetic world.

In contrast to that flouting of content limitations, the poems of *Fervor*, in their formation and poetic technique, generally follow Borges' statement that "the two wings" of Ultra poetry should be free verse and the image. As in his earlier poems published in Spain, he continues to use the fantastic, even startling, new type of metaphor which harks back to Gómez de la Serna's *greguerías* and to the theories of Huidobro and Reverdy.

Borges shows, in the poem "Un patio" ["Patio"], his ability to express his thematic concerns—in this case both his love for Buenos Aires and his observations on time—within the ultraist idiom. For Borges the *patio* has a special importance. In an essay from this period with the appropriate title "Buenos Aires," he carefully describes a typical house of the city and singles out the patio as "full of patrician qualities and of primitive efficacy, since it's cemented in the two most fundamental things that exist: in the earth and the sky." The poem elaborates this unique duality.

Un Patio

Con la tarde
se cansaron los dos o tres colores del patio.

La gran franqueza de la luna llena
ya no entusiasma su habitual firmamento.
Hoy que está crespo el cielo
dirá la agorería que ha muerto un angelito.
Patio, cielo encauzado.
El patio es la ventana
por donde Dios mira las almas.
El patio es el declive
por el cual se derrama el cielo en la casa.
Serena
la enternidad espera en la encrucijada de estrellas.
Lindo es vivir en la amistad oscura
de un zaguán, de un alero y de un aljibe.

[Patio

With afternoon
the two or three colors of the patio got tired.
The full moon's great frankness
no longer makes enthusiastic its habitual firmament.
The angry sky will tell a fortune today,
that an angel died.
Patio, bedded sky.
The sky is the window
through which God watches the souls.
The patio is the slope
down which the sky is slid into the house.
Serene
eternity waits at the juncture of the stars.
It is lovely to live in the dark friendship
of entryway, eaves and cistern.]

In its formation the poem displays "the two wings" of ultraist technique with its free verse and its unbroken series of images. In the first group of three images (lines 1–6) Borges uses personification, the most frequently occurring poetic recourse in *Fervor*: the colors *got tired*, the moon's *frankness* no longer *makes enthusiastic* its "*habitual* firmament," and the *angry* sky will *tell a fortune*. In the second grouping of three metaphor-based images, each begins with an anaphora, restating the title (lines 7–11). The patio (is) the *bedded* (as in river bed) *sky*, it is "*the window* through which God watches the souls" and it is "*the slope* down which the sky is slid into the house." For the final images he returns to personification: "*serene* eternity *waits* at the juncture of the stars"; and in the last lines the three parts of the patio, the entryway, eaves and cistern offer "dark friendship."

In versions of this poem republished after 1943, Borges eliminates lines five and six and lines eight and nine; such a removal of almost all of the other references to God or divinity in fact represents one of the major elements in his revisions of this first book of his. That a confessed near-atheist would remove references to divinity causes no surprise; but the question does arise as to why he included them in the first place, even as a young man. Two possibilities suggest themselves: one is the latent expressionist influence and its "search for God" component; the other is an apparent modishness for religious elements, which receives support from the ultraists' intentions to do away with symbolist mythological tropes. Of the four worn-out *modernista* adjectives pointed out for scorn in the *Prisma* manifesto (ineffable, divine, blue, mysterious), for example, only "divine" escapes execution in Borges' essay "Ejecución de tres palabras" ("Execution of three words") from *Inquisiciones* [*Inquisitions*]. And in an essay from *El tamaño de mi esperanza* [*The Measure of My Hope*] (1926), "Historia de los Angeles" ["History of Los Angeles"], he underscores the aversion to symbolist tropes, but singles out the divine exception:

> Man's imagination has come up with a number of monsters (tritons, hippogriffs, chimeras, sea serpents, unicorns, devils, dragons, "lobisones," cyclops, fauns, basiliscs, semigods, leviathans, and a host of others) and all of them have disappeared except for the angels. Nowadays what verse would dare to mention the phoenix or to provide a path for a centaur? None; but for any poetry, however modern it might be, it is not out of place to be a nest for angels and to glow with their light. I always imagine them at nightfall, in the late afternoons of the suburbs or out in the open country, in that long and quiet instant in which things stand out alone with their backs to the sunset and in which the different colors seem like memories or presentiments of other colors.

A certain faddishness might then explain the inclusion of divine references in the *Fervor* poems in general (God was "in" that season), but "Un patio" loses strength especially with the second omission. Since the first set of three images merely sets the tone of the poem the following series of three metaphors in the original version have the important function of showing the patio's uniqueness and centrality through the anaphora which reinforces its role; and that reinforcement comes not only from the repetition, but also from the progressive description of the patio's cosmic capabilities. The first of the metaphors explains succinctly the special role for the patio which Borges expresses in a more prolix manner in another *Fervor* poem, "Cercanías" ("Neighborhoods"): "the Moham-medan patios/full of ancestrality and efficacy,/since they are cemented/in the two most fundamental things that exist:/in the earth and the sky."

In "Un patio" Borges expresses this linking function of the patio in his three word metaphor ("patio, cielo encauzado"); the bed, earthbound, holds the sky. As holder of the sky, the patio becomes God's opening into the lives which the house holds, and by means of the patio the sky "slides into" or pervades the house. The sky, which he has just linked with the house through its patio, represents what is timeless for Borges. In his many later treatments of the topic of time, Borges as essayist shows time to be a human phenomenon, and therefore limited to the earth. But the sky is free from the limitations imposed by earthly temporality, a situation which Borges infers when he follows the sky-patio metaphors with the personified status of the eternity which waits serenely in the juncture of the stars. As a result of these two images, which associate the patio with the sky, eternity becomes an aspect of the patio (representative here of "lo criollo" and "lo bonairense"). Thus far Borges has led the reader through a progressive description of the patio—as holder of the afternoon's colors, as the moon's habitat, as the sky's bed, as the conductor of the sky into the house itself, and as a result of this last function his patio endows the whole house with an eternal character.

At this point in the poem it looks as if Borges implies that the eternity admitted into the house will affect its inhabitants as well ("God looks on their souls," after all), and possibly will allow them all an escape from his recurrent nemesis, time. But after this grand progression through the cosmic characteristics of a Buenos Aires house, the final two lines of the poem serve as a typically Borgesian disclaimer: it's nice to live in the dark friendship of an entryway, eaves and a cistern. He has had to give up his cosmic idealizations and has returned to the mundane reality of his familiar home.

Borges uses ultraist technique to present this cosmic-mundane, metaphysical and affectionate interrelationship. Such an intellectual exercise looks like an abandonment of avant-garde ideals, but this procedure represents instead an admirable, if unsanctioned, expansion of the poet's scope, which he achieves while still maintaining accepted avant-garde criteria. The various metaphors for the patio in the poem, made up of unexpected and distant relationships whose "justesse" is established by Borges' metaphysical logic, demonstrate how he uses ultraist technique at a highly sophisticated level.

A more complex and ambitious expansion of poetic expression, but one which still remains within the ultraist mode, occurs in one of the love poems from *Fervor*. "Ausencia" ("Absence") departs from accepted ultraist norms in more ways than the obvious depth of personal emotion which gave the poet his reason for writing it. Borges ridiculed all poetry categorized under the rubric of "rubendarismo" in his ultraist manifestos, and that implied that he was reacting against everything within *modernismo's* all-encompassing umbrella—with its romantic, parnassian and symbolist elements. But Borges shows in this poem a strong affinity for, and possibly a heavy influence from the highly original avatar of Symbolism, Stéphane Mallarmé. The title alone is enough to make the connection to this poet, and the whole poem continues development of the absence theme. "Peindre non la chose, mais l'effet qu'elle produit" (Do not paint the thing itself, but the effect that it produces), Mallarmé's dictum, summarizes the intent of "Ausencia." "The thing," the beloved, is "the absent one," and Borges evokes a series of descriptions of absences in order to ironically underscore the concreteness of their effect.

Ausencia

Habré de levantar la vida inmensa
que aún ahora es tu espejo:
piedra por piedra habré de reconstruirla.
Desde que te alejaste,
cuántos parajes se han tornado vanos
y sin sentido, iguales
a luminarias que arrincona el alba,
cuántas sendas perdieron su fragancia!
Tardes que fueron nichos de tu imagen,
músicas donde siempre me aguardabas,
palabras de aquel tiempo,
habéis de ser quebradas
y a mis manos,
reacias y con dolor.
El vivo cielo inmenso
clama y torna a clamar tu dejamiento.
¿En qué hondonada empozaré mi alma
donde no pueda vigilar tu ausencia
que como un sol terrible sin ocaso
brilla, definitiva e inclemente?
Tu ausencia ciñe el alma
como cuerda que abarca una garganta.

[Absence

I will lift up the immense life
that even now is your mirror:

stone by stone I will reconstruct it.
Since you went away,
so many places have turned shallow
and meaningless, similar
to burning lamps that daybreak corners,
so many paths have lost their fragrance!
Afternoons that were niches of your image,
melodies where you always awaited me,
words of that time,
you all will be broken
in my hands,
reluctant and with pain.
The immense living sky
clamors and clamors again your remoteness.
In which ravine will I throw my soul
where it would not be able to guard your absence
which glares, as a terrible sun without setting,
definitive and inclement?
Your absence girdles the soul
like a cord that encircles a throat.]

The first two lines of the poem could qualify as a "greguería" or as any ultraist's fantastic image; its formation occurs through metonymy and metaphor and the result has the subtlety and suggestive qualities of the best symbolist creations. The poet, instead of referring to the loved one directly, selects an aspect of her, saying he will have to lift, or resuscitate, "the immense life." Her life is her mirror (already Borges uses what will later become one of his own tropes); again he refers not to the real woman but to her image reflected in his mind. Despite the intangibility or irreality of the absent one, the process chosen for reconstructing her memory—"stone by stone"—shows the concrete effect the absence has on him. But conversely, concrete objects in the poem (places, lights, paths) have been drained of any significance.

The next two metaphors (lines 9 and 10) create ethereal effects; intangible afternoons were niches, or solid containments: but for only her image, another intangible which becomes even more etherealized when he describes her as awaiting within the music (Mallarmé's "au creux néant musicien"—in music's hollow void). These intangibles of the senses—afternoons, music, words—again have a concreteness for the poet. All of these elements (words, music, afternoons, paths, lights, places) are the "stones" with which he has reconstructed the "mirror" of the absent one. Despite their vagueness (vanos, sin fragancia) or intangibility these recollections form a concrete effect for the poet, and "they have to be broken" by his hands.

Relief does not come with the breaking of the mirror, that infinite reflector of life. An even more vast and limitless reflector (much like Mallarmé's "tout l'abîme vain éployé—the whole vain abyss outspread), the personified sky, echoes ("proclaims and again proclaims") its own pangs at the loved one's leaving. For the last two images Borges reiterates the real effect of the intangible "ausencia" by bridging it, through simile, to two destructive agents: the sun ("shining without setting, definitive and inclement") and the strangling cord. The last simile, in fact, sums up the whole poem; the effect of one intangible (the absence) overriding another (the soul) has the physically strangling result.

Other examples of Mallarmean metonymy are found in "Sábados" ["Saturdays"] where "our two solitudes" blindly seek each other, and only "the whiteness of your flesh" survives the afternoon ("nuestras dos soledades en la sala severa/se buscan como ciegos./Acallando palabras momentáneas/hablan la angustia y tu pudor y mi anhelo./Sobrevive a la tarde/la blancura de tu carne [In the stark hall our two solitudes/blindly seek each other./Silencing momentary words,/the anguish and your prudence and my longing speak./The whiteness of your flesh/survives the afternoon]"). And, in the so vague as to be unreal comparison in "Calle desconocida" ["Unknown Street"], night is compared not just to the coming of music but to "hoped for" or "awaited" (thus absent) music ("y la venida de la noche se advierte/antes como adveni-miento de música esperada/que como enorme símbolo de nuestra primordial nadería [and the coming of night is recognized/like an awaited music/not as a symbol of an essential insignificance]").

"Ausencia" develops its Mallarmean theme into a vivid and suggestive evocation of the poet's romantic turmoil (this poem more than adequately reminds that even the "cold" and "philosophical" Borges of many later essays and stories was young once). The pattern of alternations between non-concrete to concrete effects ("mirror" to "reconstitute," "afternoons-music-words" to "broken," "absence-soul" to "cord-throat") and the ending with three straight punishing images (the sky screams, the sun glares, the cord encircles) gives cumulative reinforcement to the poet's anguish. Centering the poem around the poet's personal emotional situation goes against the whole avant-garde trend toward "dehumanized" and unsentimental art; but at the same time the *greguería*-like images shine within "Ausencia" as excellent examples of avant-garde technique. Although influence from Mallarmé does not pervade the entire collection, the examples shown provide sufficient evidence that, for Borges, a poem which offers a well-wrought setting for the images it contains justifies the theoretical compromise involved in using the vagueness of symbolist suggestion to evoke the effects of love.

Borges continues to defy the ultraists' desire to avoid personal emotion as a basis for poetry in his second published book of verse, *Luna de enfrente* (*Moon across the Way*) of 1925. As in *Fervor de Buenos Aires*, love is one of the central themes ("Antelación de amor" ["Anticipation of Love"] and "Dualidad de una despedida" ["Duality of a Departure"] stand out), along with other topics he has previously established: affection for Buenos Aires and a preoccupation with time ("time will go on living me/death — dark and unmoving storm — will scatter my hours" underlie several of the poems. And concern for historical or familiar past continues from "Rosas" ["Roses"] and "Inscripción sepulcral" ["Carved on a Tombstone"] in *Fervor* to "Los llanos" ["The Plain"], "El General Quiroga va en coche al muere" ["General Quiroga Rides to His Death in a Carriage"], "Dulcia linquimus arva," and "El año cuarenta" ["The Year Forty"] in *Luna de enfrente*.

Although he does not continue with poems in the Mallarmean vein, the personal tone which was so apparent in "Ausencia" becomes more intense in his second book. In fact, the increasing appearance of his own sentiment in the love poems, in ancestral reminiscences (especially in the last four verses of "Dulcia linquimus arva"), and most jarringly in a post-adolescent world weariness, translates into a confessional poetry which blatantly violates the third anathema in Borges' own *Nosotros* article of 1921. "Casi juicio final" ["Almost the Final Judgment"] (where he announces, "I have been and I am"), and "Versos de catorce" ["Verses of Fourteen"] (written, as the title indicates, in fourteen syllable verses, or Alexandrines, and thus defying the ultraists' desire to use only free verse) both show an unusually egotistic side of Borges, as does "Mi vida entera" ("My Whole Life"), which shows more than a trace of influence from Paul Valéry: "I am that awkward intensity which a soul is. . . ./I have crossed the sea/I have known many lands; I have seen a woman and two or three men/I have loved a haughty and pallid girl who had an Hispanic tranquillity/. . .I have savored numerous words/I believe deeply that that is everything and that I will never see, nor will I do, new things."

This confessionalistic tone, besides creating a greater variance with ultraistic thematic conventions, also undermines the general level of quality for the whole book.

Except for those self-centered pieces, the rest of the poems in *Luna* well represent Borges' modified avant-garde approach, wherein he injects a sensitive thought process into the ultraist framework. All except for "Versos de catorce" and "El General Quiroga va en coche al muere" are in free verse and contain more than a sufficient supply of ultraistic fantastic images. In fact, "Singladura" stands out as a virtually perfect ultraist creation, despite its being an almost completely revised version of a poem which Borges originally published in Spain in 1921 (only the title and one of the images remain from the original). The 1925 version occasioned most likely by his trip back to Spain two years earlier contains, like the original version, an unbroken series of images, most of them formed by metaphors like those in the opening verses: "the sea is an innumerable sword," "the sea is solitary, like a blind man," "the sea is a wild language that I cannot manage to decipher." As those images would indicate, the whole poem evokes the poet's frustration and sense of solitude when he is separated from Buenos Aires by the sea. Reconciliation with that situation comes through the image, as fantastic or unreal as those from the beginning of the poem, retained from the original poem: "la luna nueva se ha enroscado aun mástil [the new moon has curled up to a mast]." This Disneyesque vision of an affectionate moon hugging the mast leads into an expansion of the same image: "la misma luna que dejamos bajo un arco de piedra y cuya luz agraciará los sauzales [the same moon that he have left under an arch of stone and whose light will grace the willows]"; through watching the moon at sea he finds a mental link to the remembered vision of the mood at home. Borges acknowledged in the prologue to *Luna de enfrente* that, with regard to the book's title, "the moon . . . is already an emblem in poetry." He had to be aware of the incongruousness of using the moon as an affectionate symbol and as the central element of a creationist image when it had been so associated with Leopoldo Lugones (by way of Laforgue, in his *Lunario sentimental* of 1909), whom the ultraists had been holding up as representative of the *modernista* establishment. After the grandiose scope of his comparisons for the moon and the sea, which place them in a highly derealized poetic environment, Borges ends "Singladura" with an ironic return to an everyday calm (as he did in "Un patio") when he says, "I share the afternoon with my sister, like a piece of bread."

A more important poem, "Los llanos" ["The Plain"], with its historical and *criollista* [creole] theme which also dovetails into the concern for time, illustrates the high level of poetic expression which Borges' ultraism can reach. Its formal elements make it, like "Singladura," a true work of avant-garde art. Borges could hardly increase the density of metaphors; they predominate as a technical element in the poem, and they succeed in creating, as Guillermo de Torre had urged, a level of reality which goes "más allá" from [beyond] that of the world of ordinary consciousness. And he achieves that higher level of reality in this poem in spite of, or perhaps because of, his refusal to avoid an "anecdotal" content. Achievement of the vanguardist objectives in "Los llanos" comes through a tight and intelligent structuring of the poem, with metaphors used as the links in its chain of construction.

"Los llanos" has a symmetrical structure. The first five lines deal with the *llanura*, the plain; the following twelve lines present the central concern of the poem (notwithstanding the title, "The Plain"), which is the empire of Juan Facundo Quiroga; the final five lines, which formally balance the first group of verses, express the effect of this man's empire on Argentina's history.

Los Llanos

La llanura es un dolor pobrísimo que persiste.
La llanura es una estéril copia del alma.
El arenal es duro y enceguecido y en él no brilla
    la videncia del agua.
¡Qué cansados de perdurar están estos campos!
Esta flagrada y dolorida ausencia es toda la Rioja.
Por este llano urgió su imperio hecho de lanzas
    Juan Facundo Quiroga.
Imperio forajido, imperio misérrimo.
Imperio cuyos vivos atambores fueron cascos de
    potros redoblando ciudades humilladas
Y cuyas encarnizadas banderas fueron los cuervos
    que una vez muerta la pelea se abaten
Imperio que rubricaron facones criollos encruele-
    ciéndose en las gargantas.
Imperio cuyos únicos palacios fueron las desgarradas
    y ávidas llamas.
Imperio errante. Imperio lastimero.
Aquella torpe vida en su entereza se encabritó
    sobre los llanos
Y fueron briosa intensidad la espera de los combates
    ágiles
Y el numeroso arremeter detrás de las profundas
    tacuaras
Y la licencia atestiguando victorias
Y el saquear desbocado
Y la estrella caliente que trazan el varón y la
    mujer en juntándose
Todo ello se perdió como la tribu de un poniente
    se pierde
O como pasa la vehemencia de un beso
Sin haber enriquecido los labios que lo consienten.
Es triste que el recuerdo incluya todo
Y más aún si es bochornoso el recuerdo.

[The Plain

The prairie is a very poor pain that persists.
The prairie is a sterile copy of the soul.
The sandy ground is hard and blind and in it
    the clairvoyance of the water does not shine.
How tired of endurance these fields are!
This flagrant and pain-filled absence is all of the Rioja.
On this plain urged his empire made of lances
    Juan Facundo Quiroga.
Outlaw empire, miserable empire.
Empire whose living drums were horses' hooves
    beating on humiliated cities
And whose flesh-covered flags were the crows
    flying over once the fight is done
Empire that the creole knives sign cruelly into being
    on throats.
Empire whose only palaces were the torn
    and avid flames.
Errant empire. Pitiful empire.
That clumsy life in its fortitude rose on its hind legs
    above the plain
And there came the spirited intensity, the expectation
    of agile combats
And numerous attacks behind the profound
    'tacuaras'
And license witnessing victories
And looting, out of control
And the warm star that the male and the
    woman sketch in uniting
All of that was lost as a tribe of a sunset
    is lost
Or as the vehemence of a kiss passes
Without having enriched the lips that consented to it.
It is sad that memory retains it all
And even more if it is a shameful memory.]

    The first five lines reflect the title of the poem, "The Plain." The first three
verses form a series of metaphors for this plain, which first is equated with
a persistent pain, a pain which afflicts the poet's (and the nation's) conscience,
a connection made by the second metaphor of the plain as also a sterile copy

of the soul. The *arenal*, the sandy land of the plain, is *hard*, a word which
echoes the effect of the word "estéril" (sterile) of the previous line, but which
also connotes a benumbed emotional state; "cansado" in the next line reinforces
this sense of total exhaustion. Beyond a hardening, a blindness ("enceguecido")
results from this situation which is too painful to bear. The image with which
the line ends reflects both of these aspects of the plain: the absence of water
keeps it hard (dry) and does not provide the reflective, visual function ("videncia,"
clairvoyance) which could counteract the blindness. After these expressions
of the pain, hardness and sterility inherent in this land, the attribution in the
succeeding line of tiredness as a characteristic of the countryside comes as no
surprise. This tiredness again reflects the emotional and physical state of the
poet onto the plain. In the last of these introductory lines he declares in a
metaphor, one which stands out even among Borges' many fantastic images
for its flagrant unreality, that this beaten and pained absence is, or refers to,
the whole Rioja region. Adjectives of such violent effect applied to the empty
state ("ausencia")—not to just a barren or waste land, but to a complete absence—
create an image whose sharply incongruous and illogical relationships exemplify
the poetic possibilities on the route to the "más allá." Although an absence,
a vacuum, cannot be described as beaten or pained, that Mallarmean word
evokes (in the same way, although Borges' context is bitter, as Mallarmé's
"L'absente de tous bouquets") in *infinite* expression of what is lacking due to
Quiroga's destruction.

Each of the first five lines contains a specific reference to the title: *the plain,
the sandy ground, these fields*, and *La Rioja*. Repetition of terms continues into
the sixth verse, serving as a link to the beginning of the central section of the
poem, which begins with the words "on this plain." The first section has
established the bitter tone and the poet's angry sentiments toward the activities
which he is about to relate in the body of the poem. This lack of subtlety
is underlined by the harsh and unrelenting frequent repetitions of the terms
"la llanura" and "Imperio" (Empire) at the beginning of many lines; a repetition
which also helps to emphasize the connection between the title—*Los llanos*—
and the central theme, Quiroga's empire. The anaphora and use of polysyndeton
reflect the extension and ever-continuing vastness of the pampa which parallels
the extensiveness of Quiroga's empire and its cruelty.

Throughout these plains, then, Quiroga "urged" his empire "made of lances."
There are two images here. One, the graphic construction of an empire made
out of spears, emphasizes through metonymic exaggeration the harsh cruelty
of this man; this in itself is a double image, the spears standing for the soldiers
who created the empire, while "hecho de lanzas" also evokes the results of their
destruction. More striking, though, is the verb "urgió" applied to Quiroga's

relationship to this empire. This term gives the impression that he sits astride it as he does his horse, spurring it on—an image that is paralleled seven lines later when "that whole life" *se encabritó* (rose on its hind legs) over the plains. With these descriptions Borges makes the "empire" a living, breathing beast which hovers menacingly over the plain.

Many of the metaphors in the body of the poem reinforce the vision of the cruel beast. The empire's "living drums were horses' hooves beating on humiliated cities," an image whose relentlessness is drummed into the reader by the rhythm which the anaphora in the poem produces; and the empire's destruction is symbolized by the "flesh covered flags," the crows flying over the battle fields. In the next image (line 10), a particularly gripping one, Borges personifies the knives, which parallel the lances of which the empire is made (line 6), by means of two verbs of action. These knives "rubicaron" the empire, an action which has double significance due to the expressiveness of that verb. "Rubicar" means both "to sign" and "to cover with red color," and here it indicates that they leave their bloody seal. They leave this mark of remembrance by "encrueleciéndose" (becoming cruel) on the throats of the victims, a verb which literally vivifies the action. The destructive nature of the empire—it is made of lances—is reinforced by Borges' ironic metaphor of its only palaces being the flames left by Quiroga's henchmen.

Now comes the portrayal of the empire, a beast raising itself over the plains, causing such depravities, all of which are described as having "spirited intensity," a description which also fits the restless behavior of a wild stallion. The word "desbocado" which characterizes this destruction has two meanings which apply both to the humans who are committing the atrocities (it can mean "foul-mouthed"), and (with its meaning of "runaway") to the image of the beast which represents their destructive force.

The beastly empire and its cruelty have an ephemeral existence, however, and the final five lines describe its effect, beginning with "all of that was lost," an abrupt statement of complete finality backed up by two comparisons. The loss of Quiroga's violent empire is like the disappearing of an Indian tribe from the West or like the passing of the "vehemence of a kiss" which—in spite of the possible physical and emotional violence inherent in those acts, a parallel to the incongruousness of the "pain-filled absence"—leave no trace. But, with equal abruptness, Borges returns to the present—the last two lines of the poem, like the first five, are in the present tense—to declare that, like the "poor pain that persists," memory retains it all. In these lines he includes the emotional effect of this disappeared past on himself and on the nation. The sadness he expresses here has a double edge for Borges, for he realizes that memory, which he describes elsewhere as a refuge or "remanso" (backwater) from time's flow, can inflict its own pain. This injection of personal feeling again goes counter to his ultraist injunctions against the poet's use of his own emotions in his poem; but the sadness and shame expressed in these lines parallels and ties up the emotions which he had attributed to the plains in the beginning of the poem, thus completing the structural, thematic and emotional balance of the piece. Achieving such a balanced poetic creation clearly takes precedence over ultraist prescriptions for technique, although Borges continues to use the image in almost "industrial quantities" in this and other poems in *Luna de enfrente*.

The third book from the twenties, *Cuaderno San Martín* [*San Martin Copybook*] (1929)—the title is a brand-name of a notebook—marks the end of Borges' publication of poems in book form until the appearance of *El hacedor* [*Dreamtigers*] in 1960 and *El otro, el mismo* [*The Self and the Other*] in 1967; besides the end of his youthful poetic production it represents the end of poetry as Borges' primary means of expression for the next four decades. The brevity of the book very likely indicates a lessening interest in poetry in general, as well as a significant weakening of the Ultra influence on his work. In any case the ultraist epoch has ended by the time *Cuaderno San Martín* appears; *Martín Fierro* ceased publication in 1927, which corresponded with a drastic curtailment of avant-garde activity in Buenos Aires.

The vanguard's recession scatters imagistic remnants in its wake, leaving some firm traces of its influences even on Borges' collection from late in the decade. "Arrabal en que pesa el campo" (Suburb on which the Countryside Weighs), omitted from the 1954 edition, continues creation of images through personification ("the moon is more alone," "phonographs confess their pain") and through metonymy, in an unusually sensual passage: "in Villa Ortuzar/the male's desire is sad in the afternoon/when hips stroll by on the sidewalk." Of the twelve pieces which comprise *Cuaderno San Martín*, the one which most reflects what remains of the ultraist in Borges is "La Chacarita," the first of two poems grouped under the title "Muertes de Buenos Aires" ("Deaths of Buenos Aires").

Not only the remnants of the avant-garde elements evident in this poem make it an especially interesting example of the last poetry from this period; it also contains both of the themes which predominate in the other pieces from this book, namely nostalgia for the past and death. "La Chacarita" is the name of the cemetery in Buenos Aires where indigents are buried and which stands in contrast to the cemetery called "La Recoleta," the subject of the second poem of the pair, and the resting place of Buenos Aires' aristocracy, among them Borges' ancestors. The origins of the cemetery for the poor receive a very personal and image-filled treatment; again Borges lets sentiment intrude into the poem's metaphors. This personal approach, non-ultraist in a strict sense, applies to most of these poems written after the avant-garde fever has subsided. Borges' poetic sensibility in this regard overrides his original theories, but his vestigial ultraist "fervor" surfaces in this poem's images, which are still startling because of the terms which they link together in unexpected ways. In this respect Borges continues to follow Guillermo de Torre's quest for the "más allá"; and the discussion of this poem, paraphrasing its descriptive process, should demonstrate how he interweaves the metaphoric transformations into its fabric.

La Chacarita

Porque la entraña del cementerio del sur
fue saciada por la fiebre amarilla hasta decir basta;
porque los conventillos hondos del sur
mandaron muerte sobre la cara de Buenos Aires
y por que Buenos Aires no pudo mirar esa muerte,
a paladas te abrieron
en la punta perdida del oeste,
detrás de las tormentas de tierra
y del barrial pesado y primitivo que hizo a los
        cuarteadores.
Allí no había más que el mundo
y las costumbres de las estrellas sobre unas chacras,
y el tren salía de un galpón en Bermejo
con los olvidos de la muerte:
muertos de barba derrumbada y ojos en vela,
muertas de carne desalmada y sin magia.

Trapacerías de la muerte—sucia como el
        nacimiento del hombre—
siguen multiplicando tu subsuelo y así reclutas
tu conventillo de ánimas, tu montonera clandestina
de huesos
que caen al fondo de tu noche enterrada
lo mismo que a la hondura de un mar,
hacia una muerte sin inmortalidad y sin honra.

Una dura vegetación de sobras en pena
hace fuerza contra sus paredones interminables
cuyo sentido es perdición
y convencido de corruptibilidad el suburbio
apura su caliente vida a tus pies
en calles traspasadas por una llamarada baja de

barro
o se aturde con desgano de bandoneones
o con balidos de cornetas sonsas en carnaval.
(El fallo de destino más para siempre,
que dura en mí lo escuché esa noche en tu noche
cuando la guitarra bajo la mano del orillero
dijo lo mismo que las palabras, y ellas decían:
"La muerte es vida vivida,
la vida es muerte que viene.").
Mono del cementerio, la Quema
gesticula advenediza muerte a tus pies.
Gastamos y enfermamos la realidad: 210 carros
infaman las mañanas, llevando
a esa necrópolis de humo
las cotidianas cosas que hemos contagiado de
        muerte.
Cúpulas estrafalarias de madera y cruces en alto
se mueven — piezas negras de un ajedrez final —
        por tus calles
y su achacosa majestad va encubriendo
las vergüenzas de nuestras muertes.
En tu disciplinado recinto
la muerte es incolora, hueca, numérica;
se disminuye a fechas y nombres,
muertes de la palabra.
La noche piensa "nunca";
un silbido — agresor de infinitud — cruza con su
        malevo.
Chacarita:
desaguadero de esta patria de Buenos Aires, cuesta
        final,
barrio que sobrevives a los otros, que sobremueres,
lazareto que estás en esta muerte no en la otra vida,
he oído tu palabra de caducidad y en ella no creo,
porque tu misma convicción de tragedia es acto de
        vida
y porque la persuasión de una sola rosa es más que
        tus mármoles.

[Chacarita

Because the guts of the cemetery of the South,
    satiated by yellow fever, said *enough*;
because the tenement houses of the Southside
    send death over the face of Buenos Aires
and because Buenos Aires was unable to look at the carnage,
they opened you with shovels
in the city's lost western edge
behind duststorms
and the heavy, primitive district that made the teamsters.
There was no more than the world
and its custom of stars rising above a few huts,
and the train left from a shed in Bermejo
with what death forgot:
dead men with slack beards and sleepless eyes,
dead women, soulless flesh, without magic.

Death's deceits—dirty as man's birth—
continue thickening your subsoil; so you muster up souls
for your compound, your hidden pile of bones
that fall to the bottom of your buried night
as if into the depths of a sea,
toward a death without immortality, without honor.

Hardened vegetation, garbage in torment,
presses in on the interminable walls
that mean perdition
and, convinced of its own corruption, the slum
hurls its hot life at your feet
in alleys shot through with low flames of dust,
or is confused with the accordion's deceit
or bleatings of dazed carnival cornets.

(Destiny's verdict forever,
which goes on within me, I heard that night in your night
when the guitar and the words joined
under the player's hands—and they said:
"Death is life lived,
life is death coming.")

The mocker of the cemetery, La Quema
calls newly arrived death to your feet.

We spend and infect reality, 210 cartloads
to insult the mornings, bringing
to that necropolis of smoke
the everyday things which we have contaminated with
    death.
Clumsy wooden domes and raised crosses
are moving—black pieces in a final chessgame—
through your streets
and their sickly majesty covers up
the shame of your death.

In your disciplined enclosures
death is colorless, hollow, numerical;
subsides into dates and names,
deaths of the word.
Night thinks "never";
a malevolent whistle—infinite aggressor—
    crosses.

Chacarita:
drain of this patria of Buenos Aires, final hill to
    climb,
district that outlasts the others, and outdies them,
pesthouse of our death, not of the other life,
I have heard your feeble word and I don't believe it
because your very conviction of tragedy is an affirmation of life
and because the persuasion of one single rose is greater than that
of your marbles.]

The attachment which the poet feels for the cemetery is brought out by
the frequent use of personification, which Borges continues to favor. In a poem
about the effects of death, this method has particular force, creating images
which are fantastic but humanized, however incongruously. In the first image,
in which the entrails of the "cemetery of the South" were *satiated* until it *said
enough*, the cemetery becomes the effigy of an over-indulging person who has
been forced to stuff himself past the point of satiety, an almost Rabelaisian
description. The "conventillos del sur" ("tenement houses of the Southside")
have the ability to *send* death onto Buenos Aires' *face*, and this city is not able
to look at that death; in all these instances personification occurs through nouns
denoting human physical properties (entrails, face) and through verbs of action.
La Chacarita itself is even more completely personified, addressed as a person

throughout the poem ("a paladas *te* abrieron"). Other elements which appear in this strophe are also given human attributes: the "barrial" (district) *made* the "cuarteadores" (teamsters), the stars seen above the huts have their own *world* and *customs*, the train leaves with death's *forgettings*.

A conspiracy between two of these personified elements, death and the cemetery, forms the basis for the images in the second strophe. Death's deceits keep "multiplying its subsoil," which is an inventive way of euphemizing, through hypallage, the increase of cadavers beneath the ground. These bodies form the "tenement house of the souls" (like Valéry's "édifice dans l'âme" in *Cimetière Marin*) below ground, for which La Chacarita *recruits*, and which becomes part of its "buried night" where death has strictly personal limitations, lacking immortality and honor.

From these general impressions of the dead within the cemetery Borges turns to personification of the place itself, beginning with the image of garbage which surrounds the walls and which has taken on the characteristics of the souls within. "Sobras en pena," ("garbage in torment," an effective play on "ànimas en pena [tortured souls]") has both a heavenly and an extremely mundane application. This garbage *presses in on* the cemetery's walls, and the city *drains* its life through the streets, described in expressionist terms as "flames of dust" or "bleatings of cornets."

Borges has so far been leading up to the central issue of the poem, expressed in the words of a song which he heard one night at a gathering after passing by the cemetery, as he explains in an "annotation" at the end of *Cuaderno San Martín* (1929 edition): "la muerte es vida vivida, la vida es muerte que viene" (death is life lived, life is death which is coming). He has inferred this coexistence of death in life by demonstrating that death is devious and that it can be treated in abstract and euphemistic terms; but the cemetery, which the city passes by at festival time and dumps its garbage on, will claim us all. As the poet points out, this couplet is "destiny's verdict for ever" (for mankind, that is: "which goes on within me," as he says), as opposed to the fleeting aura of timelessness in the carnival. He heard this song "esa noche en tu noche" (the cemetery's night that he has previously described as "your buried night"), as if he were hearing this judgment from within the state of death itself.

A series of images shows the certainty of that observation: the fire (la Quema, the public incinerator) at the cemetery which eats up "the everyday things which we have contaminated with death" takes on the appearance of a mimic who makes faces threatening death to the onlooker; wooden domes and crosses of a funeral procession are seen as pieces in a final chess game which move through the street trying to cover the "shame of our death" with their "sickly majesty." In the next strophe, however, when confined within the cemetery, death becomes devoid of these emotions, being reduced to a "colorless, hollow, numerical" state and perceived only in terms of names and dates. Additional personified images complete this all-encompassing vision of death; "night *thinks* 'never'," which the "*buried* night" of the cemetery declaims through someone's *malevolent* whistle.

At this point the poet should supposedly be convinced of the ultimately victorious nature of death. But Borges the ironist, the negator of time, stubbornly and with good humor declares that, in spite of the overwhelming evidence that he (and the cemetery) present, he will not believe that death must overpower life. In his final address to La Chacarita he sums up her status with a series of metaphors. The cemetery is a "drain" of the "patria [native land]" of Buenos Aires; the final hill to climb; a district which "sobrevives" and "sobremueres" as well, a play on words ("survive" and "surdie") which is similar to, and given in the same spirit, as the earlier "sobras en pena"; and finally, the cemetery is a "lazareto," a place of quarantine. Borges says that he does not believe the cemetery's "palabras de caducidad" (feeble words), and with a bit of sophistry explains that "your very conviction of tragedy is an affirmation of life." And finally, in the face of all the evidence of death's pervasiveness he insists on declaring that the persuasion of a rose, a symbol of the fleeting nature of time and of beauty within life as well, has greater effect (or more appeal to him, at least) than death's marble, which represents what is cold and detached. In other words, *carpe diem*.

With their predominance of fantastic images within a free verse structure, "La Chacarita" and the poems selected for commentary from *Fervor de Buenos Aires* and *Luna de enfrente* all tend to represent those poems which most adhere to the esthetic, or to the spirit, of Ultra; as previously indicated, some of the poems from this period, especially those after 1925, demonstrate less influence from Borges' theories on his own work. Borges the young poet, especially with regard to his choice of themes, rose above the restrictions which Borges the theoretician sought to impose on his also youthful followers. In an almost uncanny way, the Jorge Luis of 1929, the artist, was functioning as a creator who had already adopted the attitudes which he, as a reflective older man, was to formulate at age 70. In the prologue to a book of verse, *Elogio de la sombra* (*In Praise of Darkness*), published four decades later in 1969, Borges' (lack of) theories catch up with his art.

> I am not the possessor of an esthetic. Time has taught me some
> tricks . . . such tricks or habits certainly do not make up an esthetic.
> Besides, I don't believe in esthetics. In general they are no more

than useless abstractions; they vary for each writer and even for each text and they can be nothing more than stimuli or occasional tools.

These observations differ markedly from the pronouncements made by the young theoretician who as an *ultraísta* framed his precepts in the defiantly positive tone that a youthful revolutionary was expected to have, even if his revolution was an artistic one. Now, grown old, the poet couches his observations in a negative tone and speaks with caution. His early poems show that this distrust of rigid rules for art, as stated in this more recent (anti-)esthetic, was already something which the young artist felt. As unprofound as it may seem, the explanation for this has to be that Borges' artistic sensitivity simply overrode certain aspects of his own theories. Even though an active and enthusiastic participant in the ultraist school could never have made the pronouncement that esthetics vary for each author and for each text, as the older Borges does forty years after their dust has settled, the young ultraist *artist* felt and worked according to this freedom from esthetic restrictions. Eduardo López Morales strongly expresses this very idea, saying that with regard to Borges' early poetry and theories: "I believe, with Marx, that practice is the criterion for the truth; and Borges' literary practice denies his speculations." López Morales comes to that conclusion after rather myopically affirming, flatly, that Borges' *Fervor de Buenos Aires* "*is not* a book of ultraist poems" (his italics); but it is true that in only a few of the pieces from his earliest years did Borges practice in extreme form what he and Guillermo de Torre were preaching as an artistic ideal.

The bulk of his artistic production from the early years rises above the few examples of excess and slavishness to avant-garde theory. Many of the poems do contain excellent examples of the ultraist technique, though instilled with a personal sensitivity which greatly enhances their poetic value; and these can stand comparison with any of the later work. The same themes found in *Fervor de Buenos Aires, Luna de enfrente* and *Cuaderno San Martín* recur in the later poems along with a few new concerns. Referring to *Elogio de la sombra*, Borges states that "to the mirrors, labyrinths and swords which my resigned reader already forsees, two new themes have been added: old age and ethics." True, but the old familiar topics of Argentina, Buenos Aires, family, love, and time reappear frequently also. And while the later poems show a technical expertise and masterful handling of language whose almost lapidary perfection often surpasses the early work, they rarely have the enthusiasm, humor and audacity of image which give life to much of the earlier work. The early poems do have their rightful position as an important aspect of Borges' total output, both as forceful and sensitive poetry in their own right and as an initial step in the artist's remarkably cohesive body of literary creation.

In his poem "Invocación a Joyce" ["Invocation to Joyce"] from *Elogio de la sombra* Borges sums up his attitude toward the avant-garde *Littérateurs*.

> Dispersos en dispersas capitales,
> solitarios y muchos,
> jugábamos a ser el primer Adán
> que dio nombre a las cosas.
> Por los vastos declives de la noche
> que lindan con la aurora,
> buscamos (lo recuerdo aún) las palabras
> de la luna, de la muerte, de la mañana
> y de los otros hábitos del hombre.
> Fuimos el imagismo, el cubismo,
> los conventículos y sectas
> que las crédulas universidades veneran.
> Inventamos la falta de puntuación,
> la omisión de mayúsculas,
> las estrofas en forma de paloma
> de los bibliotecarios de Alejandría.
> Ceniza, la labor de nuestras manos
> y un fuego ardiente nuestra fe.

> [Scattered over scattered cities,
> alone and many
> we played at being that Adam
> who gave names to all living things.
> Down the long slopes of night
> that border on the dawn,
> we sought (I still remember) words
> for the moon, for death, for the morning,
> and for man's other habits.
> We were imagism, cubism,
> the conventicles and sects
> respected now by credulous universities.
> We invented the omission of punctuation
> and capital letters,
> stanzas in the shape of a dove
> from the librarians of Alexandria.
> Ashes, the labor of our hands,

and a burning fire our faith.
(*In Praise of Darkness*, tr. Norman T.
di Giovanni)]

This is a faithful, if somewhat oversimplified, recollection of the artists who formed the literary vanguard of the twenties, and of whom Borges is a part: "I am they," he says later in this poem. By his use of the present tense to include himself he seems to be no longer adamantly refusing to admit his participation in the activities and creations of those years. It now appears that he also recognizes all of that era as a milestone in the development of modern artistic production, even if much of its present status is due to the veneration by the "credulous universities." This leads to the central perception in "Invocation to Joyce," that the production of the avant-garde artists has been reduced to the ashes left by the "fuego ardiente" of their spirit (Borges the ultraist would have applauded that image—"ardiente" means both ardent and burning—if not the sentiment). Yet he finds in the *oeuvre* of James Joyce one set of literary masterpieces which has validated the modernist period and its struggles toward innovation in art, as these lines later in the poem indicate: "what does my lost generation matter/that vague mirror,/if your books justify it?"

Joyce's work most certainly merits the exalted position which Borges awards it in this poem. Obviously, however, the entire preceding discussion of Borges' early poetry has had the intention of indicating the qualifications which make it, too, a major work which justifies the period, and which also has a "fuego ardiente" burning with an enduring brightness. Borges kindled a spirit of poetic reform within his fellow "nueva sensibilidad [new sensibility]" poets, and the work that they produced stands as a creative testimony to their dedication in upholding avant-garde artistic principles.

Borges and Derrida

Before the third chapter of the first part of "La Pharmacie de Platon" Derrida has three epigraphs, two from Borges and one from Joyce. The Joyce fragment is identified as coming from *A Portrait of the Artist as a Young Man* and reads as follows: "A sense of fear of the unknown moved in the heart of his weariness, a fear of symbols and portents, of the hawk-like man whose name he bore soaring out of his captivity on osier woven wing, of Thoth, the god of writers, writing with a reed upon a tablet and bearing on his narrow ibis head the cusped moon." This passage is sandwiched in between the two Borges quotes, which are given—*hélas*—in the French translation and whose source is not indicated. The first Borges quotation reads: "Universal history continued to unroll, the all-too-human gods whom Xenophanes had denounced were demoted to figures of poetic fiction, or to demons—although it was reported that one of them, Hermes Trismegistus, had dictated a variable number of books (42 according to Clement of Alexandria; 20,000 according to Hamblicus; 36,525 according to the priests of Thoth—who is also Hermes) in the pages of which are written all things. Fragments of this illusory library, compiled or concocted beginning in the third century, go to form what is called the *Corpus Hermeticum* . . . ." It was not an easy task to find this passage for it sounds like the quintessential Borges. The quotation is taken from "La esfera de Pascal" ("Pascal's Fearful Sphere"), an essay contained in *Otras inquisiciones [Other Inquisitions]* (1952). The second Borges quotation—the last of the three epigraphs—reads as follows: "Another school declares that *all time* has already transpired and that our life is only the crepuscular and no doubt falsified and

English translation published in this volume for the first time. © 1986 by Roberto González-Echevarría. Originally appeared as "Borges y Derrida" in *Isla a su vuelo fugitiva* by Roberto González-Echevarría (Madrid: Porrua, 1983).

mutilated memory or reflection of an irrecoverable process. Another, that the history of the universe—and in it our lives and the most tenuous detail of our lives—is the scripture produced by a subordinate god in order to communicate with a demon. Another, that the universe is comparable to those cryptographs in which not all the symbols are valid. . . ." This quotation (which, again, was not easy to locate) is from "Tlön, Uqbar, Orbis Tertius," the celebrated story by Borges that opens *Ficciones* (1944). Because Derrida has alerted us to the significance of such outside, "liminal" elements as epigraphs, I am going to speculate briefly on the possible meaning of these fragments from Borges and Joyce in relation to "La Pharmacie de Platon," as an indirect way to make some observations about the relationship between Borges and Derrida. I am looking at these matters from the point of view of a practicing critic and historian of literature, not as a philosopher, and I am obviously concerned with the situation of critical discourse in the wake of Derrida and Borges.

Chapter three, part one of "La Pharmacie," the section prefaced by the three epigraphs, has to do with the presence in Plato's *Phaedrus* of the Egyptian myth of Thoth, alluded to through the figure of the messenger Theuth. Derrida apparently wants to explain how Theuth reflects the story of Thoth, and how his presence in Plato falls within a certain structure of Western thought, one in which writing is condemned as being false and secondary, as opposed to voice, which is thought to be the origin, the carrier of truth and the bearer of "presence." Thoth is the god of writing, the secretary, the son of the sun-god Rê or Ammon, whom he replaces. He is the moon-god or god of reflected light, therefore the god of "secondariness." Thoth is portrayed as being systematically opportunistic, siding with Osiris sometimes, while at other times he is against him. He is also the god of death. Thoth not only supplants living language, but is in addition in charge of the lugubrious task of weighing the heart and soul of the dead; he is the accountant god, who is besides inventor of games of chance and cryptograms. Thoth is, then, the father's other, and at the same time the subversive moment of his replacement: "Le dieu de l'écriture est donc à la fois son père, son fils et lui." (That is to say, "the God of writing is at once his father, his son, and himself.") Writing is possible in that supplanting of the father with a simulacrum of presence. The father is the voice; writing its representation. But isn't Thoth all there really is? Isn't the figure of the father the simulacrum, and writing a play of differences, one through which representation takes distance from a phantasmatic a priori? While Thoth is a rejected form of signification within Western metaphysics, he may very well be the only possibility of signification. Throughout "La Pharmacie" Derrida speculates about the presence of this scapegoat, this *pharmakos* lodged within the very fabric of language and representation.

This scandalous conception of writing, which corrodes the very foundations of our thought from Philology to Semiology, persists in what Derrida calls *textuality*, his theory of writing as a system of supplements that differentiate from one another without mutually cancelling each other. In a very circuitous fashion Derrida seems to be suggesting that the foreign, oriental mythology brought into the *Phaedrus* is not foreign at all, but an integral part of Plato's own discourse—a significant supplement, as it were, that needs to be placed outside, yet really belongs inside. Both at the closest and most minute textual level and in the broadest possible sense these ideas are the ones at stake in the relationship between Borges and Derrida.

Let us return to our three epigraphs. It should be clearer now how they are related. In the first two there is a direct allusion to Thoth. In the third the allusion is not as direct, but it is nevertheless clear enough: the "subordinate god" could be no other than Thoth, the god secretary, Rê's amanuensis. The "cryptographs" could also very well be an allusion to Thoth, who not only "invented" graphic representation but also, as we saw, cryptographs. This is obvious. The question remains, what is the meaning of these allusions? Do these epigraphs have solely a tangential, ancillary function? Do they merely reflect the meaning of the chapter? Is Derrida giving us here the "sources" of his ideas? But, how can we speak of sources within his system? Let us restore the quotations to their "original" context and see if this critical exercise helps us in beginning to answer some of these questions.

"Pascal's Fearful Sphere," from which the first quotation is taken, is a three-page essay in which Borges traces a metaphor found in Pascal through the history of Western thought and literature. The metaphor, that God is like a sphere whose center is everywhere, is traced from Plato, through Dante, to Pascal. Borges closes the essay with his well-known dictum: "Quizá la historia universal es la historia de la diversa entonación de algunas metáforas." "Perhaps universal history is the history of the diverse intonation of a few metaphors." The translation in *Labyrinths* reads: "It may be that universal history is the history of a handful of metaphors." If in "La Pharmacie de Platon" Derrida is placing the irreducible mechanisms of language above/before thought (not the other way around), "Pascal's Fearful Sphere" already advanced that same argument. Metaphor here comes to replace thought. Borges' detour through Hermes Trismegistus and the mythical origins of the *Corpus Hermeticum* is a way of slyly hinting at a marginal, heterodoxical tradition that also disseminated the metaphor. This process is analogous to Plato's excursion to Egypt in the *Phaedrus*.

The quotation from *A Portrait* is somewhat more complex in relation to its source. The fragment comes from a point near the end of the novel, when

Stephen Daedalus is about to become a writer, appropriately so, as the quotation alludes to a transition from symbols to the god of writing. It is clear that in order to write Stephen has to conquer his fear of "symbols and portents," in other words, received meanings, doctrine, liturgy. All these are part of the world of his father, the world that he has endured at school, in church, and at the university. It is even more appropriate that his meditation should be about his name. There is in the fragment a revealing metamorphosis of Icarus, son of Daedalus, into Thoth, son of Rê, a kind of distancing of the Greek, logocentric tradition by moving into the Egyptian myth of the god of writing. (It is difficult not to remark that in the figure of Thoth, the pointed beak of his ibis head looks like an instrument of writing, as if voice had been turned into a piercing nib.) Icarus falls in his flight to the sun (Rê provides here a nice transition by being the sun-god) and becomes Thoth, who supplants the father. The last sentence in *A Portrait of the Artist as a Young Man* harks back to this substitution, which is carried out not without trepidation and a sense of guilt: "27 April: Old father, old artificer, stand me now and ever in good stead."

The quotation from "Tlön, Uqbar, Orbis Tertius" comes from the list of various philosophical schools in Uqbar. The two schools retained in the quotation are those that argue for a conception of Uqbar as something *added* to the universe after all life had ended. Like writing, Uqbar is a supplement that has replaced the world—a third world, so to speak, without the political connotations. As in the other two quotations, this one introduces a foreign— and how—mythology to upset the logic, the logocentric logic Derrida would say, of Western discourse.

There is obviously a certain propriety to the epigraphs, in that they anticipate ideas or figures contained in the body of the text of "La Pharmacie de Platon." The propriety extends even to the fact that these texts are *outside*. But there is more. Why, for instance, the pattern Borges-Joyce-Borges? Why the repetition? Or, is it a repetition? How do the epigraphs differ? While all three quotations allude to Thoth, and all, in a sense anticipate the logic of the supplement, their sequence embodies that very logic. The quotation from "Pascal's Fearful Sphere" refers to the mythic origins of writing, to the foundation of the library in Alexandria. Hermes Trismegistus *dictated* "a variable number of books. . . ." He stands here as the voice of the father, who has generated the library. In the quotation from Joyce, as we saw, we are in the realm of the son, as he transforms himself from Icarus to Thoth, from ephebe to the god of writing; his fear of symbols and portents, the sign of the father, leads him to writing. The quotation from "Tlön, Uqbar, Orbis Tertius" takes us into the realm of the supplement, not only in the details that we already saw, but more clearly still if we think of the story itself. The article on Uqbar (from which supposedly the author gathered the information) does not appear, according to the narrator, in volume 46 of the *Anglo-American Cyclopedia*, but:

> The tome Bioy brought was, in fact, Volume XLVI of the *Anglo-American Cyclopaedia*. On the half-title page and the spine, the alphabetical marking (Tor-Ups) was that of our copy, but, instead of 917, it contained 921 pages. These four additional pages made up the article on Uqbar, which (as the reader will have noticed) was not indicated by the alphabetical marking. We later determined that there was no other difference between the volumes. Both of them (as I believe I have indicated) are reprints of the tenth *Encyclopaedia Britannica*. Bioy had acquired his copy at some sale or other.

Uqbar, then, is the supplement, a world in which, as with the productions of Thoth, books "of a philosophical nature invariably include both the thesis and the antithesis, the rigorous pro and con of a doctrine." Borges is repeated in the third epigraph, but not quite, in the sequence Borges-Joyce-Borges. The second time he takes the place of the first Borges, but exceeds him: "Le dieu de l'écriture est donc à la fois son père, son fils et lui."

We can see now that these three epigraphs—at the very center of the first part of the "Pharmacie"—occupy an appropriately important place. They are outside the text, being a mere supplement, yet appear as its source; but by anticipating what the text says they turn the text into a supplement. The Borges-Joyce-Borges epigraphs, furthermore, play in the "Pharmacie" a role similar to that of the Thoth myth in the *Phaedrus*; a foreign mythology that is incorporated into the arguments put forth by the text, but that really belongs to its own structure.

Derrida has brought together in Borges and Joyce two key figures in modern literature who had however been joined already by history. As is known Borges wrote one of the very first important essays on *Ulysses*. But their conjunction here is suggestive because of their position in relation to Derrida's text and their homologous relation to the Thoth myth and Plato's. I have written elsewhere that the importance of Joyce in Latin America stems from the fact that his relation, as an Irish writer, to the English tradition is analogous to that of Latin American writers with respect to the Spanish (and the European tradition in general). In both cases the relationship may be understood in the sense suggested by Derrida's epigraphs, as a supplement that repeats the original tradition, by taking its place, by re-writing it from within, but always as if it were from without.

Derrida dares to indicate, in the complex manner shown here, that Borges is one of his sources; that the representative of a recent, marginal literature, is within the central tradition, corroding it yet making it possible. Of course, like Borges, Derrida likes to point to the presence of heterodoxical traditions, like the Kabbalah, in Western discourse. Neither Borges nor Derrida takes the hegemony of Graeco-Roman discourse for granted; both affect a certain Judaism in their contact with texts, and Borges likes to imagine: "Had Alexandria triumphed instead of Rome, the bizarre, troubled stories that I have summarized here [he has been writing on Gnosticism] would be coherent, majestic and common. Statements such as Novalis's 'Life is a disease of the spirit,' or Rimbaud's desperate 'True life is absent, we are not in the world,' would glow in the canonical books."

Latin American writers like Borges himself, Lezama, Carpentier, Sarduy, Puig, and others have been writing from such a strategic marginality. This accounts, I believe, for the historical coincidence of the recent boom of Latin American literature with the explosion of French critical thought. There is, of course, a *petite histoire* that explains this coincidence, having to do with the presence in Paris of writers like Sarduy, Paz, García Márquez, etc. But a larger history looms behind it. If Borges becomes a cult figure for Foucault, Derrida or Barthes, it is due to the kind of systematic marginality that I have analyzed here. After all, if one were to assume an entirely historicist position one could say that from its elusive beginning Latin American literature has exhibited some of the characteristics of writing as Borges and Derrida define it. Perhaps the best example are the works of Garcilaso de la Vega, el Inca. Garcilaso's main work, the *Royal Commentaries* (1609, 1616) is, as the title implies, a text that sets itself up strategically as secondary, as commentary; Garcilaso wishes to merely correct and annotate, he says, the work of Spanish historians of the Incaic empire. Having command of the language of the region Garcilaso is able to question a good deal of what those historians had written, but he does so always insisting on the secondariness of his work. His text has been preceded by those of Spanish historians, by the oral history of the Incas that he heard revealingly from an uncle (a father substitute), by Christian history, which he claims includes in its providential design Peru. In addition, Garcilaso's text is not written in his mother tongue (Quetchua), which is quite literally his mother's, but in his father's, that is in Spanish. Garcilaso's text is made up, then, of a paternal language to which it does not belong—or that does not belong to the author—and commentaries about a prior text that is multiple. Had Cuzco won, one could say paraphrasing Borges, the stories that are mere appendages in the *Royal Commentaries* would appear in the canonical books. A similar situation obtains in writers like Carpentier, Borges, and others for whom Spanish was not the first language and whose works are composed of fragments and commentaries of a central tradition, presumably Western.

But can we endow Borges with such a determining power in history? In other words, can we turn his texts, and with them the whole of Latin American literature, into the original supplement, if I may be allowed the oxymoron? Isn't it a crude, logo- and ethnocentric gesture to invert the situation and turn marginality into a panacea? I believe that it would run counter to the logic of our three epigraphs from "La Pharmacie," or at least with the logic of my hermeneutical exercise with them. The same question arises on the level of literary history: Is Borges the source or even a source of Derrida? How can one postulate an anteriority within Derrida's system? Is Borges the blind father of post-structuralist tradition? But if he is not the source, why is Derrida signalling in his direction through the device of the epigraphs?

The second Borges epigraph in chapter three of the first part of "La Pharmacie"—as we saw—repeats the Borges of the first quote, yet exceeds him. It would be a violation of Derrida's thinking to turn Borges, a Borges, into a logocentric father, into the possessor of the transcendental signified, hoarder of Negativity. For Derrida there will always be the spacings, the deferrals, textuality not as a relationship between an authoritative text and its fragmented commentaries, but always already the fragments, *grams* or *differances*, as he calls them. Borges may appear under the two fragments surrounding Joyce's, but these are two different traces, out of which we could not construct, or reconstruct, a hypostatized BORGES, who could account for Derrida's text. The ambivalent position of the fragment already suggested such a denial.

But if this is the case in both Borges and Derrida—the disappearance of anteriority and authority, of a transcendental signified be it a Text or an Author—are we not facing a large, radical rupture or break with modern tradition? In other words: Doesn't the absence of such a text or such an authority defuse the mechanism of the most encompassing trope in the modern tradition— irony? Irony is possible when the presence of an authoritative and truth-bearing system of signs is postulated; modern textuality is generated in the ironic distancing from that source, but if there is no magnetic field to give us a textual north, fragments free-float without the sense of separation, the nostalgia for knowledge present throughout the modern tradition.

A radical reading of Borges/Derrida would, I am sure, suggest that we have come to such a break, even if Derrida is loath to accept "decisive ruptures." But have we really? That the danger that we may have come to such a break is present in the minds of critics in the wake of Derrida/Borges there can be no doubt. My friend and colleague Geoffrey Hartman speaks in a recent book not only of *saving the text* (the title of his book) but winds up the volume with a remarkable meditation on the *word as wound* that I would entitle, *the critic as medicine man*. Hartman's investment in Romanticism is too great not to feel threatened by Derrida. I wonder, however, if Hartman's gesture, which by alluding to word not only as wound but as cure as well (cure for a wound that would be the spacing, the gram, the differance) would endow it with a balsamic quality rather than a signifying one, is not really the same as Derrida's and Borges'. Are not Borges and Derrida in fact themselves investing their efforts in favor of a language with its own substantiality, the Romantic dream of words that do not designate objects but are themselves objects? In Derrida this Romantic countergesture is to be found in his dense, allusive, Joycean style, in Borges, in the stories, whose seductive (curing) quality remains in spite of the negativity they imply. Lönnrot's death at the end of "Death and the Compass" is a hero's death—he is a minor tragic hero in search of the sort of original Text that Borges constantly denies. In spite of their hypercritical appearance, Borges and Derrida may very well have labored not to deconstruct literature, but to reconstruct it.

Chronology

1899   Jorge Luis Borges is born on August 24 in Buenos Aires to Jorge Guillermo Borges and Leonor Acevedo de Borges.

1906   Publishes a translation of Oscar Wilde's "The Happy Prince" in the local newspaper.

1912   Publishes "El rey de la selva" ("King of the Jungle"), a short story.

1914   Accompanies his family to Europe; they take up residence in Geneva as war erupts, and Borges attends a Geneva *lycée*, learning French, German, and Latin.

1916   The Radical president Hipolito Irigoyen takes office in Argentina, where his party retains power until 1930.

1918   Graduates from *lycée* and travels to Spain, where he comes under the influence of the *Ultraísta* movement and publishes several poems.

1921   Returns to Buenos Aires with his family. Publishes a volume of poetry, *Fervor de Buenos Aires* (*Buenos Aires' Fervor*), with financial assistance from his father. Helps edit the magazine *Prisma*, a "billboard review."

1922   Helps found *Proa*, a little magazine.

1923   Spends year in Spain as the family returns to Europe.

1924   Helps found the second *Proa*.

1925   Publishes a volume of poetry, *Luna de enfrente* (*Moon across the Way*), and a book of essays, *Inquisiciones* (*Inquisitions*).

1926   Publishes another book of essays, *El tamaño de mi esperanza* (*The Measure of My Hope*).

1928   More essays: *El idioma de los argentinos* (*The Language of the Argentines*).

1929   Awarded second prize in the annual Municipal Literary Contest of Buenos Aires for his third volume of poetry, *Cuaderno San Martín* (*San Martin Copybook*). Purchases the *Encyclopedia Britannica*, eleventh edition.

1930   The Argentine Radical government succumbs to right-wing miliary coup. Publishes a book of essays, *Evaristo Carriego*.

1932   *Discusión*, a book of essays, published. Argentina returns to civilian government, though Conservatives retain political control.

1933   Becomes literary editor for weekly arts supplement of the newspaper, *Crítica*.

1935   Borges' grandmother, Frances Haslam de Borges, dies. He publishes a collection of narrative prose, *Historia universal de la infamia* (*Universal History of Infamy*).

1936   Publishes *Historia de la eternidad* (*History of Eternity*), a book of essays.

1937   Publishes, with Pedro Henrique Urena, *Antología clasica de la literatura argentina* (*Classical Anthology of Argentine Literature*). Borges' father dies. Borges assumes position as assistant librarian in a small municipal library.

1938   Suffers head wound and septicemia and is hospitalized for several weeks.

1940   Publishes, with Silvina Ocampo and Adolfo Bioy Casares, *Antología de la literatura fantastica* (*Anthology of Fantastic Literature*).

1941   Publishes *El jardín de senderos que se bifurcan* (*The Garden of Forking Paths*), a collection of eight stories.

1942   *The Garden of Forking Paths* is nominated for the National Literary Prize, but does not receive it. *Sur* publishes a special issue, "Desagravio a Borges" ("Vindication of Borges"), in which twenty-one writers take his part. Publishes, with Adolfo Bioy Casares, a book of humorous detective stories, *Seis problemas para don Isidro Parodi* (*Six Problems of Don Isidro Parodi*), using joint pseudonym, H. Bustos Domecq.

1944	Publishes *Ficciones*, a book of largely essayistic fiction. Awarded the Prize of Honor from the Sociedad Argentina de Escritores.
1946	General Juan Domingo Perón assumes presidency by majority vote. Borges is relieved of his library post but offered position of poultry inspector, which he declines.
1947	Publishes *Nueva refutacion del tiempo* (*A New Refutation of Time*).
1949	*El Aleph* (*The Aleph*), a book of stories, is published.
1950	*Aspectos de la literatura gauchesca* (*Aspects of Gauchesca Literature*) published.
1951	The first translation of a book by Borges, *Fictions*, is published in Paris.
1952	Publishes *Otras inquisiciones* (*Other Inquisitions*), a book of essays. Eva Perón dies.
1953	With Margarita Guerrero, publishes *El Martín Fierro* (*Martin Fierro*).
1955	Perón government falls to centrist army coup. Borges appointed director of the National Library, though he is now nearly blind.
1956	Publishes new edition of *Ficciones*, containing three more stories.
1957	Named Professor of English Literature at the University of Buenos Aires. Publishes, with Margarita Guerrero, *Manual de zoologia fantastica* (*Handbook of Fantastic Zoology*).
1960	Publishes *El hacedor* (*Dreamtigers* in English edition), containing prose and verse.
1961	With Samuel Beckett, receives the International Publisher's Prize (Prix Fomentor). Teaches at the University of Texas for a semester.
1962	The first English collections of Borges' writing, *Labyrinths* and *Ficciones*, are published in New York.
1963	Lectures in England, France, Spain, and Switzerland.
1967	Marries Elsa Astete Millan (widow of Ricardo Albarracin Sarmiento) in September.
1967–68	Teaches at Harvard as the Charles Eliot Norton lecturer.

1968   Publishes expanded version of the *Manual de zoologia fantastica* as *El libro de los seres imaginarios* (*The Book of Imaginary Beings*). Receives honorary doctorate from Oxford University.

1969   Publishes *El informe de Brodie* (*Doctor Brodie's Report*), a book of stories; and *Elogio de la sombra* (*In Praise of Darkness*), a volume of poetry. Lectures in Israel.

1970   Divorced.

1971   Receives honorary doctorate from Columbia University and Jerusalem Prize.

1972   Publishes *El oro de los tigres* (*Gold of the Tigers*), a book of poetry and prose.

1973   Perón regains the presidency; Borges resigns his post at the National Library.

1974   *Obras completas* (*Complete Works*) is published, in one volume.

1975   Publishes *El libro de arena* (*The Book of Sand*), a collection of stories; *La rosa profunda* (*The Deep Rose*), a volume of poetry; and *Prologos* (*Prologues*), a collection of prefaces. Borges' mother dies, age 99. Perón dies; replaced in presidency by his widow, Isabel.

1976   Publishes *La moneda de hierro* (*The Iron Coin*), a volume of poetry. Publishes, with Adolfo Bioy Casares, *Cronicas de Bustos Domecq* (*Chronicles of Bustos Domecq*). Government of Isabel Perón succumbs to right-wing military coup.

1977   Lectures throughout Argentina.

1978   Spends year in Europe.

1981   Receives honorary degree from Harvard University.

1982   Delivers William James lecture at the New York Institute for the Humanities.

1983   Awarded the T. S. Eliot Award for Creative Writing by the Ingersoll Foundation.

Contributors

HAROLD BLOOM, Sterling Professor of the Humanities at Yale University, is the author of *The Anxiety of Influence*, *Poetry and Repression*, and many other volumes of literary criticism. His forthcoming study, *Freud: Transference and Authority*, attempts a full-scale reading of all of Freud's major writings. A MacArthur Prize Fellow, he is the general editor of the *Chelsea House Library of Literary Criticism*.

THOMAS R. HART, JR., is a Professor of Romance Languages at the University of Oregon, Eugene. He is the author of *Gil Vicente, Casandra and Don Duardo*, and *La alegoria en el Libro de buen amor*.

PAUL DE MAN was Sterling Professor of French at Yale University and the author of *Blindness and Insight*, *Allegories of Reading*, and *The Rhetoric of Romanticism*.

LOUIS MURILLO is Professor of Spanish at the University of California at Berkeley. He is the author of *The Cyclical Night: Irony in James Joyce and Jorge Luis Borges* and *The Golden Dial: Temporal Configuration in Don Quijote*.

RONALD J. CHRIST is Professor of English at Rutgers University and the author of *The Narrow Act: Borges' Art of Allusion*.

JAIME ALAZRAKI, Professor of Romance Languages and Literature at Harvard University, is the author of *Jorge Luis Borges*; *Poetica y poesia de Pablo Neruda*; *La prosa narrativa de Jorge Luis Borges*; and *Versiones, Inversiones, Reversiones*.

JAMES E. IRBY, Professor of Romance Languages at Princeton University, is the author of *La influencia de William Faulkner en cuatro narradores hispano americanos*.

CARTER WHEELOCK is Professor of Spanish and Portuguese at the University of Texas at Austin and the author of *The Mythmaker: A Study of Motif and Symbol in the Short Stories of Jorge Luis Borges.*

EMIR RODRÍGUEZ-MONEGAL, former Professor of Spanish and Portuguese at Yale University, is the author of *Narradores de esta America*; Neruda, el viajero inmovil; *El arte de narrar, dialogos, El boom de la novela latinoamericana*; and *Jorge Luis Borges: A Literary Biography.*

ALICIA BORINSKY is Professor of Spanish at Boston University and has written widely on Latin American literature and literary theory.

JOHN STURROCK is the editor of *Structualism and Since: From Lévi-Strauss to Derrida* and the author of *The French New Novel* and *Paper Tigers: The Ideal Fictions of Jorge Luis Borges.*

NANCY B. MANDLOVE teaches in the department of Foreign Languages at Westminster College in New Wilmington, Pennsylvania.

SHLOMITH RIMMON-KENAN, a Senior Lecturer in English at the Hebrew University of Jerusalem, is the author of *The Concept of Ambiguity: The Example of James.*

RICARDO GUTIÉRREZ-MOUAT is Associate Professor of Modern Languages and Classics at Emory University.

THORPE RUNNING is Professor of Spanish at St. Johns University, Collegeville, Maine. He is the author of *Borges' Ultraist Movement and Its Poets.*

ROBERTO GONZÁLEZ-ECHEVARRÍA, Professor of Spanish and Portuguese at Yale University, is the author of *Alejo Carpentier: The Pilgrim at Home*; *Isla a su vuelo fugitiva: en savos criticos sobre literatura*; and *Relecturas: estudios de literatura cubana.*

Bibliography

Alazraki, Jaime. *Jorge Luis Borges*. New York: Columbia University Press, 1969.

Ayora, Jorge R. "Gnosticism and Time in 'El Immortal.'" *Hispania* 56 (1973): 593–96.

Barrenechea, Ana María. *Borges the Labyrinth Maker*. Ed. and trans. Robert Lima. New York: New York University Press, 1965.

Barth, John. "The Literature of Exhaustion." *Atlantic Monthly* 220 (August 1967): 29–34.

Botsford, Keith. "About Borges and Note About Borges." *Kenyon Review* 26 (Autumn 1964): 723–37.

Britton, R. K. "History, Myth, and Archetype in Borges's View of Argentina." *Modern Language Review* 74, part 3 (July 1974): 607–16.

Burgin, Richard. *Conversations with Jorge Luis Borges*. New York: Holt, Rinehart and Winston Inc., 1969.

Carroll, Robert C. "Borges and Bruno: The Geometry of Infinity in 'La muerte y la brújula.'" *Modern Language Notes* 94 (1979): 321–42.

Caviglia, John. "The Tales of Borges: Language and the Private Eye." *Modern Language Notes* 89 (1974): 219–31.

Cheever, Leonard A. "Glimpses that Can Make Us Less Forlorn: Wordsworth, Borges, and Neruda." *Research Studies* 47 (1979): 37–44.

Christ, Ronald J. "The Art of Fiction: Jorge Luis Borges." *Paris Review* 40 (Winter–Spring 1967): 116–64.

———. *The Narrow Act: Borges' Art of Allusion*. New York: New York University Press, 1969.

Chrzanowski, Joseph. "Psychological Motivation in Borges's 'Emma Zunz.'" *Literature and Psychology* 28 (1978): 100–104.

Costa, Rene de. "A Note on Narrative Voice in Borges's Early Fiction." *Modern Philology* 76 (1978): 193–96.

Dauster, Frank. "Notes on Borges' Labyrinths." *Hispanic Review* 30 (April 1962): 142–48.

Davidson, Ned J. "Aesthetic Persuasion in 'A New Refutation of Time.'" *Latin American Literary Review* 14 (1979): 1–4.

di Giovanni, Norman Thomas. "'Streetcorner Man' Revisited." *Western Humanities Review* 26 (1972): 213–18.

————; Daniel Halpern; and Frank MacShane, eds. *Borges on Writing.* New York: E. P. Dutton & Co., Inc., 1973.

Doxey, William S. "Borges' 'Caballo' Labyrinth: The Intricacy of Beauty." *Journal of Modern Literature* 7 (1979): 548–52.

Dunham, Lowell and Ivar Ivask, eds. *The Cardinal Points of Borges.* Norman: University of Oklahoma Press, 1971.

Enguidanos, Miguel. "Imagination and Escape in the Short Stories of Jorge Luis Borges." *Texas Quarterly* 4 (Winter 1961): 118–27.

Flores, Angel. "Magical Realism in Spanish American Fiction." *Hispania* 38 (May 1955): 187–92.

Foster, David Williams. "Borges' *El Aleph:* Some Thematic Considerations." *Hispania* 47 (1964): 56–59.

Fraser, Howard M. "Points South; Ambrose Bierce, Jorge Luis Borges, and the Fantastic." *Studies in Twentieth-Century Literature* 1 (1977): 173–81.

Gallagher, D. P. "Evident Words." *Review* no. 8 (1973): 18–23.

Gass, William H. "Imaginary Borges." *The New York Review of Books* (November 20, 1969): 5–8.

Gold, Barbara K. "Labyrinths in Borges' 'House of Asterion.'" *Helios* 8 (1981): 49–59.

Gyurko, Lanin. "Rivalry and the Double in Borges' 'Guayaquil.'" *Romance Notes* 15 (1973): 37–46.

Harss, Luis and Barbara Dohman. "Jorge Luis Borges, or the Consolation by Philosophy." In *Into the Mainstream.* New York: Harper & Row Publishers, Inc., 1967.

Hulme, Peter. "The Face in the Mirror: Borges's 'La busca de Averroes.'" *Forum for Modern Language Studies* 16 (1979): 292–97.

Irby, James E. "Introduction" to *Labyrinths.* Ed. Donald A. Yates and James E. Irby. New York: New Directions Publishing Corp., 1962.

Irby, James E. "Introduction" to *Other Inquisitions.* Trans. Ruth L. Simms. Austin: University of Texas Press, 1964.

Keller, Gary D. and K. S. Van Hooft. "Jorge Luis Borges' 'La Intrusa': The Awakening of Love and Consciousness/The Sacrifice of Love and Consciousness." In Lisa E. Davis and Isabel Taran, eds., *The Analysis of Hispanic Texts.* Jamaica, N.Y.: Bilingual Press, 1976, 300–19.

Kerrigan, Anthony. "Introduction" to *Ficciones.* Ed. A. Kerrigan. New York: Grove Press, Inc., 1962.

King, James Roy. "Averroes' Search: The 'Moment' as Labyrinth in the Fictions of Jorge Luis Borges." *Research Studies* 45 (1977): 134–46.

King, Lloyd. "Antagonism, Irony, and Deceit in Two Stories by Borges." *CLA Journal* 23 (1980): 399–408.

Kinzie, Mary, and Charles Newman, eds. *Prose for Borges.* Evanston, Ill.: Northwestern University Press, 1972.

Levine, Suzanne Jill. "A Universal Tradition: The Fictional Biography." *Review* no. 8 (1973): 24–28.

Lewald, H. Ernest. "The Labyrinth of Time and Place in Two Stories by Borges." *Hispania* 45 (1962): 630–36.

Magliola, Robert. "Jorge Luis Borges and the Loss of Being: Structural Themes in *Dr. Brodies' Report." Studies in Short Fiction* 15 (1978): 25–31.

Maloff, Saul. "Eerie Emblems of a Bizarre, Terrifying World." *Saturday Review* (June 2, 1962): 34.

Maurois, André. "Preface" to *Labyrinths.* Ed. Donald Yates and James E. Irby. New York: New Directions, 1962.

McBride, Mary. "Jorge Luis Borges, Existentialist: 'The Aleph' and the Relativity of Human Perception." *Studies in Short Fiction* 14 (1977): 401–3.

Murillo, Louis. *The Cyclical Night: Irony in James Joyce and Jorge Luis Borges.* Cambridge, Mass.: Harvard University Press, 1968.

————. "The Labyrinths of Jorge Luis Borges: An Introduction to the Stories of *The Aleph." Modern Language Quarterly* 20 (September 1959): 259–66.

Naipaul, V. S. "Comprehending Borges." *The New York Review of Books* (October 19, 1972): 3–5.

Rodríguez-Monegal, Emir. *Jorge Luis Borges: A Literary Biography.* New York: E. P. Dutton & Co., Inc., 1978.

Rosenblum, Joseph. "'The Immortal': Jorge Luis Borges's Rendition of T. S. Eliot's *The Waste Land." Studies in Short Fiction* 18 (1981): 183–86.

Rudy, Stephen. "The Garden of and in Borges' 'Garden of Forking Paths.'" In Andrej Kodjak, Michael J. Connolly, and Krystyna Pomorska, eds., *The Structural Analysis of Narrative Texts.* Columbus, Ohio: Slavica, 1980.

Shaw, Donald L. *Borges: Ficciones.* London: Grant and Cutler, 1976.

Sosnowski, Saul. "'The God's Script'—Kabbalistic Quest." *Modern Fiction Studies* 19 (1973): 381–94.

Stabb, Martin S. *Jorge Luis Borges.* New York: Twayne Publishers Inc., 1970.

Steiner, George. "Tigers in the Mirror." *The New Yorker* (June 20, 1970): 109–19.

Sturrock, John. *Paper Tigers: The Ideal Fictions of Jorge Luis Borges.* New York: Oxford University Press, 1977.

Updike, John. "Books: The Author as Librarian." *The New Yorker* (October 31, 1965): 223–46.

Wheelock, Carter. *The Mythmaker: A Study of Motif and Symbol in the Short Stories of Jorge Luis Borges.* Austin: University of Texas Press, 1969.

Wood, Michael. "Borges's Surprise!" *The New York Review of Books* (June 1, 1972): 32–33.

Yates, Donald. "Behind 'Borges and I.'" *Modern Fiction Studies* 19 (Autumn 1973): 317–24.

Acknowledgments

"Introduction" (originally entitled "Poetic Misprision: Three Cases") by Harold Bloom from *The Ringers in the Tower: Studies in Romantic Tradition* by Harold Bloom, © 1971 by The University of Chicago. Reprinted by permission of The University of Chicago Press.

"Borges' Literary Criticism" (originally entitled "The Literary Criticism of Jorge Luis Borges") by Thomas R. Hart, Jr. from *MLN* 78, no. 5 (December 1963), © 1963 by The Johns Hopkins University Press. Reprinted by permission.

"A Modern Master" by Paul de Man from *New York Review of Books* 3, no. 6 (November 5, 1964), © 1964 by the Estate of Paul de Man. Reprinted by permission of Patricia de Man.

"Three Stories" (originally entitled "Borges 3") by Louis Murillo from *The Cyclical Night: Irony in James Joyce and Jorge Luis Borges* by Louis Murillo, © 1968 by the President and Fellows of Harvard College. Reprinted by permission of Harvard University Press.

" 'The Immortal' " (originally entitled "Summation: 'The Immortal' ") by Ronald J. Christ from *The Narrow Act: Borges' Art of Allusion* by Ronald J. Christ, © 1984 by Ronald J. Christ. Reprinted by permission of the author.

"Kabbalistic Traits in Borges' Narration" by Jaime Alazraki from *Studies in Short Fiction* 8, no. 1 (Winter 1971), © 1971 by Newberry College. Reprinted by permission.

"Borges and the Idea of Utopia" by James E. Irby from *The Cardinal Points of Borges*, edited by Lowell Dunham and Ivar Ivask, © 1971 by the University of Oklahoma Press. Reprinted by permission.

"Borges' New Prose" by Carter Wheelock from *Prose for Borges*, edited by Charles Newman and Mary Kinzie, © 1972 by Northwestern University. Reprinted by permission of Northwestern University Press.

"Symbols in Borges' Work" by Emir Rodríguez-Monegal from *Modern Fiction Studies* 19, no. 3 (Autumn 1973), © 1973 by Purdue Research Foundation, West Lafayette, IN. Reprinted by permission.

"Repetition, Museums, Libraries" (originally entitled "Repetition, Museums, Libraries: Jorge Luis Borges") by Alicia Borinsky from *Glyph* 2 (1977), edited by Samuel Weber and Henry Sussman, © 1977 by The Johns Hopkins University Press. Reprinted by permission.

"Odium Theologicum" by John Sturrock from *Paper Tigers: The Ideal Fictions of Jorge Luis Borges* by John Sturrock, © 1977 by Oxford University Press. Reprinted by permission.

"Chess and Mirrors: Form as Metaphor in Three Sonnets" (originally entitled "Chess and Mirrors: Form as Metaphor in Three Sonnets of Jorge Luis Borges") by Nancy B. Mandlove from *Kentucky Romance Quarterly* 27, no. 3 (1980), © 1980 by The University Press of Kentucky. Reprinted by permission.

"Doubles and Counterparts: 'The Garden of Forking Paths'" (originally entitled "Doubles and Counterparts: Patterns of Interchangeability in Borges' 'The Garden of Forking Paths'") by Shlomith Rimmon-Kenan from *Critical Inquiry* 6, no. 4 (Summer 1980), © 1980 by The University of Chicago. Reprinted by permission of the University of Chicago Press and the author.

"The Center of the Labyrinth" (originally entitled "Borges and the Center of the Labyrinth") by Ricardo Gutiérrez-Mouat from *Romance Notes* 21, no. 2 (Winter 1980), © 1980 by the University of North Carolina. Reprinted by permission of the Editor.

"Borges' Ultraist Poetry" by Thorpe Running from *Borges' Ultraist Movement and its Poets* by Thorpe Running, © 1981 by International Book Publishing, Inc. Reprinted by permission.

"Borges and Derrida" by Roberto González-Echevarría, © 1986 by Roberto González-Echevarría. English translation published for the first time in this volume. Originally appeared as "Borges y Derrida" in *Isla a su vuelo fugitiva* by Roberto González-Echevarría (Madrid: Porrua, 1983). Printed by permission of the author.

Index